CRIME CITY

Manchester's Victorian Underworld

Joseph O'Neill

MILO BOOKS

First published in March 2008 by Milo Books

ISBN 978 1 903854 77 8

Typeset by Jayne Walsh

Printed in Great Britain by
Cox & Wyman Ltd, Reading, Berkshire

MILO BOOKS LTD
The Old Weighbridge
Station Road
Wrea Green
Lancs PR4 2PH
United Kingdom
www.milobooks.com

Contents

Prologue   7

1   Manchester   9

2   The Irish   21

3   Crime   44

4   Squalor   53

5   Criminals   76

6   Pubs   101

7   Vice   124

8   Down and Out   147

9   Conmen   172

10   The Good, the Bad and the Dangerous   195

11   Killers   222

12   Police   237

13   Punishment   257

Epilogue: Bang! Bang!   269

Prologue

Every city gets the criminals it deserves. Manchester in the second half of the nineteenth century was no exception.

The city was a furnace, forging a new world and a new man, transforming all those poured into its great crucible. There had never been anywhere like Manchester and this unique place created a unique underworld, unlike London's and totally different from those of other emerging industrial centres. The city sucked in people not only from the surrounding countryside but also from every impoverished and persecuted country in the world and flung them together into an explosive mix.

To understand the Manchester underworld at this time you must first understand Manchester. In particular you must know something about the Manchester Irish. They were the city's largest group of immigrants and throughout this period many blamed them for all the city's ills, especially its crime.

In reality Manchester's underworld rested on more than Irish immigrants. Its foundations were five stout piles driven into the bedrock of the city: the rookeries, the pub, the pawnshop, the lodging house and the workhouse. These were the criminals' natural habitat, where they flourished in good times and foundered in bad. They were also the places where they rubbed shoulders with the poor – respectable and not so respectable. Though these five pillars underpinned the Manchester underworld they were by no means the exclusive preserves of criminals. Many of those living in the lodging houses of the rookeries, for instance, were decent people struggling against overwhelming odds. The pub was a small oasis of delight in the lives of the honest poor. For most working people the pawnshop was all that stood between them and the workhouse. But the criminal world ran parallel to that of the poor. Like the shoreline and the sea it was often impossible to say where one ended and the other began.

Ranged against this amorphous threat stood the police, the courts and the prisons. Manchester boasted a number of famous policemen, masters of their profession. Two of the most celebrated, Jerome Caminada, a detective with a national reputation, and James Bent, a decent and humane man, known for his work with the Manchester poor, gave long and distinguished service. Yet, despite their efforts and those of many other dedicated peelers, the police laboured under many handicaps which severely hindered their fight against crime.

Similarly, the courts did little to stem the tide of crime, especially violent crime that flowed unchecked through the streets of the city. The notion that nineteenth century courts inflicted savage retribution on those guilty of even minor misdemeanours does not stand up to scrutiny. As we shall see, the courts in Manchester were often indulgent of those guilty of violence and other serious crimes.

Strangeways, whose grim profile gives the city a skyline as distinctive as that of Paris, then embodied the most advanced thinking in penology. But it held no terror for the criminal. Like the workhouse, its inmates enjoyed a life better than that outside.

Respectability was far more effective than the police, courts and prison in containing crime. It kept poor people from drifting into the ways of the criminals they lived with. But chiefly the shortcomings of the underworld kept crime in check. There were famous criminals in Manchester during this period whose imagination, audacity and inventiveness made them a major threat to the city. But they were the exception.

For the most part Manchester criminals were like all criminals – pathetic, inadequate individuals. More than any other group, the murderers demonstrate this. Few killed as part of a criminal strategy. Some were inept criminals, killing for piffling gain. Most did it because it was the only way they could express their rage, frustration or resentment. They lived when boot and fist were the idiom of anger.

And Manchester was an angry city. It was not a city, more an assault on the senses. There had never been anywhere like it.

1

Manchester

A New World

Manchester made the world. Our industrial past, the chrysalis from which a city of penthouses and tapas bars is now stirring into existence, was the birthplace of industrial society. Manchester made the world in its own image and likeness. The city was the prototype, the herald of a new world that changed human existence more than any war, revolution or invention before or since. It was the most dynamic metropolis in the country. Not only was it at the heart of the cotton industry, it was the hub of a worldwide trade that was Britain's biggest earner.

But Manchester's birth was no easy delivery. The city came into the world screaming and those who witnessed it did so with fascination and horror. Blood-stained streets were a permanent feature of the city. For decades Manchester was the arena for a clash between the two classes spawned by the Industrial Revolution: the new, callous rich and the dispossessed, angry poor. The Peterloo Massacre of 1819 confirmed this in the popular imagination. When the local elite set the yeomanry on a peaceful demonstration, killing innocent women and children, their flailing swords secured the city's place in the annals of class conflict. Ten years later the violence with which the army crushed rioting in 1829 further heightened tensions in the city and the bitterness persisted in less sensational incidents throughout the century. For instance, the MPs elected in 1832, Mark Phillips and Poulett Thompson, were caricature reactionaries – hostile to any improvement in factory conditions, opposed to the extension of the franchise and adamant that the poor must be kept in their place.

As well as the battleground of bosses and workers, the city was also the focal point for the force that was challenging the old establishment – the anti-Corn Law League. Manchester was also the centre of Nonconformity, the vibrant ideology that eschewed the Anglican landowners' Church and equated hard work with doing God's will.

It is obvious why everyone seeking to understand what was going on in the world came to Manchester. Though this monstrous creation baffled them, they instinctively sensed that it was of monumental importance. In 1843 Thomas Carlyle, Victorian England's most authoritative commentator, described the city as 'wonderful, fearful and unimaginable'. He sensed the city was transforming the world, describing it as 'the type of a new power on the earth'.

Charles Dickens and Benjamin Disraeli and every other commentator trying to make sense of what was happening to the world regarded Manchester as a living experiment. What they saw was of monumental significance. When Karl Marx and Friedrich Engels evolved their theories of how the capitalist world would develop, it was while they were walking along Oxford Road and drinking in the Crescent pub in Salford. The horrors and injustices they cited were Manchester's horrors and injustices. When they wrote of a dehumanised race, reduced to units of labour and deprived of all dignity, they were talking about the people of Manchester.

Ancoats, at the heart of the city, was Manchester in microcosm. It was the pumping heart of the industrial nation, the first industrial suburb. Its narrow streets, walled in by mills which became the model for the American cotton industry, echoed to musical Italian, harsh German and nasal Polish, as well as the flat Manchester vowels. Its mills were the most advanced in the world – the Murray Mills were the first to use steam power. They formed the backdrop against which the industrial working class came into existence. The names of these streets – Cotton Street, Loom Street, Silk Street, Bengal Street – are redolent of an age when Britain was the world's only superpower. There could be no starker contrast than that between the Empire's opulence and Ancoats' squalor.

More than anywhere else Manchester epitomised the liberal spirit of the age – parliamentary reform, free trade, the Charter. The city stood for the rising middle class who wanted to replace the landed aristocracy as the country's rulers. Yet there was nowhere where the 'dark satanic mills' were more a reality. These mills gave Manchester its key place in British industry. Britain's, and the world's, greatest industry during the nineteenth century was cotton. For the best part of a century, cotton was king and Manchester was Cottonopolis. The mills of Ancoats, Harpurhey and Strangeways led the industry. Most are now gone, the rest turned into apartments for the aspiring young. Yet their image has passed into the national consciousness, largely because L.S. Lowry painted these inner city streets when cotton, like a consumptive, still had the bloom of health though it was in its death throes. Lowry captured an enigma – individuality overlaid with a grim uniformity.

Nineteenth century Manchester was also an enigma: the precursor of a new world wealthier than any preceding civilisation, one of the most important urban centres in the world and the powerhouse of the liberal ideas that were transforming society. Yet it was also a city awash with crime, vice, drunkenness, poverty and violence.

It is no wonder Manchester exercised such power over the nineteenth century mind. It attracted all manner of inquirers – economists, historians, social investigators and curious foreigners – and most recorded their impressions. There are as many descriptions of the city as there were visitors, but they agree on three things: Manchester was ugly and it was evil. But most of all it was dangerous.

The spectacular ugliness of the place struck them all. Manchester was not just ugly – it was extravagantly repulsive, an affront to the senses, an assault on nature. As early as 1808 one visitor found this 'abnormally filthy' city violated his senses. Looking down into the stinking Irwell, he remarked that 'the water of the river is as black as ink'.

Writing in the *Manchester Guardian* of the Ancoats of 1849, Angus Bethune Reach speaks of 'dingy streets, unsunned courts and gloomy culs de sac' with open gutters. He tells of the mills, each with its cinder-paved courtyard and steaming engine house. Even the chapels were shabby. And cutting through it all, like frenzied slashes through flesh, are railway viaducts and canals, with their sprawling wharves, coal yards and stagnant barges.

Fifteen years earlier, Alexis de Tocqueville, the great political thinker and one of the shrewdest observers of American and European society, spoke of the same area as if it were some strip of murdered nature: 'A thick black smoke covered the city. The sun appears like a disc without any rays.' He saw men toiling in a permanent 'semi-daylight'. And Dickens used Manchester as a source for Coketown in *Hard Times*. 'It was a town of red brick... machines and serpents of smoke, a black canal, a river that ran purple with dye, buildings that rattled and trembled all day.'

It is hardly surprising that the city was so ugly. Unloved, thrown together without foresight or care, grimly practical, brutally functional, once its buildings served their purpose they were discarded and left to moulder. Its attraction was severely practical. Like its people, it had no truck with the superfluous.

It existed for work. It provided jobs for each wave of immigrants washed up on its grim streets. For Irish and Jews, Germans and Italians it was only a means to an end, a refuge from poverty or persecution. Many of its blow-ins resented being there, cursing the colonial power that had driven them from home or enticed them with empty promises.

Many regarded the city as no more than a staging post. They hoped to fill their pockets and return home. Nowhere is this more evident than in the city's old cemeteries. As you amble between the florid headstones, the lettering obscured by lichen, their inscriptions and memorials tell us that though the bodies of these exiles lie in Manchester clay, their hearts are in Sicily, Connemara and Cracow. But observers sensed that Manchester was more than a tangle of offensive sounds, rank smells and distorted images. They agreed on a second characteristic of the city. It was evil. In creating Manchester, man had lifted the lid on hell and called up a devil.

Alexis de Tocqueville realised the city had a malevolent life of its own, beyond human control. 'A thousand noises rise... the footsteps of a busy crowd, the crunching wheels of machines, the shrieks of steam from the boilers, the regular beat of looms, the heavy rumble of carts – these are the noises from which you can never escape in these half-lit streets.'

This new force was the source of countless evils, the most obvious of which was the disintegration of social cohesion. This separation of the classes was greater in Manchester than anywhere else. The propertied classes, the purveyors of culture, religion and responsibility – civilisation – had no influence over the slum-dwellers.

Disraeli spoke of the two classes. 'How,' he asked, 'are manners to influence men if they are divided into two classes – if the population of a country becomes a group of hostile garrisons?' This cultural and social apartheid began long before anyone deplored its effects.

The flight to the city's suburbs had started by 1795. By the 1830s Manchester's warehouses were far more impressive than her mills and by the beginning of the 1840s the city centre's substantial middle class dwellings had all given way to commercial buildings. When Leon Faucher, a French economist and later government minister, visited the city in 1844, he wrote his famous *Manchester in 1844: its present condition and future prospects*. He found that Manchester was divided into two separate parts – one which was healthy and attractive, where the respectable lived and another that was vile and poisonous, where the poor and dangerous existed. This divide increased in the following years with the result that by the 1860s hardly any wealthy people lived in the city.

Writing in the *Manchester Guardian* in 1864 Edward Brotherton, the Victorian philanthropist, was merely repeating what many others had said before. 'The intelligent classes,' he said, 'know nothing of the poor parts of the city.' If they did, 'they would find thousands of children who must almost of necessity grow up idle, reckless and many of them criminal.'

The fear he voiced was stoked by growing concern about the garrotting epidemic of 1862 and 1863. Again the local press sent its intrepid reporters into the depths of the slums, seeking the source of this latest threat – and once more they lighted on the low lodging house. The *Manchester City News* of 12 March 1864 found there were 472 lodging houses in the city; of these 147 were the resort of known thieves, 244 were occupied by vagrants and 'poor travellers' and seventy-two by hawkers, foreigners and the Irish.

Little had changed in the fourteen years since Reach had investigated the lodging houses of Angel Meadow. The same ragbag of fallen humanity lived there. According to Reach, prostitutes, their bullies, vagrants, cadgers, tramps, thieves and the low Irish huddled together in moral and physical squalor. Contemporary observers were unanimous in their belief that there was a close link between living conditions and sexual immorality. In particular, they had in mind the overcrowding that forced whole families to sleep in a single room. Sharing beds remained a part of working class life for a long time after the middle class came to believe that separate rooms were vital to maintain the privacy and delicacy essential to decency.

The city also led to the breakdown of the family on which a healthy society depended. When Hippolyte Taine, the French philosopher and one of the most distinguished intellectuals of his day, visited Manchester in 1872, he saw a mass of workers, most of whom 'married young, had six children, drank and saved nothing. The wife was a bad housekeeper in becoming a good factory hand.'

This disjunction of family relationships led to a coarsening of human instincts. Engels was not the last to comment on the appalling neglect of children, which was a feature of Manchester life. Though the overall death rate among children was staggering, that for illegitimate children was eight times higher. The death rate was high in all cities, yet many observers commented on the callous indifference that marked Mancunians' attitude to the suffering of children, especially their own. This is to some extent reflected in the 1868 figures for missing children. That year 5,410 were reported lost. Of these 3,247 were found and restored to their parents.

But what of the rest? In many ways Manchester was a frontier town, where all the old certainties died and restraints were thrown off. By the 1850s the city had a reputation for its raucous nightlife, a tumult of drink, violence and vice. The streets hummed with industry during the day and at night with the throng of drunks, thieves, gangs and tarts. Finally, visitors agreed the city was dangerous. In 1843 when Carlyle was mesmerised by Manchester, he summed up the threat it represented by saying it was 'built on the infinite abyss'.

The first to describe this threat was Dr James Phillips Kay. He was a leading member of the Manchester Statistical Society, a group of prominent citizens who sought to apply scientific developments 'to promote the progress of social improvement'. He was Senior Physician to the Ardwick and Ancoats Dispensary. In his famous 1832 account of the Deansgate area he chiefly addressed the conditions which threatened the lives of the poor. But he also spoke of 'a mass of buildings, inhabited by prostitutes and thieves'. Moral and physical squalor were mixed, like shades of filth in a midden. In Parliament Street, almost 400 people shared a single privy. Salford's equivalent was the area around Gathorn Street. Almost fifty years later, Alfred Alsop, another middle class explorer who sometimes ventured into 'unknown Manchester' – of which his class were as ignorant as of darkest Africa or the Amazon rainforests – found a city that had changed little from Kay's time.

Despite the vogue for slum exploration, it was not necessary to enter these places in order to know what they were like. All you had to do was inhale. They exuded an overpowering stench of refuse and human waste. This was more than a matter of offended sensibilities, though. Squalor killed. In the 1840s there was one death in every thirty-two of the Manchester population, compared to one in fifty-five in Sussex and Cornwall. What this means is that average life expectancy in Manchester was twenty-four years at a time when the national average was forty.

For most of the nineteenth century, Ancoats was the death black spot of Manchester. It had its own poisoned microclimate: a pall of smoke glowered over its grey streets, acid rain fell on the soot-streaked walls and a plague of disease choked off the breath of its people: bronchitis, influenza, pneumonia and asthma hovered in the damp air. It is hardly surprising that by the 1870s life expectancy had dropped to less than twenty. And as if all this were not bad enough, the city decided to dump all its shit on Ancoats.

For most of the nineteenth century Manchester had no sewage policy. Ashpits and communal cesspits were the city's only provision for human waste and the city council decided their contents should be hauled to Ancoats. Heavy or prolonged rainfall, a common occurrence, meant these pits overflowed into the cellars that still housed large numbers of families. What was even worse was that until 1870 much human waste ended up in the River Irwell, for many still a source of drinking water.

Even when street cleaning was introduced the best streets were cleaned once a week and the alleys, courts and narrow streets where the poor huddled, once a month. No wonder cholera was a regular summer visitor to the city. Though it cut great swathes through the population, it was not the main killer. Consumption (pulmonary tuberculosis) – the hacking cough, breathlessness and the clot of blood vivid on a white handkerchief – was the main killer. It culled most of its victims from the inner city of Ancoats, Hulme, Chorlton-on-Medlock and Ardwick. It was only the piping of fresh water from the Longdendale Reservoir in the 1850s and Thirlemere in the 1890s that wiped out cholera and typhoid.

Manchester's death pallor was obvious to all. When Queen Victoria visited in 1851, she had no need to consult mortality data. 'What a painfully unhealthy-looking population! Men as well as women,' she exclaimed.

Yet the filth of the city was only its most obvious threat. Poverty was equally dangerous. In an age beset with fear of revolution, this concentration of destitute wretches was a ticking time-bomb.

The Essence of Hell

In the 1840s Manchester was the poorest place in Britain, worse than the much documented East End of London which drew gasps of indignation from the social investigators who witnessed the destitution of its residents. Throughout the nineteenth century the average wage in Manchester was well below subsistence level.

When in 1888 the *Lancet* sent an investigator to study the conditions of Manchester tailors, he found that their pay was 6d an hour – as it had been for the previous twenty years. A report of 1889 found that forty per cent of working men in Salford were in 'irregular employment'. Clinging to a precarious existence on a weekly income of less than four shillings, their poverty was a result of the erratic nature of casual labour, the only work available to many. During the winter of 1878 and 1879 most of those receiving poor relief were casual or seasonal workers, such as warehousemen, builders and general labourers, storemen and carters. Many were Irish or of Irish descent.

Life was precarious in other ways. Of the inquests held by the Manchester coroner in 1868, 266 returned a verdict of accidental death. Some of these were the result of the general use of open fires for warmth and cooking and candles and oil lamps for light. But many were simply the occupational hazards stalking all those working in pits and factories.

The city's industry had an insatiable appetite for labour. It vacuumed up people. First it drew them from the surrounding countryside. In the early nineteenth century it pulled in the first of the Jews who were to settle in the city, cotton merchants, who wanted to be at the heart of the industry that was driving the revolution. They congregated around Cheetham Hill. However, this rural idyll, barely a mile from the city's commercial centre, was soon a victim of the demand for labour. The grass of Cheetham's meadows was soon buried under thousands of jerry-built hovels, slums before the mortar was dry.

This was the real threat of Manchester: would it poison the surrounding countryside as it had Cheetham's meadows? Would she export her filth and disorder the way she exported her cotton? And what about those sinister aliens, especially the Irish and the Jews, who infested the bowels of the city? What would check their evil influence?

From the 1840s parts of the city were no-go areas, totally out of bounds for anyone who valued his life. The very fact that a person frequented such places was proof of criminality. According to Alsop, 'returned convicts, sharpers, smashers, thieves, harlots, gaolbirds, fortune-tellers and unlicensed sellers of beer' infested its streets. This place consisted of 'the very scum of the city, the essence of hell'. Little wonder that squalor and crime figured large in the reputation of Manchester. The city's image was so powerful that at times it seemed to take on a life of its own, attracting every type of crook and shyster because they really believed that Manchester was a rogue's paradise.

A Rogue's Paradise

Today reality comes a poor second to image. Every city and town council employs public relations consultants to generate a distinctive and positive aura. Manchester's image in the 1870s was certainly distinctive, though entirely negative.

No doubt a large part of this was the result of the popular stereotype, the caricature of the northern industrial town. But a caricature is the pearl that forms around a grain of truth. An American visitor in 1825 found Mancunians gruff and charmless. They lacked courtesy to strangers and 'cared little for the civilities which others expect and which produce a favourable impression'. This 'up yours' attitude has persisted to our own day, when Oasis'

Manchester

Liam Gallagher is a famous exponent of the city's characteristically belligerent approach to social interaction. In some circles it carries a certain macho kudos.

In the nineteenth century, however, this indifference to social niceties was seen as a part of Manchester's obsession with money. 'Money seems to be their idol – the god they adore and in worshipping this their deity they devote but a small portion of their time to those pursuits which expand the mind,' observed another American. There is something vividly contemporary about this – the author could be describing the population of any city or town in Britain today.

Other facets of the popular image have endured too. Then as now, Manchester was the rainy city, set in a sodden, inhospitable landscape in an uninviting part of the world. Its people were said to be aggressively practical, adamantly non-intellectual – people of concrete action, hostile to abstract ideas. These traits sit well with the Mancunian man's lack of sentimentality, his aversion to things of the imagination, his grim pragmatism.

The Mancunian was a pallid little person wearing a dirty brown shop-coat, the smell of engine oil on his breath, feathers of cotton and calico in his hair. Capable of neither poetry nor oratory, his attempt at a love letter came out as, 'Your of the 11th ult. duly came to hand, in which per advice...' At best, he was a grubby factory foreman or a low commercial type. And his city, lacking in grace and dignity, crass and boorish, vulgar and seedy, was a reflection of him.

Unflattering as this is, it was not the most disparaging aspect of the popular image of the Manchester man. At worst, he was a slum-dweller. He was a subterranean creature, shut off from nature by a cocoon of filth. The air that enveloped him was grey with grit and smoke. Noxious fumes and toxic gases obscured his sky. The rivers that ran under his streets were poisonous effluent, reeking heavens high. A carrier of disease, a threat to order, he was also a criminal.

Strangely, the Irish did not feature in the popular image of Manchester. Though Mancunians blamed them for all the city's problems – particularly crime – and they formed one of the largest concentrations of Irish people in the country, to the outsider the Manchester-Irish were invisible.

2

The Irish

A Very Picture of Loathsomeness

The Irish have been in England since the early fifteenth century. Right from the start their hosts despised them as parasites: the original spongers. This image as an unwelcome burden stuck and was complemented by an array of equally unfavourable attributes until the Irish came to represent every problem that beset nineteenth century Britain.

From the early eighteenth century many came to England and Scotland to labour on the grain and hay harvest. But from the early nineteenth century many stayed and found permanent work in the burgeoning towns around Manchester. By the early 1800s there were about 5,000 in the area and, contrary to the popular image of the Irish as mindless brawn, most were skilled weavers. As the Irish cotton industry expired under English competition, destitute weavers from Cork, Belfast and Dublin brought their skills to Manchester.

Improvements in travel boosted the number of Manchester Irish. In 1818 the first steamer, *Rob Roy,* linked Belfast and Glasgow and by the 1820s there were frequent, regular and cheap services from Cork, Belfast and Dublin to Liverpool and the west coast ports. Those prepared to travel on deck could cross for 3d., a sum within the means of even a pauper. By the 1850s they were an established community and their children, though born in England, regarded themselves as Irish.

Many served as officers and men in the armed forces. By the 1870s one in three regular army soldiers was Irish-born and in

1871 95 per cent of the York garrison was Irish.

The first Irish to settle in Manchester made their home in the north east of the city, Newton, later known as Irish Town, and Angel Meadow. Situated between the River Irk and St. George's Road (later Rochdale Road), over 20,000 people huddled in cramped houses and cellars. Wherever the Irish settled they marked their territory by building a church and in 1829 they built St. Patrick's Catholic Church, Livesey Street. Soon they spread to nearby Ancoats.

The third area they colonised was Chorlton-on-Medlock, where they opened St. Augustine's Church in 1820 and in 1832 the *Manchester Guardian* first referred to it as Little Ireland. It wasn't long before this obscure area of Manchester gained an international reputation and became a magnet for every social commentator of the day. By then the cholera outbreak of 1832 – significantly called 'Irish fever' – branded Little Ireland as the centre of a plague that decimated the population.

Though Little Ireland was to shape the image of the Irish slum, it was the smallest Irish settlement in the city and the shortest-lived. The houses dated from the 1820s and by the late 1840s the development of the railway had swept them away. Dr James Phillips Kay was the first to investigate the conditions there, where the plague had begun. What he discovered horrified the middle classes, who had no knowledge of the life of the poor. Kay discovered one-room cellars, home to sixteen people and a host of animals. He saw rooms so small that it was impossible to stand upright, the ceilings black with cockroaches and every inch of the floor covered with bodies huddled on beds of fetid straw. He found hordes of people living without water, ventilation, sanitation or light. Filthy water from the River Medlock frequently flooded these houses and factory smoke choked off the light and poisoned the air. Average life expectancy was fifteen years.

Kay came to the conclusion that all this was the fault of the Irish immigrants. They had brought 'their debased habits with them' and 'infected' the host community. They were a tribe of savages. Worse, they led their neighbours astray, encouraging them to squander their money on drink and become a burden on society. From this time the image of the Irish as ignorant, unskilled and idle paupers wallowing in filth, crime and drink who, nevertheless, also managed to depress wages and corrupt the health and morals of the native workers, became a fixed part of the English mindset.

Engels, the author of *The Condition of the Working Classes in England*, in 1844, married Mary Kelly, a Manchester Irish woman and a Fenian (see The Boys Who Broke the Van, below), yet this did nothing to soften his opinion of the Manchester Irish and his description of Angel's Meadow reinforced the image of the Irish as a tumour in the body of the city. 'It is not surprising,' Engels wrote, 'that a social class already degraded by industrialisation should be still further degraded by having to live alongside and compete with the uncivilised Irish.' Idle and lacking in character, they were incapable of undertaking any task that involved 'regular apprenticeship and unremitting labour'.

Faucher agreed. When he visited the Irish settlements in the mid-nineteenth century, he noted that the people there were the poorest in the city. Their homes were dirty and derelict. They distilled illicit spirits in their cellars. When Leon Faucher's *Manchester in 1844* was published, it repeated the charge that the Irish brought down the rest of the community. He criticised them for their idleness and lack of ambition, yet, paradoxically, he also accused them of taking the jobs of English workers.

When Reach visited Angel Meadow in 1847 it was densely populated with hovels pressed up against factories and warehouses. He further strengthened the hostile image of the Irish. He described the Irish colony as 'the lowest, most filthy and most wicked locality in Manchester ... inhabited by prostitutes, their bullies, thieves, cadgers, vagrants, tramps and, in the very worst sties of filth and darkness, those unhappy wretches, the low Irish.' Visiting a cellar that was home to Irish immigrants he noted that the room measured only twelve feet by eight and the ceiling was so low that all the occupants permanently stooped. In a corner, a dozen famished figures huddled round a fire. The family made

matches and piled the shavings in a corner where two children
used them for their bed. A further twelve people lived in the cellar. More than anything else the cellars fascinated and horrified
the public: 18,000 people lived in Manchester cellars in the 1830s
and about a third were Irish. The more gruesome the accounts of
their lives, the greater the public interest.

In 1836 a visitor to Manchester described the cellars as 'the
very picture of loathsomeness, receptacles of every species of vermin which can infest the human body'. Most were dark, damp,
ill ventilated and dirty. And newly arrived Irish immigrants, the
poorest of the poor, occupied the worst. The most squalid cellars
were in closed courts or under back-to-back houses. Many were
single rooms, between six and nine feet square. They had no lighting, water or sanitation. Many of the streets had no drainage or
sewage with the result that the cellars were often ankle deep in
human waste. Often the bare earth formed a floor.

Generally the rent for a cellar was half that of the house above.
Many Irish cellar dwellers worked in the worst paid jobs and
could afford nothing else. Many were casual labourers, hawkers
and street vendors. Large numbers worked as porters in Manchester's Smithfield Market or as dealers in second-hand clothes.
However, half the Ancoats Irish cellar-dwellers worked in the
cotton mills. This type of work required good time-keeping,
manual dexterity, regular attendance and good concentration – all
the things the Irish reputedly lacked. But the fact that the Irish
cellar-dwellers were much like their English neighbours did not
stop their hosts seeing them as a threat. They were not regarded
as a settled part of society but as dangerous outsiders.

In fact, the Irish were in many ways no different from other
newcomers. They were mainly young. The census of 1841 high-
lighted a feature of the city that was to remain constant until
the end of the century: over forty per cent of the population and
more than fifty per cent of Salford's were under twenty. Most
were previously 'farm servants' – agricultural labourers who depended on seasonal farm work. Most of these were not Irish but
came from the surrounding counties of Lancashire and Cheshire.

The Irish

No matter where they came from, they needed shelter and this stimulated growth in the building trade. The city was desperately short of housing and this resulted in overcrowding and home-lessness. To make matters worse, much of the new housing was substandard – prone to dampness, with insufficient privies and lacking light and ventilation. None of the houses of this type had running water. After 1850, however, the housing situation began to improve. Fewer of the new houses were back-to-back and the number of people living in cellars fell.

About this time a survey of the cellars around Oldham Road in the St. George's (Angel Meadow) area revealed many cases of overcrowding. One cellar housed nine people, another ten – seven slept on the floor. Many of the cellars in these houses were filthy and without furniture. Cesspits and middens were overflowing and many streets had only two sets of privies. Lots of these hous-es had pigsties at the front door and sometimes the occupants brought their precious animals – their most valuable possessions – into the house at night. Though there were several slaughter-houses in the area, the inhabitants often slaughtered pigs and cattle for their own consumption in the alleys.

The majority of the Irish living in this area were what today we call economic migrants: they came to improve their lives, or in the words of one, 'to get a meal every day'. But many were escap-ing a previous life. Women with bastards, petty criminals, those who had disgraced their families and those fleeing the police em-braced the city's anonymity. Others hoped to find seasonal work in England. For these, Manchester was supposed to be a tempo-rary base, a stopover with a relation or a neighbour from home. But having arrived, something deflected them from their plan. Perhaps they chanced upon a job and stayed. Or the large and established Irish community may have been more appealing than journeying on alone to where they knew no one. Many navvies, who moved around the country in search of large construction projects, fell into this category.

Once an Irish family settled in Manchester they often be-came the focal point for further immigration – their family and neighbours moving from Ireland to join them. They provided a welcoming smile, accommodation and help to find a job. Yet they never lost the sense that they were outcasts and this created strong communal ties that bound the Irish together. Nor was it only their hosts who drove them together in shared opprobrium. There were those who, though strangers themselves, sought to subject them to the oppression they had hoped to escape.

Orangemen set up England's first County Grand Lodge in Manchester early in the nineteenth century. The country's first anti-Catholic riot of the nineteenth century, directed at the Manchester Irish, followed in 1807 with subsequent attacks in 1830 and 1834 further heightening tension. Prejudice also afflicted the Irish in a less spectacular manner. It confined them to the worst jobs and kept them poor. The 1836 commission into the state of the Irish Poor in Great Britain heard that they were 'prevented from advancing from feelings of jealousy. A manufacturer would prefer employing English to Irish simply on the grounds of they being Irish and not being worse workmen.' A host of witnesses testified that the Irish were more industrious and showed a far greater capacity for sustained labour than their English counterparts. Their critics were on firm ground when they complained that the Irish forced their competitors onto poor relief by working for less.

Relations with the police were also poor. Analysis of court records shows that Irish immigrants committed a disproportionate number of minor offences. In 1836 there was much evidence of the production and drinking of illicit alcohol, though the extent to which the Irish were more given to drink than the host community is hard to decide. Drinking on a Saturday night was common among the Irish, but not on other nights.

Hostility to the police also united them. The 1840 Little Ireland riot was only one extreme example of antagonism flaring into violence. When the police entered the area to stop the customary Sunday morning gambling and arrested two young boys – William Donnelly and Patrick Connelly – for playing pitch and toss, they set off what the newspapers described as 'a most desperate battle between nine policemen and scores of Irish'. Two officers suffered serious injuries.

The Irish saw the police as enemies and regarded any who entered Little Ireland as fair game. The Irish had a reputation for resisting arrest as a matter of principle and would, in the words of one peeler, 'struggle until the shirt had been torn from their backs' – by which time a crowd of locals would have gathered to help their countryman.

The influx of impoverished Irish in the early 1840s further strained relations with the host community and confirmed the popular belief that the Irish were parasites. Between 1841 and 1843 Manchester poor law unions removed 2,647 Irish from the township on the grounds that they had no right of settlement and therefore no right to relief.

The Irish formed a large proportion of the poor. Poor relief figures suggest they also made up a high proportion of the city's paupers. Half of those seeking relief from the New Bridge Workhouse were Irish, mostly from Ancoats. They formed the bulk of Smithfield Market's workforce and most of the street sellers, hawkers and domestic servants in the area. Poverty bound the Irish together, as did their powerful sense of kinship, but starvation put great strain on this loyalty in the mid-1840s.

As conditions in Ireland deteriorated, culminating in the Famine of 1847, the pressure to emigrate became irresistible. The influx of destitute, disease-ridden spectres during the 1840s heightened the hostility of the host community and confirmed their belief that the Irish were a threat. In the short-term they threatened to overwhelm the city's poor relief provision. In 1847 Manchester Poor Law Union reported that 1,500 Irish had arrived over a few weeks. This was at a time when droves of immigrants from surrounding Lancashire were also descending on the city. Of Manchester's population of 400,000 in 1851, fifty-five per cent were born elsewhere and seventy-two per cent of those were twenty or under. Of these, 52,500 were Irish-born. This made the Irish by far the largest group of newcomers. In 1851 Lancashire had the highest proportion of Irish-born people of any mainland county, about thirteen per cent. Almost eight out of every ten Irish in the North West lived in Manchester and Liverpool.

Those who came in the 1847-51 period were largely rural and destitute. Half a million of those who arrived from Dublin from 1847-53 were paupers. This put an extra poor rate burden on those with a £12 house and posed a threat to the labourers at the bottom of the economic pile, for the Irish worked for less than a subsistence wage. A report to the Manchester Board of Guardians for May 1847 blamed Irish immigrants for the introduction of typhus, scarlet fever, smallpox and measles. The same applied to Salford. In 1800, the old Salford had a population of a mere 7,000. By 1900 it had soared to 220,000, an increase unmatched anywhere in the country. The result was cramped back-to-back houses. By the late Victorian period the Irish formed one third of the population and were a major source of cheap labour.

From the 1850s Manchester was an enclave of Irish political separatism second only to London. In addition to the settled Irish community there was a constant flow of 'harvestmen' who passed through every year on their way to Cheshire, Yorkshire, Lincolnshire and the east of England. The Famine influx coincided with a general influx from rural areas and economic distress in the textile industry. The new arrivals crammed into Ancoats and Irishtown. The 1851 census shows that forty-two per cent (fifty if their children are counted) of the Angel Meadow population were Irish-born. Once there they generally married their own: four-fifths of marriages were between two Irish people. By 1861 the Irish-born made up one in five of the city's population. They sought to solve the housing problem that resulted from their poverty by multiple occupancy. On average the density of population in all-Irish or mainly-Irish houses in Angel Meadow was ten persons compared to 6.4 for non-Irish households. It was common for as many as thirty people to occupy a single house.

But their priests and not the cramped housing held the Irish together. Invariably Irish and Irish-speakers, like most of their parishioners, they were the exile's last link with home. They had much in common with their congregation and identified with them against English employers and authorities.

The priests frequently visited Ireland and returned with news of home. Father Daniel Hearne, a renowned Irish Town priest, incensed by the deterioration of conditions in Ireland and the onset of the Famine, became progressively more radical in his politics. The ideas of the Young Irelanders captivated him and in expressing his support for them he aroused opposition from other clergy and even sections of his congregation, eventually forcing him to withdraw from Irish Town and then Manchester, returning to Ireland.

Yet this did nothing to reduce the role of the church and its ancillary institutions as the focus of the Irish community's life in the city. Between 1832 and 1860 nine new churches opened in Manchester. In the 1750s an old dye house near the River Irwell, just off Parsonage Street, served as the city's only Catholic church. For fear of a raid, sentinels stood at the top of the steps leading to the building. In 1753 services moved to a room just off High Street – Roman Entry. In 1762 the first Catholic baptismal register opened.

St. Chad's became Manchester's first post-Reformation church. It opened in Rook Street, behind Mosley Street, in 1774. The priest was Fr. John Orrell and ten years later its congregation numbered over 500. St. Mary's Mulberry Street opened in 1794 by public subscription, which also paid for it to be rebuilt in 1848 after the roof collapsed.

St. Augustine's in Granby Row served Little Ireland. It opened in October 1820 at a cost of £10,000. St. Patrick's in Livesey Street appeared in 1832 to serve Irish Town. Appropriately it was built in the shape of a T (cruciform) after the style so often found in Ireland. The belfry was the first erected in a Catholic church in Manchester since the Reformation. In erecting a belfry it became the first Catholic church to break the law, its congregation the first to carry the crucifix in public procession through the streets of the city. It soon had a convent, the first in the city since the Reformation, and its school was the first Catholic school for girls in Manchester.

The Church consolidated and extended the Irish character of the area. St. Patrick's served the Catholics of Angel's Meadow which soon sprouted other institutions: a Convent of the Presentation Order, St. Patrick's Boys' School, St. Bridget's Orphanage and, in 1845, a community of Christian Brothers. Partly because the Irish were putting down roots, large scale anti-Irish disturbances diminished after 1855. The Irish were winning a grudging acceptance. Yet competition in the workplace between unskilled workers and the Irish remained intense.

This competition was nowhere more acute than in the building trade. It was the one key industry that remained almost untouched by mechanisation and mass production methods. Apart from the introduction of the machine-made brick, it remained as labour intensive as ever. It employed almost three-quarters of a million workers in 1871 and was the fourth biggest employer of labour in the country. It was a magnet for Irish immigrants. It provided work for the unskilled, offered an outdoor life to farm boys, allowed them to work with family and fellow countrymen and gave those with a background in the Irish building trade the opportunity to exploit their experience. In 1851 there were about 20,000 building workers in Manchester and Salford and a very large percentage were Irish. The qualities that endeared Irish workers to their employers were precisely those that antagonised indigenous workers competing with them for employment. Among employers they had a reputation for hard work and it was said that they could toil at a pace that no Englishman could sustain. John Wallis, a prominent London master builder, told a Royal Commission he preferred Irish workers because of their conscientious attitude and their courteous manner. His only complaint was that many of them went home to Ireland at harvest time.

The findings of the 1836 Royal Commission suggest that the Irish were in the forefront of trade union activity and conspicuously active in all the major building disputes in Manchester from 1833 to 1870. The records of the Manchester Bricklayers Labourers' Union confirm this. In 1856 it had 900 members, organised into nine lodges. All the officials were Irish, as were the great majority of members. The Union was part of community life, for its trustee and treasurer was Canon Toole, parish priest of St. Wilfred's, Hulme, an area with a sizeable Irish community.

The Irish in England had a strong tradition of cooperation. Their suspicion of the British government, which regarded them as aliens in their own land, gave rise to a culture of cooperative self-reliance. Then, just as the Irish were putting down roots and winning a degree of acceptance in Manchester, the city was the scene of events that cast them in the role of murderous aliens.

The Boys Who Broke the Van

The Irish Republican Brotherhood – the Fenians – a secret revolutionary organisation sworn to establishing an Irish republic by force of arms, was, in the view of one historian, 'probably the most powerful and far reaching conspiracy the world has ever known'. It became a real threat to Britain in the years after 1865 when Irish Americans with military experience in the American Civil War stiffened its ranks. These, together with others who had been driven from home and forced to settle in Britain and America, provided leadership for the movement both in Ireland and in areas with a large Irish population such as Manchester. In 1867 the Irish community in Manchester was in the vanguard of the struggle for Irish independence.

The Fenian rising of 1867 petered out in Ireland almost before it began. John Joseph Corydon, the informer, foiled a bold Fenian plan to capture Chester Castle.

Colonel Kelly, the driving force behind the Fenians' struggle for Irish independence, and his aide-de-camp, Captain Deasy, escaped to England. They were determined to continue the rising and planned to bring together the Fenian leaders in a council of war. Manchester was their first port of call. It was there that misfortune befell them, the first in a chain of events which led William Allen, Michael Larkin and Michael O'Brien to the scaffold.

As they left a meeting in Shudehill, near the city centre, Kelly and Deasy realised that a group of policemen were watching them. They stepped into the shadows of a doorway, waiting for them to pass. But the police cornered them and, after a fierce struggle, captured them both. The British authorities couldn't believe their luck. The Fenian leader had fallen into their hands and the movement was about to be smashed. But they reckoned without Edward O'Meagher Condon, Kelly's comrade from the American Civil War. He sped to Manchester to mastermind a rescue.

The British government didn't appreciate the strength of Fenianism. Its leaders may have lacked political sophistication but there was no shortage of courage and audacity. And among the population of Manchester there were many prepared to risk everything for their leader. On Wednesday 18 September 1867, two warders pushed Kelly and Deasy into a Black Maria parked outside the magistrate's court, ready to return them to Bellevue prison. Just before leaving the court, the authorities changed the arrangements for the transportation of the prisoners. Instead of one of the policemen riding on top taking the keys to the Black Maria, they gave them to the sergeant inside the van. This was the tragic Sergeant Charlie Brett.

The van left the centre of the city by Hyde Road, a long, straight highway with a scattering of houses interspersed by open land. When Condon planned the rescue, he had immediately seen the potential of the spot where the railway crossed the road: it was perfect for an ambush. As soon as the van entered the bridge arch, pistol shots exploded. Shrieks filled the air. The police scattered under a torrent of stones. An iron bar, hammers and a sabre pounded the van. A rock thudded against the roof. A shot pinged off the door lock and there was a scream. Sergeant Brett clasped his face, but the blood spurted through his fingers. A prisoner stuffed the keys through a ventilator and Kelly and Deasy, their hands manacled, leapt from the van.

A roar went up as the warders from Bellevue prison appeared. A horde of hostile civilians hurtled round the arch after Kelly. The mob caught O'Brien, who had the job of covering Kelly's retreat, and kicked him senseless. They also took Larkin, Allen and

Condon. Later police arrested the unfortunate Michael Maguire at home. Though he was not a Fenian and had nothing to do with the rescue he was to become the final member of the group of 'principal offenders'.

The effrontery of the rescue outraged the Manchester authorities. Fenian fever swept the country. The mayor armed the police and swore in thousands of special constables. Kelly had a price on his head and the police, fired with anti-Irish feeling, combed out the Irish areas of the city and arrested hundreds of suspects. But Kelly remained free. On one occasion he dressed as a priest and walked through a troop of armed policemen heading for the house he had just left. He then escaped to New York where, in 1908, he died in his sleep.

The Government was determined to make an example of the prisoners. They established a special commission, led by the Lord Chancellor, Justice Blackburn, to try them in Manchester. The court room and the whole city bristled with armed military. There was no proof that any of the accused fired the shot that killed Brett, yet the jury convicted all five of murder and the judge sentenced them to hang. Though each swore he had not fired the shot, they all accepted their fate with such heartbreaking courage and dignity that it is impossible to read the court records without being moved. They proudly affirmed their part in Kelly's escape. All except one.

Among this heroism and valour, there was the hapless Maguire. He stood in the dock because of his striking resemblance to an unknown participant in the rescue. Witness after witness picked him out. But he had an alibi. His innocence was so obvious that the journalists who reported the case sent a petition to the Home Secretary, Gaythorne Hardy, who granted a free pardon.

Condon also escaped the gallows. His American citizenship saved him. But for Allen, only nineteen years old, Larkin, a married man with four children and O'Brien, a veteran of the American Civil War, there was no reprieve, despite protests from Europe, America and many liberal and socialist groups in Britain, including radical MPs and the thousands of English working men who gathered at Clerkenwell, a centre of working class radicalism, to sign a petition for clemency.

During the weeks between the rescue and the execution, Manchester was under martial law. Such was the resentment against the Irish that none was safe outside his own locality. The authorities expected another rescue bid and the city became an armed camp. In the days before the execution bosses put their workers to defending mills and warehouses and the government stationed field guns in Stanley Street, and blocked all roads leading to the New Bailey prison, the place of execution. A detachment of infantry looked out from the railway bridge abutting the prison and the prison walls bristled with cannon muzzles. Shortly before the executioner brought the three condemned men from their cells, a company of 72 Highlanders, stationed inside the prison, marched to the temporary platform that had been built inside the wall of the gaol. There was to be no rescue.

Instead the executions spurred a great upsurge of nationalistic and anti-English feeling. This showed itself in massive demonstrations or commemorations not only in Manchester but everywhere in the world where there was an Irish community. No action of the British authorities in the nineteenth century deepened the bitterness between Ireland and England more than the hanging of Allen, Larkin and O'Brien. *The Freeman's Journal* expressed the opinion of the Irish community when it said Britain had executed them because they were Irish and had totally overlooked the political nature of their crime.

Brett's death also had reverberations. It gave rise to an upsurge in anti-Irish feeling, expressed in the way the English press depicted the Irish as ape-like brutes, slaves to irrational anger and savage passions. Every significant Fenian outrage, particularly the Clerkenwell explosion of 1867, a botched prison-break that left twelve dead and 126 seriously injured, further inflamed anti-Irish sentiment. Fourteen years later, an explosion at the Salford barracks killed a child and maimed her mother, and again raised the spectre of the murderous Fenian.

The tragic case of nine-year-old Ellen Higgins illustrates the extent of anti-Irish feeling. In June 1869, Ellen and several other children were walking along Little Peter Street in Manchester when a group of youths, identifying them as Catholics, stopped them and told them to take the green ribbons from their hair. The boys attacked them and kicked Ellen so brutally about the body and head that she sustained severe injury to her internal organs, though it was brain damage that actually killed her. The incident attracted very little media attention and no expression of official outrage. The death of a child was by no means unusual at the time and the press had no interest in stressing the sectarian dimensions of the murder.

Part of this anti-Irish sentiment was due to the anti-Catholic bigotry, which ran through every facet of Victorian society. In addition there was a great deal of racial bigotry – as displayed in the many anti-Irish cartoons which depicted the Irish as barely human. This anti-Irish feeling, however, declined in the 1880s. Other groups, particularly the Jews, became the object of popular resentment. There were still isolated attacks on Catholic churches – as late as 1902 a Gorton mob tried to burn down a Catholic church. The absence of a strong Orange presence, however, meant that full-scale confrontations were infrequent. The events of 12 July 1888, when 100 Orangemen attacked the Canal Street area of Miles Platting, a well-known Irish area, were unusual. It took forty peelers almost an hour to quell the disorder.

Generally, however, animosity was less overt. Whit – with its tradition of Catholic and Anglican walks – was a time of friction, when the Rochdale Road area, from Oldham Road to Collyhurst Road, was frequently the scene of pitched battles. The opposing sides were boys from the Lancastrian School, Marshall Street, Rochdale Road and those from St. Joseph's Catholic School in the same area.

As the century progressed, and the percentage of Irish-born people in the city declined, there nevertheless remained an enduring Irish subculture. Partly this was due to religion. Nearly all working class Catholics were Irish or of Irish descent. Second and even third generation Irish remained strongly tied to their culture and their faith. They also continued to figure prominently among the city's criminal class. Of those arrested in 1870, 9,000 were English and 3,500 Irish – a disproportionate number of Irish,who made up one in ten of the population but almost four out of ten of those arrested.

By the 1880s the city's Irish were no longer concentrated in a few areas but spread throughout all the poorer areas, which they shared with the indigenous population and other immigrants. It is true that Hulme had a distinctively Irish flavour, but the real focus of Irish Manchester was in the north, especially Ancoats, Collyhurst, Angel Meadow and, to a lesser extent, Miles Platting.

St. Michael's ward, in the centre of Ancoats, was one of the most Irish areas in Manchester. A contemporary account describes it as 'a district of dull, depressing streets in which are crowded together the houses of market porters and other labouring men'. In sharp contrast the suburban areas of Withington and Chorlton-cum-Hardy – areas which eighty years later were to become centres of the Manchester Irish community – had fewer than one in twenty Catholic residents. The majority of these were Irish domestics.

Economically, the Irish remained at the bottom of the heap. For most of the nineteenth century few obtained the relatively secure work offered by the mills. The general feeling among employers was that the Irish lacked the discipline, regular habits and intelligence required of a good factory worker. Consequently, NINA – No Irish Need Apply – attached to job advertisements, was common. Most Irishmen still found work in unskilled, insecure and badly paid labouring jobs. This is reflected in the large number who ended up in the city's workhouses and prisons. The single most important employer of the Irish was Smithfield Market in Ancoats.

There were some Irish merchants and stallholders in Smithfield but most of those who worked there were porters and labourers. There was also an army of Irish street traders and hawkers of all kinds who relied on the market for a precarious livelihood. As late as 1900 about one in five of those living in St. Michael's ward depended on the market. As hawkers and street traders the Irish replaced the Jews. Contemporaries maintained they achieved this because they were the only people prepared to work longer and accept a lower profit margin than the thrifty Jews. None but the Irish, it was said, could live on the meagre pittance they eked out.

The nucleus of the Irish community was the church. The majority of Irish Catholics were practising – they went to church every week. This marked them off from the rest of the working class community. Among Anglicans living in Ancoats church attendance was almost an eccentricity. One of the things that bound the Irish to the Church was its links with home. The vast majority of Manchester priests were both Irish and nationalists. This was evident in the North East Manchester by-election of 1891 when only one of the constituency's Catholic priests failed to campaign for the Home Rule candidate.

The Church in Manchester celebrated its links with Ireland. It commemorated the feast of St. Patrick with Masses, entertainment in the church hall, the blessing of shamrock and, until the 1890s, a Catholic rally held in the Free Trade Hall. In all this the parish school was an adjunct of the Church. Until the Great War virtually all Catholic children received their education in Catholic schools. And it was this combination of faith and national identity that made the city's reaction to the Irish so ambivalent.

The Most Formidable Weapon

Manchester held out its hand to greet the Irish. Then it hit them in the face. Anti-Catholic bigotry was endemic in every level of British society and for most of the nineteenth century Irish and Catholic were synonymous. Manchester and Salford were deeply imbued with anti-Popish venom.

There were very few indigenous Catholics in Manchester. With the exception of a few Eccles families, the famed Lancashire Catholics of the sixteenth century, who remained committed to the faith despite state persecution, were not Mancunians. The city was a centre of Protestantism until the Irish influx of the nineteenth century diluted its Reformation zeal. Their hosts attributed many of the reputed faults of the Irish to their pernicious faith, to which they were uncritical adherents. However, this was not their only deficiency. The English also dismissed them as racially and intellectually inferior to the Anglo-Saxons and claimed they were totally incapable of governing themselves. They represented a lower form of civilisation. There were many in the great conurbation who were ready to put up a fight against these pernicious invaders.

Salford's anti-Catholic organisations tell us a lot about the conurbation's attitudes. Hugh Stowell, Vicar of Christ Church, Acton Square, was typical of the paranoid anti-Catholicism common in the mid-nineteenth century. Nothing alarmed him more than the re-emergence of Catholicism in the twin cities, making the area a principal centre of the faith in England. The new Catholic pro-cathedral of St. John's, on Chapel Street, symbolised this threat. Built on a grand scale, with the tallest steeple in Lancashire, it was an affront to the good Protestant people of the city. Stowell's anti-Catholic rants appeared in widely circulated penny leaflets. His arguments became the accepted wisdom among large sections of the working class and spawned a number of anti-Catholic organisations, including branches of the Auxiliary Irish Society of London and the British Reformation Society.

In the 1830s militant anti-Catholics formed the Salford Operative Protestant Society to spread their ideas among workers. The Manchester equivalent was the Protestant Tradesmen's and Operatives' Association. Both organisations were extremely voluble and the local press provided sympathetic coverage. Dr Giacento Achilli, a renegade Dominican friar and one of the first anti-Catholic rabble-rousers, was an avid proponent of these societies' efforts to impregnate popular culture with anti-Popery. He often attracted large crowds, which he regaled with tales of virtuous Protestants rotting in Papal dungeons.

The Famine of 1848 saw an influx of starving Irish paupers

choke off the city's charity and gave a great boost to anti-Irish hatred. Verminous, plague-ridden and prepared to work for starvation wages, they were a threat to the poor of Manchester with whom they were in competition for unskilled work and cheap housing. For those at the bottom of the economic pile, life was already a hand-to-mouth affair. Now these newcomers threatened to snatch the bread from their hand.

Others ploughing the same furrow of bigotry in the 1850s were Signor Alessandro Garazzi, the Reverend Count Wlodarski and Baron and Baroness de Camin, all of whom had the background and aura of third-rate music hall acts. Many of their meetings sparked violence and, in the 1850s, a number of anti-Catholic riots – in Stockport and Hulme in 1852 and Wigan in 1859.

The ranks of the militant anti-Catholics contained a number of national figures. Thomas Hughes, author of *Tom Brown's Schooldays*, and Charles Kingsley, one of the most prolific of Victorian writers, played a role in promoting anti-Catholicism nationally. All this trickled down to the English poor, drove a wedge between them and the Irish and by the 1860s created a strong anti-Irish tradition in parts of Manchester and Salford. Many blamed the Irish for the cotton famine of the 1860s that plunged Lancashire into destitution, forcing hundreds of thousands of people onto poor relief. Extreme anti-Irish, anti-Catholic bigotry showed itself most blatantly in violent attacks on the Irish population. Resentment and rivalry were there from the start. Isolated instances of small-scale violence occurred throughout this period.

The most infamous instance, however, was in 1868 when William Murphy brought his anti-Catholicism circus to Manchester. Murphy was the son of an Irish schoolmaster from Kilrush, County Clare. Soon after joining the Protestant Electoral Union he became its star turn, promoting its militant anti-Catholic agenda. Its aim was to create religious violence. His strategy was always the same. He hired a hall as near to the heart of the Catholic community as possible and delivered a series of inflammatory lectures. These culminated in a no-women, no under-twenty-ones diatribe on the supposed secrets of the confessional. This gave

Murphy an opportunity to deliver a pornographic harangue on the iniquities of the Catholic clergy, who allegedly used the confessional to corrupt girls and young women by asking intimate questions in order to put obscene ideas into their heads. Now a member of the Orange Order and the Protestant Evangelical Mission, he sparked violence wherever he went. Riots in Plymouth, Wolverhampton, Birmingham and Rochdale made him front page news. To quell the disorder in Wolverhampton the authorities called out the military and thereby ensured Murphy an enthusiastic reception wherever he spoke.

The Birmingham riot was one of the most violent. His meetings there attracted crowds of up to 100,000 which he incited to attack Catholic churches, schools, convents and homes throughout the city. A crowd of between 50,000 and 100,000 people gathered, causing considerable damage to property. Overwhelmed, the Mayor had to reinforce the police with 400 soldiers, including 100 cavalry together with 600 special constables. Far more important, however, was the new intolerant atmosphere these incidents created and the accompanying inter-communal violence. This soon reached Manchester and its environs, the centre of Catholicism in the north of England. In January 1868 it took the authorities two days to quell an anti-Catholic riot in Stalybridge.

In March 1868 a crowd of 6,000 gathered on Rochdale's Cronkeyshaw Common to hear Murphy's tirade. The authorities, however, arrested him and thereby prevented the planned series of lectures in the town. However, this did nothing to stop religious violence in Rochdale. A Protestant mob attacked St. John's Church and the parochial house, the home of Fr. John Dowling, in Ann Street, where a force of Catholics had gathered to repulse them. On release from prison Murphy set up camp at railway sidings on Milkstone Road, where he continued to inflame his followers. It wasn't long before the mob, brandishing burning crosses, descended on The Mount (Mount Pleasant) and other Catholic areas. Again St. John's was the focus of the assault.

Inevitably Murphy's visit to Ashton-under-Lyne in 1868 resulted in disorder. Two hundred Irishmen took pre-emptive action: they attacked a meeting of Murphyites and Orangemen. Not to be outdone in violence, Murphy gathered a counter-mob of 500, armed with scythes, pokers, swords, bayonets and revolvers. As they descended on the town's Irish quarter, over 100 Irish Orangemen, many from Ashton, swelled their ranks. They swept aside the police barrier and as they stormed the rows of terraced houses, women filled their aprons with stones as they prepared to defend their homes. But they were no match for the rabid hordes who smashed windows and kicked in doors, before making bonfires of the contents of the houses. They gutted 111 homes, destroying every stick of furniture.

Sectarian hatred did not inspire all the rioters. According to newspaper reports, many were local 'layabouts' and 'bullyboys', delighted to take advantage of the opportunity to give vent to their resentment against Paddies and Popery. When they reached St. Anne's they broke into Fr. Crumbleholme's presbytery and wrecked it. The church was next. They smashed the altar, stripped the building of statues and paintings and destroyed them all. They then smashed the windows and the contents of the parish school. From there they marched on St. Mary's, where the parish priest, Monsignor James Provost Beesley was saying evening Mass. When he heard of the advancing mob, he sent the women home while he and twenty parishioners prepared to defend the church by barricading themselves in. Though they withstood the siege for two hours, the church suffered such extensive damage that it was later demolished. The damage to houses, shops, church and the parish school was such that many years later one observer likened it to the devastation on parts of the Western Front during the Great War.

The bitterness of the riots lingered long after the event. Catholics were indignant that, according to them, the police made no attempt to quell the mob and seemed to be concerned only to restrict them to their part of the town. When the police, aided by troops, eventually restored order, the anti-Catholic elements felt aggrieved. They alleged that a Father Daley of Rochdale shot and wounded one of the leaders of the riot, Rueben Bailey. The Assize

Court jury acquitted the priest by the narrowest of margins, but Bailey's supporters used the case to fuel anti-Catholic feeling.

When Murphy announced his intention to visit Manchester, Irishmen organised to protect Catholic buildings. The violence he sparked in Ashton, Bury, Blackburn and Rochdale had already led the Bolton authorities to ban him. St. Francis' monastery in West Gorton, in the process of construction, had recently attracted local hostility and was clearly a target for Murphy's hordes. The extent of the fear Murphy inspired is shown by the decision of Manchester's Chief Constable, Captain William Palin, to meet him at the railway station on his arrival in Manchester. He asked the rabble-rouser not to deliver his planned speech. But Murphy had more in common with Ian Paisley than his inveterate hatred of Catholics. He adamantly asserted his right to free speech, insisting that no Papist savages would prevent him alerting the British people to the dangers of Popery. Chief Constable Palin, however, was intent on making Murphy's stay as uncomfortable as possible. He searched him and found a ten-chamber revolver and a knuckle-duster, which he described as 'one of the most formidable weapons I have seen for some time'.

Murphy had hired a lecture room on Cooke Street, off Stretford Road, not 300 yards from St. Winifred's Catholic Church, but his arrest prevented him from lecturing. On 1 September 1868, William Murphy appeared before the Manchester city magistrates charged with inciting a breach of the peace. On this occasion the actions of the police prevented disorder but its anticipation heightened tensions and once more accentuated the difference between the Irish and their neighbours.

Yet for all this it is wrong to think that the Irish lived in isolated, embattled enclaves surrounded by hostility. In many ways they were distinctive and inward-looking, bound together by values not shared by their neighbours. Yet even the most Irish sections of the city were never homogeneous ghettos and their occupants were always part of a wider working class community and shared many of its values.

In particular they shared the fierce loyalty to the street and neighbourhood that was common to Mancunians. And when it came to ideas of masculinity, they subscribed fully to the belief that a man had to be hard and had to show his hardness in combat.

It's not surprising the Irish played a big part in scuttling – the violent street disorder that marked much of this period. Some of the era's most notable thugs were Irish. Among the most notorious were Broughton's Jimmy O'Neill, Red Shelley from the Adelphi, Jerry Hoddy in Greengate and Thomas Calligan, the king of the Hulme scuttlers. Apart from being Irish, there was nothing to distinguish them from their English counterparts. They shared the same fierce loyalty to the streets in which they grew up and were neither more nor less brutal than other scuttlers – and no less committed to 'hardness' as the measure of a man's worth.

The Irish gave and received the customary kindnesses that came under the umbrella of 'neighbourliness'. Yet there was a limit to this. Like stones in mortar, the Irish were part of the mix of working class culture, yet always distinguishable. The Church discouraged 'mixed marriages', between a Catholic and a non-Catholic, which in practice meant between an Irish person and a non-Irish. Irish antipathy to the English also meant that most preferred to marry 'one of their own'. But more than anything else it was the stigma of marrying an Irish Catholic that greatly reduced the frequency of such marriages. Even in the meanest Manchester and Salford slum, when overt anti-Irish violence had virtually disappeared, marrying an Irish Catholic involved a great loss of status. Nor did the absence of violence mean that the Irish lost their aura of criminality. Figures for both arrests and imprisonment show that they still played a big part in crime.

3

Crime

Looking After Yourself

No description of Manchester's image is complete without mentioning its reputation for crime. From the 1840s onwards people assumed that everyone from Manchester was a thief. It was a city of rogues, prostitutes, con men, thieves, professional beggars, frauds, charlatans, hucksters, spivs, burglars, quacks, pickpockets, counterfeiters and card sharps. There was no dishonesty, no depravity, no form of violence known to man, that was not practised on Manchester's streets.

Yet even the most prejudiced observer had to admit that not every Mancunian was an inveterate rogue. In reality there were as many fine gradations in working class society as there were pubs in Manchester.

In 1851 Victoria visited Manchester. In her journal she expressed her satisfaction with the visit. She was delighted with 'the order and good behaviour of the people', the most impressive she had seen in her 'many progressions through the capitals and cities' of her kingdom. This favourable impression echoed the mid-century optimism of middle class Manchester. The respectable working man was subscribing to the self-help philosophy and the cooperative movement and not the revolutionary societies that terrified Europe's propertied classes and threatened to undermine social order.

It is difficult to exaggerate the allure of respectability in the nineteenth century. It was the chief aspiration of all those outside the solid middle class and the aristocracy whose claim to respectability was unquestionable. Within the working class there were distinctions – as clear as the distinction between the rag picker and royalty – separating the 'respectable' working family from the 'rough' and the 'common'. The extent to which one was clean, honest, industrious, sober and chaste was the measure of respectability. These were the traditional working class values. Being feckless, idle, improvident and self-indulgent led to the loss of respectability and a downward slide into ostracism. Those who were not respectable merged into the criminal underworld. This is one of the reasons why many commentators saw crime as a moral problem.

The respectable man believed education was the way to improve himself and his family. The focus of his life outside work was the home – not the pub. He believed in moderation, especially in drink. Abstemiousness was an aspect of his commitment to thrift and self-sufficiency. He was courteous and polite, quiet and self-effacing. Yet working people were proud it was they who had made Britain the greatest industrial power in the world and built the foundations of the British Empire. Similarly, they took pride in their work and the skills it required – especially if they were craftsmen.

Respectable working people were sober and clean. They dressed modestly, went to church and restricted their sexual activity to the confines of marriage. They worked hard and their recreations were worthy – they pursued improving and healthy hobbies and didn't confine themselves to the frivolous. The respectable had proper regard for morals and morality. They were self-sufficient and independent, relying on their own resources. The respectable paid their own way, looked after themselves and their families. The philosophy of self-help was a version of respectability. The respectable did not get drunk, did not resort to obscenities, dressed tidily and kept themselves and their homes clean and neat. Most of all, they were law-abiding.

The rough or common were the opposite of all these things. Thrift and foresight were alien to them – they lived for the here and now, for drink and gambling, for a 'sing-song' and a 'bit of a do'. They squandered their money and lived a hand to mouth existence. They fought and cursed. They rejected authority and fell out with the foreman and the employer and had no respect for the police or the minister. But what most separated them from their respectable neighbours was their excessive concern with proving their masculinity. Status within their section of the working class was very much tied up with being 'hard'. This more than anything was the measure of masculinity. A man who could hold his own in a scrap and take a beating when outnumbered, while giving a good account of himself, merited respect. He would, of course, reap vengeance and thereby retain his honour and his status. He stood for no slight on his masculinity and was quick to avenge affronts. Closely allied to this was the importance of holding one's ale. A man who could drink a large quantity of beer without showing any ill effects thereby affirmed his masculinity.

The respectable maintained his status by fulfilling his role as a breadwinner. His status lay in providing for his family by his own honest endeavours. He prided himself on never having to depend on charity and on being financially self-sufficient, just as those who were not respectable prided themselves on being physically self-sufficient. Those who measured themselves by their ability to scrap were by no means eccentric. Fighting was an everyday part of working class life. A man who was challenged had to accept the challenge or else lose face and put up with relentless taunting and mockery. The fight was in public – usually the street – and watched by a large crowd.

The street was important to all working people. They were people of the streets, especially the poor and less respectable. The respectable used the streets only for travelling to and from work, church and the shops. Working people's children played there but anyone loitering in the streets, especially at night, was suspect. The noise, bustle and dirt amazed visitors to working class areas. The street was the workplace of the pedlar, the knife-grinder, the tumbler, the dustman, the sweep, the carter and the prostitute. The street was the slum-dweller's village green, the child's playground and an extension to his cramped home. How a person appeared on the street was an infallible guide to respectability. Flashy or scanty clothes, too much exposed breast, the absence of corsets, untidy hair, dirty linen – all spoke of being common.

As for boys and young men, the extent to which they went in for 'larking about' or kidding was a measure of their respectability. This took many forms but generally it involved aggressive repartee, practical jokes, illicit smoking, drinking and raucous singing and horseplay. It was a hazardous activity. Every week during the 19th century foremen in Manchester engineering works sacked an average of three apprentices for larking about. Larking about on the streets was designed to make something happen – to create excitement. It gave rise to crazes and fads, as short-lived as they were dangerous. So at one time a common lark was to push one of your mates through a shop window.

This sort of thing, together with street gambling and loitering on corners after dark, became a focus of police activity during the 1890s. The result was violence against the police. Those involved in this war of attrition with the police were at the bottom end of the social ladder, where the 'common' verged on the underworld. There was no clear-cut dividing line where one started and the other ended. One shaded into the other as imperceptibly as autumn into winter.

But regardless of their position in the social hierarchy they all shared an insatiable passion for the same thing – the spectacle of death.

Be It On Your Head

He smashed her skull like a Fabergé egg under a boot. He clubbed her with a poker – solid iron, a yard long and an inch thick – with such force that it buckled in his hand.

Sentenced to hang, Tim Flaherty plunged to his death outside Salford's New Bailey prison in the mild spring air of an April Saturday in 1868. The pushing, clawing crowd, many who had been there since the night before, were not disappointed. A fifty-strong gang of youths jeered Flaherty when he appeared on the scaffold.

'Where's your poker, Tim?' they called. 'You'll need it to poke the fires of hell.'

Throughout the night as they marched up and down singing 'When Johnny Comes Marching Home' and an obscene version of 'Glory Hallelujah', their shrill voices bounced off the prison walls. This incident captures many of the characteristics of Mancunians at this time. They were adamantly unsentimental to the extent of lacking basic human compassion. The death of a criminal was not an occasion for empathy – it was a time to delight in the prospect of a bad lot getting what he deserved. There was a great deal of bravado in this display, yet it announced to the world that they held nothing sacred and feared nothing, not even death.

This combination of callous indifference, cocky defiance and calculated disregard for the opinions of their betters sums up the spirit of Mancunians in the second half of the nineteenth century. These characteristics have endured to the present day. Yet when we look back on Victorian England, we tend to see not this brutality but stability, security and good order. Despite all the evidence to the contrary we imagine a world in which faith and morality ruled, in which people knew their place. We see the family as the centre of a well-ordered society bolstered by decency, decorum and patriotism, leavened by pride in a great Empire and a navy that ruled the waves. But it didn't feel like that at the time. For all their smug self-satisfaction and moral certainties, the Victorians were profoundly insecure. They felt they were sitting on a volcano that might erupt at any time. They saw themselves as living through a time of perilous change and uncertainty.

Communists, anarchists and socialists were at large in every country of the world, threatening kings and governments. Nowhere were they more audacious than in Ireland, at the heart of the Empire. In Manchester itself, in broad daylight, Fenians murdered a policeman and snatched their leader from the grasp of the authorities. Then there were the terrible uncertainties of trade recessions that struck the country with sickening regularity. They plunged millions into desperation and threatened the fabric of society. The cotton famine of the 1860s was only the most extreme of many, including those of 1867-1870 and 1878-1880.

And death stood at everyone's shoulder. It was ever present: the death of children, of mothers in childbirth, of great swathes of the city when typhus struck. Contagious disease was no respecter of persons. It even claimed Prince Albert, Queen Victoria's consort. A man who tore his finger on a rose bush might die of septicaemia.

Then, of course, there was crime. Crime was such an intrinsic part of Victorian life that people took it for granted. It was something people had to tolerate. For the most part they regarded it as unchangeable, like the climate. This, however, does not mean that people did not worry about it. The letters pages of local newspapers demonstrate that crime was a cause of serious concern during the whole of this period. This was particularly so in Manchester, which was widely regarded as the crime capital of Britain.

There is plenty of evidence to suggest that crime was worse in Manchester than in any comparable city. This evidence is of two types. First there are the crime statistics.

Crime statistics are notoriously difficult to interpret. When Disraeli said, 'There are three kinds of lies: lies, damn lies and statistics,' he could well have been thinking of crime statistics. Faced with damning statistics in 1868, Manchester's Chief Constable William Palin made a valiant attempt to counter the unfavourable interpretation put on these figures and the resulting criticism of the efficiency of the city force. Yet the figures prove crime was a major problem and show why the city was a criminal's paradise.

If we compare Manchester with its nearest equivalent city, Liverpool, we find that in every respect the great port was better than Manchester. Manchester had four times Liverpool's number of receivers of stolen goods and five times the number of houses used by them. In tramps' lodging houses – 'a fertile source of crime' – Manchester far exceeded her neighbour. Similarly, Manchester had two-and-a-half times as many vagrants as Liverpool.

During this period only five per cent of crimes committed in Manchester resulted in conviction, whereas for the whole of

England and Wales the figure was twenty-nine per cent and for Liverpool it was fourteen per cent. As for serious crime, the situation was even worse. In Manchester only six per cent resulted in conviction, compared with thirty-six in Birmingham, forty-five in Leeds, fifty-three in Sheffield and twenty-two per cent in London. Yet the Manchester force should have done better than that of other forces because its ratio of police to citizens was more generous and pay and conditions of service – though poor and a cause of ineffectiveness – were better than those in nearly all the northern authority forces.

In Manchester the crime rate was 1.86 per cent of the population: in other words, there were almost two crimes a year for every citizen. This was around six times the rate in Birmingham, Leeds, and Sheffield and over four times the rate in London. With one-sixtieth of the population of England and Wales, Manchester had one-sixth of all the burglaries, a fifth of the shop breakings, a third of the highway robberies and a fifth of all cases of passing counterfeit money. During the course of 1868, the year to which these statistics apply, 34,562 people passed through the hands of the police. The total number of larcenies from the person was 2,274. There were 1,074 burglaries, two murders, one attempted murder, forty-one shootings, stabbings and woundings and eleven manslaughters. During the same period, the courts heard 9,540 cases of drunk and disorderly, of which almost 7,000 resulted in conviction. Of the nearly 2,000 charged with common assault, just over half resulted in conviction. Of the 655 charges of assault on a police officer, 569 led to convictions, though the penalties imposed are amazingly lenient.

Drink-driving is not a phenomenon of the era of the internal combustion engine: in 1868 police charged 3,379 individuals in a single year, securing convictions in 2,665 cases. The courts convicted 1,000 prostitutes for being drunk and disorderly, yet only ninety-two for 'accosting wayfarers'. There were '325 houses of ill-fame', as the report puts it. This coy term refers to houses from which prostitutes operated, as opposed to brothels.

These are the facts. But why was crime such a problem in Manchester? Several commentators gave a very simple answer: the incompetence of the Manchester police. Elsewhere I shall look at the city's police force and the difficulties it encountered. For the time being it is sufficient to say that throughout most of this period several factors impeded their efficiency. Manchester also had a number of unique characteristics that made crime a particular problem. Nineteenth century criminologists agreed that density of population and high death rate – both characteristic of Manchester – went with a high level of crime. With almost eighty-four people per square acre, only Liverpool was more densely packed.

Widespread criminal activity was itself a product of cities. When people moved from settled rural communities where a web of relationships tied them to their neighbours they suddenly became isolated. Without the traditional constraints on their behaviour, in a new and hostile environment where they knew nobody cared about them, they easily fell into criminal ways. With the breakdown of the social cohesion that was so much a part of rural life came alienation. Now no one felt he had a place or a role but was cast adrift in the great impersonal city.

All those drawn into the new industrial towns felt this and not just Manchester's newcomers. What was unique to Manchester, however, was the unprecedented growth of the city and the unbridgeable gulf between rich and poor that many commentators remarked on and which gave rise to 'alarming social relationships'. Every commentator agreed: Manchester was unique. It is entirely wrong to say that what they are talking about is the beginnings of modern industrial society and that these things were true of every emerging centre of production. According to this latter view, Manchester and Birmingham, Newcastle-upon-Tyne and all the other centres of industrial society were the same. This is not so. Each had its own face, its own unique history and a distinctive personality. These differences are more interesting than the similarities.

Alexis de Tocqueville, one of the shrewdest and most widely travelled observers of the nineteenth century world, said that in

Manchester 'humanity attains its most complete development and its most brutish; here civilization works its miracles, and civilised man is turned back almost into a savage'. It is impossible to understand what de Tocqueville and others meant when they spoke of civilisation breaking down without describing life in the worst parts of the city.

4

Squalor

The Very Essence Of Hell

The shadowlands of hidden Manchester exercised a morbid fascination over the minds of the city's middle class – and there was no shortage of intrepid reporters prepared to explore what the respectable citizen shunned. Deansgate was the worst of the city's criminal enclaves. It was one of Manchester's rookeries. The core of this criminal area lay between Bridge Street and St. John's Street but this was by no means the full extent of it. To the south was a warren of interlocking streets comprising Wood Street, Spinningfield, Dolefield, Willmott Street, Hardman Street, Royton Street and Thompson Street. Deansgate was such a mixture of sin, shamelessness, squalor and depravity that it attracted the curious as well as the socially aware.

Alfred Alsop was the ideal man to tell people about the reality of Manchester's most notorious district. By 1876 he had already spent several years as the superintendent of the area's boys' home. He was no sensation-seeking journalist, hoodwinked by inhabitants putting on a show for the man from the London newspaper. He lived there and daily experienced the life of its streets. Yet his familiarity with Deansgate did not reduce its impact. Alsop never became inured to its horrors. The place, he writes, was full of 'convicts, smashers, harlots, jailbirds, fortune-tellers and unlicensed sellers of beer'. He had no illusions about his neighbours who were 'the very scum of the city, the very essence of hell'. Their breath 'is blasphemy, and their presence contaminating'.

From his home in Wood Street, where the Mission Hall and

Boys' Home floated on 'an ocean of sin, a sink of iniquity' he witnessed five or six fights every day. The creatures who clawed each other in their drunken stupor were hardly human but 'more like demons let loose, as though hell had vomited its vilest refuse upon earth'. The scenes that make up the weave and weft of Deansgate life are tableaux of depraved humanity. One minute Alsop hears a cattle dealer thrashing a prostitute, tearing clumps of hair from her head as she tries to brain him with a roofing slate. Next he sees a young man from Worsley, robbed in a brothel, his head split open with a jug, lying supine in the gutter. Then there are two drunken girls, fighting like starving mongrels, one biting off the other's ear.

In the middle of the night there is hysterical screaming from the window of a brothel: a prostitute has slashed her throat. In the early hours of the morning, shrieks and cries fill the air. 'A score of men and women, eyes blazing with passion, are fighting furiously.' Stones and bricks fly; fists, belts and clogs pummel flesh. The gutters run with blood and hair ripped from the roots. And every Sunday morning, when the last unlicensed bar has closed and the last reveller gone home, when the streets are empty and silent, several men in dark suits make their way to the only piece of open ground. They open their Bibles and each in turn preaches to the empty footpaths.

While Deansgate was at the centre of Manchester's criminal axis, it was by no means the whole of it. Off lower Deansgate, the area around Lombard Street and the Gaythorn Street district, bordered by Albion Street, Hewitt Street, Gaythorn Street and Deansgate, were notorious. Charter Street, in Angel Meadow, had a fearsome reputation as did the Canal Street area. In Salford, New Bailey Street, Bloom Street and the Chapel Street areas were known for prostitution and robbery.

What all these places had in common was that they were the oldest parts of the city, with the worst housing pushed right up against factories and mills. Pubs, beerhouses and lodging houses shouldered each other in this tangle of streets and courtyards. Charter Street, in Angel Meadow, was within spitting distance of the sprawling Manchester cotton mills. Over half the people there in 1851 lived in lodging houses and were professional or occasional criminals. Fifteen years later the area was swarming with crowds of known thieves, sometimes up to 100 strong, who gathered during the middle of the day. A number of individuals who were the focus of a great deal of criminal activity dominated the area. One such was Joe Hyde, who ran the notorious London Tavern, a meeting place for criminals from all over the country. Nearby Teddy Bob Butterworth provided accommodation in his lodging houses for professional rogues of every description. Within easy reach of the London Road lived a number of fences whose reputation was citywide. Bob Macfarlane, One-armed Kitty and Cabbage Ann were the means by which thieves disposed of much of the swag that sloshed around the rookeries.

An abundance of opportunities for theft made the city a magnet for thieves. Manchester's Chief Constable, Palin, writing in the middle of the century, was convinced that the concentration of warehouses in the city was a major reason why there was so much theft in Manchester. Each building – unlike many factories – contained great quantities of attractive and portable property that was, in his words, 'prolific of theft'. Furthermore, the city was packed with the sort of people who were most likely to commit crime: the young, the poor, the unemployed, the unskilled and foreign immigrants.

The population of Manchester was disproportionately young and poor and its economic structure ensured that a large number of people were in unstable employment. Even when in work they were unable to lift themselves out of poverty. Of those the Manchester police arrested in 1868, about half were between the ages of fifteen and thirty years old. However, criminal activity was never exclusively a young person's activity, as almost 1,600 of those arrested were over fifty; 8,000 admitted to being unemployed, as to 11,300 in employment. These figures certainly underestimate the number of people actually unemployed as 'idleness' carried a powerful stigma at this time – those who had no work were lacking in character or were in some other way deficient. Many in fact were strangers to the city, travellers drifting from place to place in search of work. The cotton industry was renowned for its use of casual labour – hiring in busy times and firing with every downturn in trade. Almost a third of those arrested were illiterate. Many were immigrants.

New arrivals in the city were mainly young people between the ages of fifteen and thirty. They sought steady, prestigious employment, such as work in the growing number of cotton mills. Even the few lucky enough to find it lived a Spartan existence, hovering just above the poverty line. In the 1870s, for instance, a man working in a cotton mill in the Manchester area might expect to earn between sixteen and twenty-eight shillings a week. A woman, girl or boy would earn between seven and twelve 'bob'. The poverty line for a man with a wife and two children was around thirty bob a week. In good times, these people just about made ends meet without falling into debt. When they were out of work or when prices rose they slid into need. Old age, bereavement, desertion, illness and injury all carried the additional dread of destitution.

The largest single occupational group of those arrested was common labourers – one in six – followed by factory hands and hawkers. Together these three groups made up almost half of all those arrested who were in employment. These figures reflect the situation in most industrial towns. Manchester, however, had far more of these people than most similar towns. It also had a bigger pool of seasonal workers than most places, many of whom worked in transport and storage, and the city teemed with carmen, porters, messengers, warehousemen and those working in the building trade, especially labourers. The casual worker was in many ways the most adaptable of workers. He tried his hand at whatever came along. He had to if he was to earn a living.

Many young men worked as navvies. There was plenty of temporary work in the mills, especially in areas like Openshaw and Gorton. The need to live near these employment opportunities forced the poor into the run-down city areas. These were the people who, in an economic world that was always precarious, suffered most in hard times. In the hungry winter of 1878 and 1879, for instance, most of those who applied for parish relief were casual labourers. Years later, during the depressed winter of 1896 and 1897, seven out of ten of those who applied for relief to Manchester's Poor Law Guardians were the casually and seasonally employed. By this time half of all the people living in the centre of Manchester were casual or part-time workers.

It is hardly surprising the centre of the city had a reputation for poverty and the percentage of paupers living there was as high as anywhere in the country. A survey of May 1889 showed that twenty-one per cent of men in Ancoats and forty per cent of those in Salford did not have regular employment. At this time half the population of Ancoats and sixty-one per cent of that of Salford were classed as 'very poor', which meant they had a weekly income of less than four shillings per adult. This is reflected in the infant mortality rate: only one in three children born in Ancoats survived to the age of five.

And Ancoats was by no means the worst area in Manchester. Most of its occupants were at least workers, either in employment or scratching a living by means which were generally honest. It was, however, the part of the city that attracted the poorest of the city's newcomers. By the 1870s it had a diverse and sizeable immigrant population. One observer remarked, with only a little exaggeration, that as he walked through Ancoats he saw 'Chinese, Lascars, Negroes, Germans, Frenchmen and ... representatives of almost every nation on the face of the earth'. In fact, Manchester was one of the few cities where the proportion of foreigners to natives was very high. Many of these were unfortunates – people escaping persecution, disgrace or the law. Others were political exiles and deserters from foreign armies. They included the German bandsmen – who hoped for work in pubs and music halls and played in the streets when times were hard – Tyrolese minstrels, Negro serenaders, pipers and flautists from Dublin, jugglers and Italian organ grinders who filled the city's drab streets with an exotic cacophony. Adding to this spectacle were indigenous elements – dog and bird fanciers, clarinettists, Lancashire bell-ringers and itinerant preachers. Many of those thronging the city streets were merely passing through. Local farmers, for instance, drove their sheep, oxen and pigs to the abattoirs on Salford's Water Street and the Cattle Market on Cross Lane.

Occasionally it is possible to get a detailed description of one of these areas as it was late in the century. A police inquiry into the London Road area provides such an account. Shepley Street, just off London Road, was typical. Numbers eight and ten were brothels. Numbers twenty-two and twenty-six were common lodging houses, separated by the Rose and Crown, the haunt of prostitutes. Yet on streets like this there also lived many respectable labourers, skilled craftsmen and shopkeepers. Invariably these people were struggling to live honest and useful lives, seeking to distance themselves from known criminals.

Mixed up with the honest workers, professional criminals and the recent immigrants trying to scrape a living in an alien environment, were the large numbers of people who lived in a twilight zone between legitimate society and the underworld. They drifted between these two worlds, never sure where one began and the other ended. Most of this amorphous group consisted of those who never enjoyed the benefits of regular employment but survived only because they were able to pick up occasional jobs. Many sometimes worked as hawkers, knife-grinders, ballad-singers and sellers of broadsheets. At other times they used the information they had gathered while shovelling coal or digging a garden to plan a robbery. While these groups languished in poverty, factory workers' incomes were generally improving. Whole leisure and consumer industries – notably the pub and the music hall – grew up to meet the needs of working men with money. And where there is money there are always those anxious to get it by illegal means.

The Irish, in this as so much else, were different. They did not share the rising income of factory workers. Few were employed in cotton mills. Many of the Ancoats Irish were day labourers in the building trade. But the single biggest employer by far was Smithfield Market. One in four of all the stallholders was Irish, as were many of the porters, labourers and the hordes of street sellers and hawkers who operated on the fringes of the market. At the best of times they were one meal away from hunger. In the last two decades of the nineteenth century a quarter of the paupers in New Bridge workhouse were Roman Catholics. During this period Irish-born offenders likewise comprised a significant fraction of Manchester's prison inmates – on average about one in three. Indeed, there were many in the final decades of the century still happy to blame the Irish for the city's crime. Among these was that bastion of liberal opinion, the *Manchester Guardian*. According to many editorials, the extent of a city's crime problem was in proportion to its Irish population. So, though the Irish-born population of England was only three per cent of the total, they made up fifteen per cent of prison inmates.

The *Manchester Guardian* again reminded its readers of the Irish peril several years later. On this occasion their reporter visited a lodging house on Charter Street, in Angel Meadow, to gather grim details with which to regale readers. As expected, he encountered all the shocking details he sought. Lodgers needed only 3d for a bed for the night, very often sleeping in buildings which had previously been pubs that had lost their licence. The pub landlord was now the landlord of the lodging house, often with the same clients. Some landlords displayed remarkable ingenuity in their efforts to maximise profits. One even removed the roof so as to cram in more lodgers.

The Irish, of course, were not the only significant minority group in the city. There was also a large community of Eastern European Jews. Fleeing pogroms and persecution, Jews from Russia, Austria and Romania fled to Manchester in the 1880s. In 1880 they numbered 10,000 rising to 35,000 just before the outbreak of the Great War, when they became the largest Jewish community in England outside London. The first Jews to settle in Manchester settled in Cheetham, then a village a short distance from the city centre. The great building boom of the 1850s transformed the area, but the Jews stayed and adapted. Many were tailors and craftsmen who welcomed the growing population as potential customers. In 1858 they built their first synagogue and in 1874 the Spanish and Portuguese synagogue – which now houses the country's first Jewish museum – and then a school on Torah Street.

As in London, most of the Manchester Jews found work in the cheap clothing and household furniture trades, centred on Red Bank, Strangeways and Lower Broughton. Like the areas settled by the Irish, these were places with plenty of cheap housing, many lodging houses and a long-standing reputation for crime and disorder. The successful and ambitious soon made enough to move out to Hightown and Higher Broughton. Also, like the Irish, the Jews attracted hostility from their hosts. Manchester's middle-class Jewish community, predating the influx of the 1880s, was less than enthusiastic about the arrival of its coreligionists. Having achieved acceptance and become an assimilated part of the business and professional community, they feared these newcomers, these 'pedlar Jews', might stir up an indiscriminate anti-Semitism.

Local newspapers complained of 'an invading force, foreign in race, speech, dress, ideas and religion'. It was common for letters and editorials to complain of 'Yids' and 'sheeneymen', who were nothing less than 'the cancer of foreign Jewry, eating away at all that is noble in our national character'. One, in a rallying cry to all who abhorred this alien influx, declared, 'We do not want them at any price. We want England for the English.' Like anti-Irish sentiment, anti-Semitism found open expression right up to the end of the nineteenth century. *Spy*, a short-lived Manchester magazine, took up the theme in 1893, bemoaning the fact that, 'Weekly fresh cargoes of penniless people are landed up on our shores… with the renewed persecution of Jews in Russia, the human rubbish heap is likely to increase.' In terms identical to those once applied to the Irish, the editorial goes on to bemoan the danger these immigrants pose to English labourers whose jobs and standard of living they threaten by working for less and enduring more.

Despite their diverse backgrounds, all the inhabitants of the poorer areas of the city had one thing in common: they lacked the traditional crafts. Many contemporaries believed this was a major cause of the crime that plagued the cities. F. Hill, in his *Crime, its Amount, Causes and Remedies*, put it down to the self-respect and sense of worth lost to unskilled men living in industrial society. Hill was a prison inspector and he maintained, 'A really good carpenter, shoemaker or blacksmith is seldom found in prison... and rarely indeed is a member of the highly-respected class of skilled agricultural labourers.'

Many also agreed that the gulf between the rich and poor which was greater in Manchester than elsewhere was a major cause of crime. The prison chaplain, W. L. Clay, an authority on all aspects of the penal system, was one of the first to point out that 'the heartless selfishness of the upper classes, their disgraceful ignorance of and indifference to the brutal degradation in which they suffer the poor to lie is the primary cause of all the crime in the country'. Others deplored the example set by the self-indulgent and sometimes dishonest rich and the way in which those on small incomes were led into crime by the temptation to ape the habits of their employers. J. Wade, a social commentator who wrote widely on many aspects of Victorian society, explained crime in terms of 'the avarice of trade... In no country are there so many worshippers of the golden calf as in England, where virtue and worth of every kind is measured by the standard of wealth.'

Captain Palin, one of the city's most renowned police chiefs, believed that the city's reputation for helping prisoners was a cause of its problems. There is no doubt that former prisoners posed a major problem. Once an offender left prison, he often had little choice but to return to crime. Few people were prepared to employ him and even if any boss was prepared to give him a chance, his workmates seldom were. In response to this problem a group of concerned citizens set up the Manchester and Salford Discharged Prisoners' Aid Society. Their findings, however, served only to fuel the dread that was sweeping through middle class society. According to the Society's research, the twin cities were home to an army of 3,000 members of the 'dangerous classes' who formed a constantly shifting mass of criminals, posing a permanent threat to property and personal safety. They were responsible for the insecurity that pervaded the city. Palin argued that the Society's hospitality attracted hordes of ne'er-do-wells. Once here, they immediately gravitated to one of the city's many pubs and beerhouses. The beerhouse was central to Manchester's popular image and large sections of the middle class blamed it for the city's high crime rate. As one visitor wrote in *The Times* in 1900, when the number of drinking establishments had been shrinking for almost thirty years, the slum districts of Manchester were 'simply flooded with beerhouses'.

Finally, it is important to point out that there was very little thought given to the prevention of crime. As late as 1886 few builders fitted reliable locks to the houses they built. The practice of shopkeepers displaying their wares in front of the shop actually increased during the nineteenth century and provided both an inducement to and an opportunity for crime. Not that any inducement was necessary. Criminals, it was said, were organised and equipped for crime and pursued their vocation with the single-mindedness of the fanatic.

A Class Separate And Distinct

Whether it's speculation over the assassination of John F. Kennedy or Dan Brown's page-turner *The Da Vinci Code*, plots are irresistible. There is nothing so enthralling as a conspiracy, an intrigue or a scheme. The more audacious and dire its consequences, the more we like it.

What could be more fascinating then than a conspiracy by society's most evil elements to make money by undermining the foundations of civilisation? The idea of the underworld, a counterculture in which crime is the only industry and all its adherents criminals, was already part of popular imagination by the 1830s. The highbrow *Fraser's Magazine* told its readers of an organised business in which recruitment and the dispersal of profits was in the hands of a controlling clique as professional as the captains of industry. Like the most forward-thinking entrepreneurs, criminals exploited new technology. Burglars and pickpockets used the new network of trains to criss-cross the country in pursuit of their trade and to avoid detection. One day they were lifting watches at the Manchester races, the next palming forged notes in Birmingham.

In 1891 W. D. Morrison, the renowned Preston prison chaplain who was an authority on the penal system wrote, 'There is a population of habitual criminals, which forms a class by itself. They are a set of persons who make crime the object and business of their lives; to commit crime is their trade; they scoff at honest ways of earning a living. They are a class separate and distinct from the rest of the community.' The Victorian philanthropist Charles Booth, in his famous survey *Life and Labour of the People of London*, sought to make a distinction between 'the lowest class of occasional labourers, loafers and semi-criminals' and 'the criminal class'. He accepted that they mixed and that the distinction is a fine one. Criminals often lived in criminal areas – the 'rookeries'. The police in Manchester called them 'rabbit warrens'. This environment was peculiarly helpful to the criminal and created considerable problems for the police. With their interlinking back yards and low boundary walls it was easy for a fleeing criminal to melt into his surroundings. Houses in one narrow street merged with those in an adjacent court, interwoven by connecting yards, cellars and lofts.

Whether concentrated in their rookeries or distributed throughout the city, the underworld exercised a powerful hold on the Victorian imagination. Fear of crime is not, despite what we may think, a product of the late-twentieth century. When in 1853 a letter-writer to *The Times* asked the rhetorical questions, 'Why do I keep loaded firearms in my home; why do most people do the like?' he was expressing not an individual's paranoia but the concerns of respectable society. When such people spoke of the 'dangerous classes' they had in mind a specific group – those who were a threat to ordered society and the 'law, moralities and taboos holding it together'. The 'dangerous classes' were 'professional parasites' and delinquents plus those who generally worked but who also supplemented their income through crime. They also had in mind those who had no fixed home.

However, the popular image of the underworld and its reality are two different things. One major difference is the degree of organisation said to characterise criminal activity. There is no evidence that Manchester criminals were in any way organised. True, there was a loose system of mutual support operating in certain areas of the city. Criminals looked out for each other. The swell mob sent as much money as possible to their imprisoned fellows and supported them immediately after their release by having a whip-round and, if they were unable to do so from their own means, organised a collection or raffle. Criminals helped those in the same line of business. As we shall see, beggars exchanged useful information about sources of charity and passed on the lore of their profession.

This system of support extended beyond what we would normally consider the frontiers of the criminal fraternity. There were in Manchester, for instance, some attorneys who provided their services to penniless prostitutes for payment in kind.

Additionally, criminals generally shared certain values, which governed their behaviour. For instance, giving information to the police was taboo. Anyone who did faced ostracism, not of the cold shoulder type but of the clenched fist and hobnailed boot variety. But this is all a long way from an organised criminal fraternity, masterminded by super criminals. No such structure existed. Manchester's nineteenth century slums were not New York in the 1950s. There was no godfather, no capos, bosses, under bosses or soldiers. There was no master plan. Instead there were thousands of individuals, each operating according to his own whims, each ploughing his own furrow oblivious to the rest. The rivalry between criminals is more striking than any cooperation. The Manchester underworld was like the wider Victorian world: there was merciless competition, on and between every level. Surviving as a criminal meant undercutting the competition – stealing more, selling for less. This applied to every aspect of the underworld.

The competition among prostitutes, for instance, was so intense that it was impossible for most of them to make a living solely by selling their bodies. Having reached what they thought was the bottom of the moral trough, they found there was no easy life. To compete most had to sell themselves for a few coppers and then either find work to supplement their income or turn to robbing customers. This is one way in which criminal life was not always an easy alternative to working for a living. This is why so many criminals did not conform to the popular stereotype of the professional malefactor – crime alone seldom provided a living.

Consequently, many criminals were amateurs, in the derogatory sense that the hardened professional used the word. They lived on the fringes of the underworld by menace of muscle or excellence of information. Those who were full-time criminals were of two types: the ones who enjoyed a reasonable degree of success and those who were incapable of honest labour, either because of physical limitations – often the result of drink – or an indelible aversion to work. Neither was guaranteed a comfortable life and certainly not in Manchester, where crime was rife and competition intense. Besides, there was the ever-present possibility of imprisonment, though as I shall show later, this was a feeble deterrent.

Criminals looked on imprisonment much as a joiner regards splinters – an irritating occupational hazard. On average, Manchester's professional criminals went to prison every two years. In between they lived off their neighbours. During the 1960s and 1970s it was fashionable among certain historians and sociologists to view the nineteenth century criminal as nothing less than the authentic voice of working class rebellion. According to this view the criminal was simply reacting against oppressive capitalism which reduced him to factory fodder. What those who expound this view conveniently overlook is that the victims of crime were generally the poor. The idea that criminals in some way redistributed wealth is ludicrous. The reality in nineteenth century Manchester was that criminals preyed on those who had least and made the lives of the poor even poorer. Working people were the ones who suffered most from crime. Most criminals operated in the areas in which they lived. Criminals were the scourge of honest people and the poor felt that the little they owned might at any moment disappear. Like hoodies on today's council estates they were a torture to those they preyed on, a major hardship in lives that were always difficult.

This applied to all nineteenth century cities and towns but what was different about Manchester, in contrast to London, for instance, was the large number of criminals who both worked and stole. The capital's convicts tended to be dependent on crime for their livelihood to a greater extent than their Manchester counterparts. Though there were fewer hardened professional criminals than in London or Liverpool, a larger percentage of Manchester's working population committed crime and hovered in the twilight between normal working class life and criminality, stepping imperceptibly from one to the other. This seems to have been particularly the case with juvenile offenders, who were responsible for a great deal of this extraneous crime.

This is a major reason why crime in Manchester proved so intractable. The criminal fraternity was not merely a stain on the fabric of the city. It was, to a greater extent than elsewhere, part of its warp and weft and therefore all the more difficult to eradicate. This is not to deny that a nucleus of hardened miscreants were responsible for most of the town's serious and skilled crime, such as the theft of lead from the new buildings springing up all over the city during the last three decades of the nineteenth century. One of Manchester's most notorious fences, One-armed Dick, operating out of his shop on Oldham Road, orchestrated a gang of youngsters who stole lead and other saleable metals from virtually every building site in the city. Jerome Caminada, Manchester's renowned nineteenth century detective, agreed. 'A great many of these [criminals] are fixed constantly in this great city. Some others come only like birds of passage – at the approach of great occasions, or during the racing or other busy season.'

According to the report of the Chief Constable for that year, 1870, there were 710 reputed thieves and 322 known to occasionally steal. In light of the poor detection rate of the Manchester police it is certain there were far more unknown thieves who 'occasionally steal'.

In terms of the nature of the crimes committed in the city, it helps to see the criminal community as a dartboard with a number of concentric rings. The outer ring consisted of those who were routinely dishonest in small matters – petty pilferers, opportunist thieves – and who dealt in insignificant amounts of money and goods of little value. Most of these worked and regarded making money on the side by stealth as acceptable. In this world there was no moral censure for crime. When a convict returned to this community it was as if nothing had happened. Most people in this group were between fifteen and twenty-five years old and made up about fifty per cent of those who came before the courts. At the centre of the dartboard, the bull's eye, were burglars and the superior pickpockets, who enjoyed an affluent lifestyle. Outside these were the sneak thieves and further out still the 'pudding-snatchers' who stole food from those leaving cook-shops, where the poor paid a few coppers to heat their food. Out towards the periphery were those who were in prison for begging.

Regardless of their criminal specialism or the extent of their entanglement in crime, criminals were far more mobile than the general population. Though initially most preyed on their neighbours, they found it advantageous to move from one place to another. The thieves of Manchester and Liverpool, in particular, frequently transferred their operations from one town to the other. One female prisoner told the prison chaplain that she had left her Manchester haunts, where she was well known to the police, for Liverpool. She returned home after a few years when she hoped they had forgotten her. Moving around the country was part of criminal life.

The poor in general were far more mobile at this time than we might imagine. In fact, the ebb and flow of population from Manchester to the surrounding countryside was an accepted feature of the period. Farmers drove horses, cattle and pigs to the city's livestock markets on a daily basis and many city dwellers had family links with the surrounding countryside. Much of this movement was seasonal, people moving to work on the harvest.

In good times the news of work in the factories, mills and warehouses sucked the poor into the city, just as changes in poor law regulations might later spit them out. The Irish and Highland crofters were always trickling into the city and many returned home periodically or permanently. There were also droves of travelling entertainers who were always on the move – street acrobats, fire-eaters, sword-swallowers, strongmen, jugglers, rope-wallahs, contortionists, stilt-dancers and the owners of performing dogs, mice and fleas. In addition there were mobile musicians, who were extremely common during the nineteenth century. Prominent among these were German bands – usually Bavarians who returned home to their farms in the autumn. The Italian organ-grinders and hurdy-gurdy men were a feature of every town and city, as were the travelling circuses – the biggest those of George Sanger and the Wombwell Company – and stage companies. In addition there were traders with covered wagons that served as accommodation and a place of business. Generally they dealt in dry goods, crockery and trinkets, all of an inferior quality. Then there were the droves of pedlars, selling everything from needles to booklets and tracts. The more dubious peddled quack remedies.

Unlike these, the Romany gypsies had genuine expertise. Renowned for their mastery of horse rearing, so long as the horse remained central to British life, their position was secure. They appeared at every fair, circus and show ground where fortune-telling, lucky dips and shies supplemented their income. Gypsies had a key role in horse racing and prizefighting, both shady activities. With their knowledge of horseflesh it is hardly surprising that they played a big part in what was an ill-regulated though increasingly popular sport. Their presence at race meetings and fairs gave them many opportunities to pass counterfeit money, while their mobility laid them open to charges of stealing animals – particularly horses – and poaching. Tinkers were a separate group. In dress and general appearance they were similar to gypsies but their lifestyle was regarded as more squalid. Their skill was in rough metalwork, such as repairing pots and pans. The gypsies looked down on them, partly because many were Irish.

The respectable public viewed all travellers – whether they were swallowing a sword or selling a safety pin – as wasters, thieves, cadgers and rogues. Part of the reason for this was that wherever a circus pitched its big top, it was never long before it attracted a host of scoundrels. Pickpockets and con men of all kinds followed the crowds, their natural milieu. As the century progressed, this mobile population declined and the British became a more settled people. The number of tramps went up and down with the state of the economy, but never disappeared. As the importance of the horse declined and the number of retail outlets increased, gypsies and pedlars declined. Yet the ebb and flow of population in and out of the cities never dried up. London, with its many refuges and workhouses, exercised a powerful pull on criminals during the winter months. In April and May, however, criminals drifted to the provinces and Manchester was one of the chief destinations in the 1850s because its guardians distributed poor relief in cash.

Professional criminals had a regular circuit. The best pickpockets, the swell mob, regularly converged on the Manchester Exchange in December, when it was packed with commercial men. Similarly, race meetings exerted an irresistible pull not only on pickpockets but on crooks of every kind. These peripatetic criminals were usually seasoned practitioners, unlike the large number of young criminals who made up a significant proportion of those who came before the Manchester courts.

Star-glazing and the Shallow Lay

Life was neither easy nor long for Manchester children born in the slums and rookeries. In the 1860s one in four died before reaching their first birthday. Even this grisly statistic is a vast improvement on the situation in the 1840s when half the children born in the city died before their fifth birthday. Like most averages, these figures conceal enormous discrepancies. Those living in the poor areas of the city were twice as likely as those in the better areas to die in their early days. Approximately one in five of the cases that came before the coroner involved children under the age of five and the bulk of these were children of the poor; children born out of wedlock were twice as likely to meet an early death.

Many reluctant parents treated their children as impediments, unwelcome burdens they shook off at the first opportunity. One Salford child summed up the position of many when he said of his mother, 'I don't think she wanted me. I don't think she did. Well, she'd had four boys and they weren't well off.' The experience of rejection was common among illegitimate children. The mother of such a child had lost every shred of respectability. The sooner she could unburden herself of the proof of her shame the better. Similarly, parents whose children got into trouble with the police or failed to get work often turned them out to fend for themselves. This is one of the reasons why children made up the majority of those who stole food, especially from stalls and displays outside shops. This was a dangerous undertaking as a thief caught in the act could expect the irate stallholder to mete out summary punishment. Unless the aggrieved grocer inflicted life-threatening injuries, he was certain to hear nothing more of the matter and would undoubtedly feel he had acted leniently in not giving the thief over to the police. Certainly no sane person would consider his actions unreasonable.

Stealing from behind a shop window, however, required more subtlety than snatching something from a stall. Thieves who went in for this often targeted tobacconists. The commonest method involved removing the glass by 'star-glazing'. To provide cover for this a group gathered in front of the window, feigning interest in a display while one of them inserted a blade between the edge of the frame and the glass. By slowly twisting the blade, he cracked the glass. Over the crack the thief attached a large brown paper plaster which he then pulled away, together with shards of glass, creating a hole big enough for a child to slip his hand through.

Children were often the victims as well as the perpetrators of crime. The most despised criminals were those who specialised in stealing from children. Mainly women, they generally operated in middle class areas, targeting well-dressed children they 'skinned' – stripped of clothes and shoes. Others specialised in shop messengers or children running errands. But it is also true that juvenile criminals often preyed on younger children, stealing parcels, food and money. Henry Wilson, for instance, who was renowned for preying on messenger boys and girls running errands, robbed at least 127 children during the early stages of his career.

A survey of Manchester in the 1840s found juvenile delinquents concentrated in the worst parts of the city. Most were petty criminals cum street vendors. The latter was often no more than a front for picking pockets and pilfering, the usual apprenticeship before graduating to more serious crimes. Ninety per cent of these children came from what the surveyor called 'dishonest and profligate' parents. Large numbers of children, then as now, were totally neglected. The major difference was that then they grew up not only without adult supervision but in abject poverty. Prior to 1870 they had little chance of any education and small hope of gaining honest employment. Those fortunate enough to find legitimate work ended up in sweatshops or as street sweepers, hawkers of cheap articles – matches and newspapers – or gathering a few coppers for holding horses. And most of these were soon sucked into a life of crime.

Prior to the last decades of the nineteenth century, childhood as we know it today hardly existed. The harsh realities of adult life – particularly the need to make a living – impinged on children at a very early age. Nor were they shielded from the reality of death. Infant mortality was so high that most children suffered the death of a brother or sister. Even children fortunate enough to get an apprenticeship were subject to the rigorous enforcement of the terms of their indenture. In 1873, for instance, one Manchester apprentice, fifteen-year-old Henry Hunter, received seven days imprisonment for not turning up for work. His case was common. Master beggars hired young children to beg for them. They pestered their victims with all the persistence of a child in Delhi or Cairo today. Scantily clad, their flesh raw in the harsh winter wind, their eyes wide with want, few could resist the pleading hands of a hungry child. Many were controlled by con men operating this 'shallow-lay' – taking advantage of people's kindness.

It is estimated that in 1850 there were 100,000 such street urchins roaming the streets of London. Several thousands roamed
the streets of Manchester and the authorities were seriously
worried about the scale of the problem. As late as 1889 a Manchester survey found 700 street children roaming around the city.
A combination of the deserted, the orphaned and the runaway,
the vast majority were illegitimate offspring whose parents drove
them out to beg and steal. Some had absconded from refuges for
homeless children, such as Barnes' House in Salford. Once on the
streets they relied on the common lodging house, whose keeper
was often a receiver of the goods these children stole. Children
made up a large proportion of the occupants of lodging houses.
Like all criminals, they were constantly on the move. They loved
the anonymity of the big cities. Some were the children of lodgers. Resident beggars and thief masters kept others they were
training up for criminal gain. But many were alone. Their attitude
to making a living was just what we would expect of a child. They
were concerned with making enough for today, for their immediate needs, with little thought for tomorrow.

Though childish in some ways, they were worldly in others.
Promiscuity was common among criminal children. A parliamentary inquiry of 1852 found many lived with prostitutes and
had venereal disease by the age of twelve. Nevertheless, as far
as the law was concerned, children were treated differently from
adults. Despite the harshness of the early-nineteenth century penal code, the courts condemned to death very few juveniles. Children were, in theory, presumed incapable of criminal intent up to
the age of seven and between the ages of seven and fourteen were
presumed innocent unless the prosecution could prove their ability to distinguish between good and evil. Children over the age of
fourteen were fully responsible for all their actions.

Yet from the 1850s the courts abandoned the punishment of
young criminals in favour of trying to divert them from a life of
crime. The Juvenile Offenders Act of 1853 and subsequent Acts
in 1854 and 1857 empowered courts to send offenders under the

age of sixteen to reformatories, as opposed to prison. This took them out of the criminal environment for two years. It cut their criminal contacts, led to a significant reduction in the number of children imprisoned and a sharp decline in juvenile crime. With the reduction in juvenile crime the number of children sleeping rough and wandering the country also fell. In 1886 one journalist wrote, 'It is almost impossible in these days to realise the extent to which juvenile crime prevailed forty years ago.' The 'steady, regular training' of the reformatory made the young person attractive to prospective employers. Even the most cynical members of the public, who rejected the possibility of reforming the young criminal, had to accept that the hard work of the reformatory ruined forever the delicacy of touch essential to a pickpocket.

In 1874 the training ships came into existence. Those sentenced to them got three years' disciplined training, which equipped them for life at sea.

Whereas reformatories provided an alternative to prison for juvenile criminals, industrial schools dealt with those who had committed less serious or even no offences. They were simply living in conditions that put them in imminent danger of becoming criminals. It is an indication of the number of children living without any positive parental influence that the courts sent 5,000 neglected Manchester and Salford children to industrial schools in the period 1870 to 1891. From 1856 it was standard procedure to commit virtually all second offenders to reformatory school, regardless of their offence. By the end of the decade all commentators agreed that the number of juvenile thieves who were hardened criminals had shrunk. The 1884 Royal Commission on the Reformatories and Industrial Schools accepted that the training of boys as professional criminals that had taken place in prisons was now a thing of the past.

Education also had a key responsibility for saving the young from a life of crime. This was an ambitious task. The Education Aid Society, in its report of 1870, spoke of the need for schools to 'civilise and humanise the great masses that have sunk so low'. Many children were no more than savages, totally lacking in any sense of right and wrong. Another report from the same period states clearly that the children it seeks to help are often 'as wild as ostriches of the desert'.

The Society was in no doubt how this came about. 'When for the first ten or twelve years of their life there has been no discipline – when cleanliness and comfort have been unknown – when no law of God or man has been considered sacred, and no power recognised but physical force, it is impossible these children should settle down to work. They seek satisfaction in the lowest sensual enjoyments. It is the story of the lives of tens of thousands.' It is hardly surprising that young criminals regarded a court appearance as a badge of honour, much as their twenty-first century counterparts regard an ASBO as a rite of passage. Imprisonment guaranteed status, especially when it merited newspaper coverage.

Dick Turpin, Jack Sheppard and other legendary desperados were young criminals' heroes. They swapped tales of their audacity round the lodging house fires and in prison cells and sang about them in the pubs, beerhouses and the penny gaffs frequented by criminals. From the mid-century hawkers sold written accounts of their exploits. And there were plenty of older criminals who regarded themselves as craftsmen, passing on their lore to the next generation, enabling them to make a living. Often, however, this was more self-interest than philanthropy. In many cases the mentor ran a lodging house and provided his charges with pencils, oranges, notebooks or other items they might peddle as a front for stealing.

Writing in 1895, Caminada tells of professional thieves who attended race meetings, not only to rob, but in the hope of 'plucking greenhorns' – recruiting accomplices from the gutter children selling newspapers and matches. An apprentice thief was totally dependent on his mentor, as no fence would accept stolen goods from anyone unknown to him. In return for this service, the boy, who often did the actual stealing, was generally well looked after – for so long as he remained a valuable asset.

Girls made up about twenty per cent of young convicts. Apart from prostitution, begging and pickpocketing, they often acted as look-outs for burglars and served as their 'canaries' – carrying tools to and from the burglary. In Manchester as elsewhere, children often provided information about targets for robbery and were essential for entering houses through small windows and apertures. Forgers and coiners used them as go-betweens. But the use of children in crime declined greatly in the second half of the nineteenth century. Yet there were still many who graduated into adolescent and young adult criminals. Then, as now, a great deal of crime was the work of young men and Manchester was a young man's city. In the middle of the century half the population was under twenty-three. They often organised themselves into groups specialising in one or two types of theft. Most attacks on the person were the work of such gangs. The very young thieves tended to be opportunists, snatching whatever they could when the opportunity arose.

The practice of juveniles preying on young children was common early in the nineteenth century and, according to the *Manchester City News,* during the economic downturn of 1864 re-emerged with such force that children went in terror of being left naked in the streets. A variation on this was robbing children of the meals they were taking to a working parent. In certain parts of the city it was quite common for gangs of youths to rob working men of their sandwiches. Additionally, many of those employees who stole from their bosses were young men.

Yet crime was by no means the preserve of the young. Many criminals continued to offend well into their seventies. Perhaps the best example of the habitual, incorrigible criminal of this period was Mary Ann Williamson who, by the 1880s, had racked up 104 convictions for theft, prostitution and drunkenness. Ann Welsh, Ann Davis – who crowned her criminal career by murdering her husband Paul Davis in 1885 – and Annie Kelly also made regular appearances at the police courts, interrupted only by frequent terms of imprisonment. All three were inept offenders, incapable of working for a living. They operated at the bottom of the criminal hierarchy.

At the other extreme were the cracksmen, the elite of Manchester's criminals.

5

Criminals

Cracksmen

He hurtled down the Victoria Station footbridge and dived over the parapet into the filthy waters of the River Irwell. His pursuers, panting in the warm night air, peered down into the darkness. Bob's legs disappeared into the tunnel running under Chetham's School, Walker's Croft and Hunt's Bank and emerged where the Irwell meets the Irk, near Moreton Street, Strangeways. It was a feat worthy of any circus acrobat and contributed greatly to Bob Horridge's mythical status among Manchester cracksmen.

Cracksmen, or burglars, were the aristocracy of the criminal world. They were well dressed and walked with a swagger, envied by the criminal fraternity, loathed by the police who knew that short of catching them in the act they were unlikely to get a conviction. For the best burglars immediately converted their haul into cash and were rarely found with anything to link them to their crimes. Sometimes referred to as 'attic thieves' or 'garret thieves', a reference to their preferred method of entry, the best specialised in fashionable houses in the most desirable suburbs. The dining hour, between seven and eight in the evening, when family and servants were most likely to be at supper on the ground floor, was when most struck. No such careful timing was needed with empty or closed-up houses, lock-up shops and warehouses. Information about the layout of a target was, however, always valuable as it reduced the considerable risk that was an unavoidable part of even the most carefully planned burglary.

Providing such information was the role of the 'putter-up', who watched houses and cultivated servants for details of the domestic routine. A cooperative window-cleaner, glazier, plumber or decorator was likely to have valuable information about the layout of prospective targets. It is hardly surprising that the victims of a burglary invariably suspected servants and tradesmen. No one did more to pollute the image of the domestic servant than the ghoulish Kate Webster. A thief, drunkard and abandoned wife, she had a volcanic temper that erupted into frenzied violence. Having failed as a thief, when she was thirty she turned her hand to domestic service in London. Her unsuspecting employer, Mrs Julia Thomas, was a woman in every respect, the antithesis of her employee. Even Mrs Thomas's closest friend conceded that she was a stern taskmaster. In fact, she delighted in humiliating servants. Before long, her mistress's vitriolic tongue lashed Kate into a fever of seething hatred. Yet, though she managed to keep her trembling fists under her apron, Kate's mask of deference cracked. What Mrs Thomas saw through the split put her in fear of her life.

Terrorised in her own home, she told Kate to get out. The maid implored a few days' grace: surely Mrs Thomas would not see her on the street? The employer relented – but only two days. Mollified, Kate seemed resigned to her fate. Then Mrs Thomas disappeared. A day later Kate tried to sell several jars of 'best dripping'. She tried to sell Mrs Thomas's furniture. Wherever Kate went, she clutched a large black bag.

A trunk washed up on the bank of the Thames. At first the police thought it was a carcass from an abattoir. But when the doctor placed the parts together it formed the body of a woman. The flesh, however, was as white as fresh lard. And the head was missing. They identified the body from the trunk. When they caught up with Kate, she denied everything. When confronted with the blood stains she had failed to erase from Mrs Thomas's kitchen and the remains of the victim's charred entrails, she blamed others – a fictitious lover and the second-hand furniture dealer. It was only while she was waiting for the hangman that she confessed and told how she'd thrown her employer down the stairs, disembowelled her with a razor, boiled her body and then butchered her. They never found the black bag. Or Mrs Thomas's head.

The trial, which opened on 2 July 1879, made Kate the object of national odium. All the major nationals and many regional papers gave it saturation coverage. The execution of a woman for murder was a rare occurrence. Prior to this the standing of domestics was low. It was assumed they were lazy and dishonest. But now many an employer thought twice before scolding a clumsy skivvy or admonishing a careless domestic. Employers turned their attention to improved security. The wise among them stored their valuables in a Chubb and Milner safe, the most advanced of its day. The company claimed, with justification, that no cracksman could pick its locks and no drill pierce its metal.

To make matters worse for the poor burglar merely trying to make a dishonest living, 1865 saw the appearance of the first burglar alarm connected to a police station. But, fortunately for the cracksman, few invested in these expensive state-of-the-art safeguards. Internal shutters and iron bars on windows were the usual precautions against burglary. And no self-respecting burglar found these anything more than a minor inconvenience. A rope and a sturdy stick made a simple tourniquet powerful enough to bend bars. The more sophisticated used the jack-in-the-box, a device very much like a modern car jack. Once the bars were sufficiently bent to squeeze through, it took the average burglar no more than fifteen seconds to cut a hole in the glass big enough for his hand.

A safer alternative was the 'treacle plaster' – similar to the 'star-glazing' plaster used by children to steal from shops. The burglar cracked the glass by applying pressure and then unpicked the plaster, leaving a hole in the pane big enough to put a hand through and open the latch. Internal shutters proved even less of an obstacle. The blade of a knife was sufficient to flick the catch. If he made a noise, the experienced burglar stopped and clamped his ear to the window frame, listening intently for any sound that told him he had disturbed the householder.

James Bent, a Manchester policeman renowned for his charitable work for the poor, knew burglars so audacious that when they suspected they had disturbed someone they simply went to the front door and knocked, claiming to have got the wrong address. The burglar then gave the householder time to get back to sleep before resuming. Once inside the safe breaker relied on the traditional tools of his trade – jacks, jemmies, crowbars and wrenches. Specialists, many based in Manchester, made these safe-cracking tools. Their new specialities, available from the 1870s, included diamond-tipped drills at £200 apiece – almost four years' wages for a policeman guaranteed to cut through the lock of any safe. Only the most accomplished cracksmen could afford such implements.

Yet until the introduction of dynamite in 1867, the cracksman's skill was in his fingertips. Even then, British cracksmen were loath to abandon their old ways and slow to take advantage of developments.

No innovations, however, reduced the demand for undersized boys, supple and brave enough to squeeze between bars and through small windows. These invaluable assets were known as 'snakesmen'. Superannuated climbing boys, having spent their apprenticeship scaling chimneys, made excellent snakesmen. Even more useful was a cooperative servant.

In the mid-century census of 1851, almost eight per cent of the entire population were servants. For women and girls the figure was thirteen per cent. To put this in context, this was twice the number of women employed in textiles, Britain's biggest employer, in which the majority of workers were women.

The temptation to take advantage of their employers was ever present. Most servants were badly paid, even by the standards of the day. Their accommodation, even in the most sumptuous houses, was Spartan. Many regarded the trifles they pilfered a perk of the job. If a servant who dealt with tradesmen could reach an agreement by which she made a few extra shillings, she felt entitled to do so. Cooks, in particular, often made mutually beneficial arrangements with grocers and butchers. Not surprisingly the consequences of being caught were serious. Any employer who suspected a servant of dishonesty was likely to resort to summary dismissal, which meant being turned out onto the street without a reference or 'a character' and therefore no hope of getting work. For a country girl brought into a strange city where she was friendless, this was a daunting prospect that led many into prostitution.

In the absence of a cooperative servant, deception was necessary. As with many things, the simple ruses were the most effective. The cab at the kerb scam seldom failed. This involved hiring a cab in which a respectable-looking lady sat outside the chosen house. An accomplice knocked on the door and concealed himself. When the domestic opened the door, the lady beckoned her to the kerb. Invariably the servant left the door ajar behind her. While her attention was distracted, the lady's accomplice slipped into the house. This scam worked several times during the 1879 spate of burglaries in Moss Side. Bent stationed a number of his men there but to no effect.

There was obviously a limit to how often this scam would work in a particular area, therefore, the prolific cracksman had to be mobile. Unknown to the local police, he avoided the danger of informers by moving on as soon as he did a job. Likewise with his swag – many Manchester burglars disposed of it in Liverpool. The most successful lived in good neighbourhoods far from their places of work. Provided they did not live an extravagant lifestyle and did nothing to attract attention to themselves they might continue accumulating money and retire in comfort. Charlie Peace, the most infamous criminal of his day, came closest to achieving this ideal. But every good burglar had to be professional and extremely careful if he were to join the happy ranks of those who retired without having seen the inside of a prison cell. As today, information was key.

A burglar who knew the household routine could avoid unpleasant surprises. By patiently watching a house, noting comings and goings, the time the beat policeman passed, when lights came on upstairs and when servants went to the shops, it was possible to discover when the house was empty. Doing this without attracting attention, however, was extremely difficult and required a degree of patience found among only the most professional burglars. Getting the necessary tools to the house and removing them, together with the proceeds of the burglary, was a hazardous operation. No professional would risk doing this himself. The best 'canary' was usually a woman, as she was less likely to attract attention. After the burglary the canary and the burglar made off by different routes. A speedy escape was important as every minute spent at the scene increased the likelihood of detection.

The great advantage of commercial premises was that they afforded the cracksman more time. This made them attractive to burglars. By the second half of the nineteenth century warehouses filled a large part of both Manchester and Salford city centres. But large warehouses were invariably difficult to break into. A common way round this was simply to walk in. A respectable-looking businessman and his colleague would visit the warehouse shortly before closing time. One left while the other concealed himself on the premises and came out when the staff had gone home. Even with the warehouse to himself, a Manchester burglar of this period was often armed. Small double and single barrel pistols were readily available. However, the availability of weapons also created problems for the burglar, because those seeking to protect their property were also likely to arm themselves. An inept burglar might find an irate householder waiting for him with a cocked gun and no qualms about using it.

Incidents in which burglars came to grief attracted considerable media coverage, specifically to discourage others. Two renowned cases took place in London in the 1850s. In the first instance two infamous London thieves, Edgar and Blackwell, tried to burgle a prestigious furrier's shop on Regent Street. Clearly their approach was not very professional as they were unaware that the owner lived on the premises. To be precise, he slept in the attic, the window of which they prised open – only to find the owner waiting for them with a gun. Edgar fell to his death. Blackwell jumped to the street, dislocating his ankle. The police found him writhing in pain. On another occasion three burglars broke into the Regent's Park home of a rich American, whose butler was in the habit of sleeping in the back parlour, snuggled up to his sporting gun. Two of the intruders surrendered after the butler peppered their colleague with buckshot.

The best burglars avoided violence and eschewed the use of firearms. Using a gun immediately catapulted their crime into a far more serious level and guaranteed a long sentence if caught. Bob Horridge, however, had no qualms about using violence. Though the most infamous Manchester burglar, he was in no way typical of his kind. Though Horridge was the product of the Rochdale Road rookery, he came of decent parents. Despite this lack of criminal breeding he was, in Caminada's words, 'one of the most accomplished and desperate thieves that ever lived in Manchester'.

By the age of thirteen Horridge was out of control. His first offence led to a six-month sentence. Immediately after his release he burgled again. This time it was eighteen months. When Horridge left prison his father resolved not to let the boy out of his sight. He set about training him in his own trade as a blacksmith and maker of fenders. The young miscreant showed remarkable aptitude and everyone who saw him working swore he was as productive as any two men. But by 1869 he was back to his old ways. Accounts of errand boys being robbed flooded into the Manchester detectives' office. Eventually one of the culprits, Ned, was caught in the act. Ned was Horridge's constant companion so Caminada decided to search the blacksmith's house, as a result of which it came to light that he had deposited a stolen watch with a jeweller. This time he got seven years' penal servitude, the most severe form of imprisonment.

Horridge was outraged. He blamed Caminada and swore he'd kill him. Yet on his release he set himself up as a smith on Style Street, Rochdale Road, where his skills made the new business a success. However, his release coincided with a rash of burglaries. In rapid succession the stock of a furrier, a silk merchant and a jeweller's all disappeared. Other burglaries in nearby towns also bore Horridge's trademark lack of subtlety. His reputation for

violence was such that thirty policemen took part in the operation to arrest him. They surrounded his house in Gould Street
but not before Horridge realised what was happening. As the
police entered the house, he broke through the ceiling plaster and
laths, climbed out onto the roof and made his way to an adjoining
street, Ludgate Hill. There he stripped the slates from the roof,
got into the loft and then burrowed his way through the bedroom
ceiling – much to the alarm of four agricultural labourers, back
from the country and enjoying a well-earned sleep. Without explanation, Horridge took the stairs like a triple-jumper and threw
open the front door, where four constables confronted him. Three
small steps rose from the street to the front door and, without
breaking stride, he leapt from the threshold, over the heads of
the peelers and sprinted into the distance. Though barefoot and
wearing only trousers and a shirt, he outran his pursuers and got
safely away.

Any ordinary criminal would have laid low for a time but Horridge was an adrenaline addict. He loved the thrill of the chase
and got immense satisfaction from outwitting the police. Shortly
after his spectacular escape from Gould Street, he and his associ-
ate, Long Dick, burgled a fancy goods shop on Thomas Street. A
passing constable spotted a light and decided to investigate. The
instant he put his foot inside the shop, Horridge floored him with
a blow in the face. The constable recovered sufficiently to grab
Dick and wrestle him to the ground. Dick got five years' penal
servitude but Horridge remained at liberty.

After a time Horridge thought it safe to return to Gould
Street. The police suspected this and searched the house. First
they searched upstairs and having found nothing started on the
ground floor. After ten minutes of fruitlessly scrutinising floorboards and walls they heard Horridge's voice from upstairs.

'Have they gone?' he asked.

Before the policemen could mount the stairs, he scrambled
through the trapdoor to the loft that ran the entire length of
the row of houses. Though the police sent for reinforcements and
searched every house in the row, they found no trace of him.

Horridge's next job was perhaps his most audacious. After watching a mill in Bradford, near Manchester, he was confident he could get away with the entire payroll.

Every Friday night a freestanding 450lb safe housed the mill's entire payroll. A watchman guarded it until 4.30am when he left the office, locked it and went to stoke the boiler. Horridge had got a key to the office. And, provided the watchman did not return before workers started arriving, he was confident he could get the £600 in gold and silver the mill paid out every Saturday. Two of his associates staged a fight outside the mill, within earshot of the boiler house. The caretaker intervened and by the time he had pacified the warring parties and sent them on their way, Horridge had completed his work. When the caretaker returned to the office, he found the door ajar and the safe gone. Horridge and another man had loaded it onto a cart. The audacity of the robbery ensured a great deal of media coverage and there was tremendous pressure on the police to make an arrest. Unfortunately, neither the bewildered watchman nor anyone else could describe the robbers. Even when the police found the safe in an old mill reservoir, it told them nothing. He had cut out its back.

The proceeds of the robbery were enough to keep Horridge in luxury for some considerable time. He disappeared until July 1880, when he carried out his most spectacular escape of all. An officer making his rounds in Redfern Street tried the door of a warehouse. Horridge was inside and characteristically floored the policeman as he stepped through the door before making off down Mayes Street and Long Millgate, where another officer and a civilian tried to grab him. He made short shrift of these two.

By now, however, the first policeman, aided by civilians, was giving chase, intent on giving him a good kicking. Horridge hurtled down a footbridge on Victoria Station approach and dived over the parapet into the filthy waters of the River Irwell and made his most spectacular escape.

His arrest, when it happened, came as an anticlimax to all those who had been breathlessly following his exploits in the newspapers. He continued his smithy business in Style Street, apparently under the impression that the police could not link him to any of his recent crimes. A plain-clothes policeman strolled into the smithy and told him he would appreciate a word.

'The Prince's Feathers. Seven tonight?' the policeman asked.

Horridge nodded. But what he was thinking no one will ever know. There are several possible explanations. Perhaps he had no idea who he was agreeing to meet and assumed it was a criminal with a proposition. It is also possible that he had started to believe his own public image and thought he was fireproof as the police had no one to identify him. Whatever the reason, he turned up for the rendezvous and went meekly into custody. The man who made more near-death escapes than 007 walked to the police station as sedately as a maiden aunt claiming her lost umbrella.

Perhaps he would have been less cooperative had he known what the judge at the Assize Court had in store for him. He handed down a sentence of seven years' penal servitude followed by another seven under police supervision. Horridge winced when he heard it. His beleaguered wife wept as she prepared herself for a long separation. But he had no intention of serving his time quietly. Within weeks of his conviction he tried to stir up a prison riot, grappling with two warders even after they shot him twice. It took a third bullet to stop him. He spent the rest of his sentence under close supervision, much of it in solitary confinement. During those empty days his resentment festered against those prisoners who hadn't backed him during the prison riot. On his release in April 1887 he sought out those who had betrayed him and took his revenge by thrashing them unconscious. Then he resumed where he had left off seven years earlier.

His imprisonment had done nothing for his technique as a burglar. He had always been careless about showing a light and was noisy. This proved his undoing when he burgled a shop on Angus Road, off Rochdale Road, only months after his release. On this occasion he and his female accomplice used skeleton keys to enter but nevertheless managed to attract the attention of a passing constable, who enlisted the support of a colleague and three civilians. Displaying no gallantry, Horridge abandoned his accomplice and tried to escape through the back door – only to be confronted, as so many times before, by two constables. This time, however, he was not prepared to rely on his athleticism. He fired two shots – one causing a glancing neck wound, the other punching a hole in the centre of the peeler's chest. Only the skill of the surgeons at the Manchester Royal Infirmary saved the life of the second officer, who suffered permanent injury. While the officer's life hung in the balance, the newspapers kept Horridge's exploits before the public. The result was a city-wide panic. Everyone went in dread of murderous Bob Horridge.

The citizens of Manchester were worrying needlessly for he had gone into hiding in Liverpool. No doubt the hue and cry would have died down enabling him to start a new phase of his criminal career in Liverpool. But his wife, Little Ada, who was under police surveillance, was careless. Horridge remained in contact with his wife and when she took the train to Liverpool, they followed her and brought her raging husband back to Manchester. This time there was no escape. The outcome of the trial was never in doubt. On 2 November 1887, the Assize Court sentenced thirty-seven-year-old Horridge to penal servitude for life. He died in prison.

More typical of the city's cracksmen was John Connolly, a professional housebreaker. He is remembered for his charm, which enabled him to recruit an army of young girls to dispose of stolen good through pawnbrokers they dazzled with their alluring smiles. Without outlets for the goods they stole neither Horridge nor Connolly would have prospered as burglars. Every cracksman needed a reliable fence.

Fences

The jury had delivered its verdict. All that remained was the sentence. In such cases the words of the judge were always the same. Only the name differed – Joe Hyde, Bob Macfarlane, Patsy Riordan or another of Manchester's notorious fences.

'Without the likes of you,' the judge invariably said, looking over his half-moon lenses, his eyes as cold as a cod's, 'there would be little theft in this city.' Everyone agreed with the judge and fully supported him in dealing out condign sentences. Thieves without fences are like beer without alcohol – largely pointless.

The market for stolen goods was far more extensive throughout the nineteenth century than today. To a great extent this was because of the scale of payment used by most fences, said to have been developed by the famous London fence, the 'great Ikey Solomons', Dickens's model for Fagin. Ikey pioneered a system of standard payments for each item, regardless of its quality. Under this system the amount paid for a gold breastpin, for instance, was the same as that paid for a silver or brass one. No doubt the result of this was to the fence's benefit. But from the point of view of the thief it meant that he could sell anything he stole.

Fences, like the thieves who supplied them, came in all shapes and sizes. In particular they varied greatly in their commitment to criminal activity. At one extreme, the fence was the leader of a criminal gang, the 'putter-up', who planned and financed everything while keeping a safe distance from the actual crime. Usually he had an alternative source of income, which served as a front for his main business. A pawnshop, pub or lodging house provided a means of maintaining criminal contacts without immediately attracting the attention of the police.

Such was One-armed Dick, a famed Manchester fence of the mid-nineteenth century. Two of his clients told a prison chaplain how he used to run a card school plying his guests with drink on credit. He set those who lost to thieving in order to repay their debt. At the other extreme was the shopkeeper who, under certain circumstances, might buy stolen goods. In between there was every shade of doubtful dealer. What they all had in common, however, was that they were in a very vulnerable position. Somehow or other they had to get stolen goods back into circulation without attracting attention. Once they bought them, they knew that if they came to the attention of the police the trail would lead back to them and not the original thief.

There were always petty criminals in the lodging houses who were prepared to act as intermediaries or fences on a small scale.

They bought items of little value, often from children, and sold them to an established fence or disposed of them personally at a small profit. The best fences, of course, were those who never came to the attention of the police and therefore left no record of their activities. These tended to be the ones who flourished and eventually operated on a large scale. They worked exclusively through dependable contacts acting on behalf of novice crooks and all those outside the closed circle of trusted associates. This was, from the police point of view, the worst of all possible worlds as it meant that stolen goods disappeared without trace. Far better that they pass through the hands of pawnbrokers who, though not scrupulously honest, might on occasion help them.

There is no doubt that many pawnbrokers found themselves in this position. When the police suspected a pawnbroker, they watched his shop until they had evidence he was handling stolen goods. He then had little choice but to become an informer or a double agent. Many small second-hand shops bought stolen jewellery and watches and immediately 'christened' them by removing identifying marks and substituting new ones or by resetting or even recutting precious stones. Experienced fences immediately melted down precious metals. Watches were disguised by putting the works into another case and melting down the original. The fences who dealt with jewellery and other valuables were near the top of their trade. The majority dealt in more mundane fare, items of little value indistinguishable from their second-hand stock.

There was hardly a dealer in second-hand goods who didn't at some time handle stolen goods. The majority of people went through their entire lives without owning a single new item. Most of those who volunteered for the Great War in 1914 received new clothes for the first time in their lives when the sergeant handed them their uniforms. Consequently, clothes made up an enormous proportion of all stolen goods. It is hardly surprising that the theft of clothes was by far the most common crime of the period.

Second-hand clothes were better value for the poor than the cheap and shoddy, mass-produced garments which were their only alternative. Everyone from the lower middle class and above sold their clothes to a second-hand dealer once they started to show signs of wear. Well made from sturdy materials, these were a good buy for working men and women. They did, however, have one major disadvantage. Clothes that had been lying in a second-hand shop acquired an indelible odour. Just as George Orwell maintained that the poor of the 1930s carried a unique odour, like cold bacon, many nineteenth century commentators maintained that the Victorian poor also had a distinctive odour: the distinctive smell of damp fustian. When mingled with the aroma of herring – toasted herring was a staple of the poor man's diet – it marked a person as poor as clearly as a workhouse uniform.

The stink of poverty, however, seldom deterred the dealer, who was prepared to buy virtually anything. The competition between dealers was cut-throat and their profit margins so minute that the money they made by buying stolen goods at a reduced price could mean the difference between making a profit and going hungry. Initially Jews monopolised the bottom end of the Manchester clothes market. Many believed they alone had the discipline, frugal habits and business acumen to survive on a minute income. But they reckoned without the Irish. The Irish reputedly had none of the qualities that made the Jews so successful in business. What they did have was a sharper and more recent memory of hunger that drove them to survive on less.

All fences, not only the Irish clothes dealers, paid only a minute fraction of the value of the goods they bought. Some paid as little as one shilling in the pound – a twentieth of the true value. What made matters worse for the amateur thief was the difficulty of contacting a fence. Most dealt only with known thieves. Newcomers had to use an established crook or other trusted intermediary and these go-betweens charged a fee.

'Leaving shops' (unlicensed pawnbrokers), chandlers' shops, 'green-stalls' (markets stalls which dealt in all kinds of household goods), marine stores and metal dealers were all likely fronts for fences. Pedlars frequently operated as small scale fences. To avoid detection, thieves often disposed of their booty in a city other than where they stole it. Police records from this period suggest that there were more known receivers in Liverpool than Manchester and they generally paid a better price. Not surprisingly, many goods stolen in Manchester found their way to Liverpool. Really distinctive and extremely valuable booty went to London. The capital was the fence's Mecca. Many of the goods stolen in England eventually found their way there because the city had outlets for every commodity and channels through which goods could be shipped abroad.

Despite all these precautions, the police had considerable success in identifying receivers – but it was difficult to convict them. Juries were reluctant to convict, often because a host of neighbours testified to the defendant's good character. The only exception seems to have been when the man in the dock was a Jew. Perhaps juries were influenced by the image of Dickens's Fagin. Maybe it was simply anti-Semitism at work. Either way juries were inclined to condemn a man simply because he was a Jew.

Yet there was at least one respect in which literature accurately reflected life. 'Flash houses' were places where experienced criminals trained their young protégés. *Oliver Twist's* Artful Dodger and Charley Bates were the fictional equivalent of the thousands inducted into crime by their elders. As *St. Paul's Magazine* put it in February 1869, 'Nearly every adult criminal, usually when in prison, always when out, is busy in training young criminals.'

Everyone who bought stolen goods was snared in the web of crime that extended into every working class community. Goods that had 'fallen off the back of a cart' were everyday currency in the poor parts of the city. Few could resist the knowing wink of a friend who, proffering a bargain, told him that if he asked no questions he would be told no lies. The man in the pub was the first recourse of the thief and the pickpocket.

The Swell Mobsmen

To those who have never been to a race meeting, a horse is a horse. They don't know the difference between a prize filly and the creature that pulls a dray. The respectable world likewise spoke of thieves without knowing that there were as many types as there are hairs on a woman's head.

At all levels, there was a good deal of specialisation among Manchester thieves. Not only did each group differ in what they stole; they also differed in their standing in the criminal hierarchy. Pickpockets, because of their skill and audacity, enjoyed great prestige. Pickpocketing was the most prevalent form of theft in both Manchester and Victorian England generally. No other crime approached it in frequency.

Pickpockets plagued every public gathering. They were among the best-travelled criminals and, like a swarm of locusts moving from one feeding ground to another, always followed the crowd. As the century progressed, the amateur pickpocket or street thief – generally a child – declined with the spread of juvenile reformatories, leaving the field to the professional.

Several developments led to an increase in the number of professional pickpockets at the top of the trade. As the size of the prosperous middle class increased, so did the scope for profitable pickings. Cheap and convenient railway travel made it easy for the pickpocket to go from one race meeting to another, from a fair to a festival and then on to a crowded holiday resort. And trains made it easy for the professional pickpocket to move on before the police got to know him. The opportunities for pickpocketing also multiplied at this time. As ever-more shopping areas and places of public entertainment sprang up, pickpockets found opportunities to fleece the unwary victims awaiting them in every town and city. What's more, the quantity of gold coins in circulation was steadily increasing, with the result that more people were carrying around substantial sums of money, generally without any precautions against theft. Even more valuable were the personal ornaments and jewellery, which became fashionable. The gold watch that pickpocket Charlie Parton stole from John Fletcher, a Manchester businessman, in a city street in 1889 was worth more than a labourer could earn in a year. As we will see, it was this watch which was to prove Parton's undoing.

However, women were more frequent targets than men. This

was largely due to prevailing fashions. The loose clothing favoured by women made it easier to reach into their pockets without being detected. When the victim was a man, it was generally his watch, shirt pin, snuffbox or handkerchief – his most valuable pieces – they targeted. A man's trouser pockets were generally a no-go area as the fashion was for high-cut pockets to the front, close to the body. Changes in women's fashions in the 1870s also made life more difficult for the pickpocket. The demise of crinoline – a stiff fabric that muffled the pressure of the thief's fingers – and the vogue for skirts cut close to the legs, all made the pickpocket's trade more hazardous.

The greatest threat to the career of a promising pickpocket, however, was imprisonment. A habitual pickpocket would sooner or later serve a long sentence that ruined the delicacy of touch on which he depended. Nothing was more destructive of a pickpocket's delicate touch than picking oakum and swinging a pick. Oakum picking, the task of unravelling old rope and straightening and cleaning the strands by hand, was a punishment introduced to British prisons in the 1840s. It resulted in callused and thickened fingers lacking the sensitivity required by a pickpocket. This was one of the few occasions on which punishment effectively eradicated a specific crime. The other major hazard for even the finest pickpocket was the experienced policeman. The likes of James Bent and Jerome Caminada believed they could spot a pickpocket by the way he walked down the street. His walk exuded arrogance. Half swaggering, half furtive, he was usually in his late teens or early twenties, sometimes in flash clothes, sometimes threadbare but never ragged. The perceptive recognised his hairstyle as the result of a gaol cropping. Weaving through the traffic, stepping out in front of vehicles, he played a game of brinkmanship in which he knew his nerve wouldn't be bettered. He was careless of all he passed, contemptuous of conventions of courtesy and safety.

He was a common sight in Manchester. Among his favourite spots were railway stations and food markets, which were conveniently near the slums into which he could at any time disappear. But no matter how skilful, more than any other criminal he depended on effective teamwork to survive and prosper. Most groups – 'mobs' – consisted of three or four men and a boy. Generally the boy specialised in women's purses, handbags and pockets and the rest of the team targeted men. The boy was often taking his first steps in a life of crime. The manual dexterity and unobtrusiveness that made children excellent 'dippers' deserted them with age, forcing them to move on to other types of street crime.

Only the best retained their aptitude long enough to reach the elite of street criminals, the swell mobsmen or the swell mob, the crème-de-le-crème of the pickpocketing fraternity. In order to attain this status it was essential to dress well. As the best boasted of earning £30 in an afternoon this was well within their means.

The richest pickings were at a race meeting, the pickpocket's ideal habitat. What could provide better dipping than a large, closely packed crowd, their attention focussed on the horses and many with their coats open to release the heat of excitement? The pull of the course was so powerful that even the most inept fancied their chances. James Bent once arrested two pickpockets at Manchester races. As both had been out of prison for only days, the court took a dim view of their recidivism and sentenced them to seven years' penal servitude. Policemen like Bent, with long experience of racecourse thieves, believed that many of them were originally youths of good character but limited means. They often started out as occasional gamblers and then became addicted. Debt led to dishonesty and often dismissal, followed by a gradual drifting into crime. In this sense they were not ordinary criminals.

But once they embarked on a career of dipping they ran a great risk of being arrested. As they invariably operated in pairs, any astute observer scrutinising a crowd could generally spot them. Besides, the Manchester force took what would today be called pro-active action. Experienced men like Caminada and Bent went in search of pickpockets at every sporting event, expecting them to be active. They were seldom disappointed. The police also watched railway stations on the day of a race meeting in the hope of spotting known or suspected thieves. In his memoirs, Caminada describes an occasion when he followed two suspects from the railway station to the Manchester course. Once there they selected a likely victim and stood each side of him as he scanned his race card. The one on his left – the watch side – moved in close to him and positioned his elbow below the victim's, preventing him bringing his arm down to his side. In an instant his companion relieved the target of his watch. They then disguised themselves by donning different clothes, hats and false whiskers. In order to get rid of the goods as quickly as possible they met their fence near the course. It was at this point that Caminada swooped, having waited for the opportunity to catch thieves and fence at the same time. On this occasion the two pickpockets got six months hard labour, the standard tariff for this offence.

Even if the police caught a racecourse pickpocket in the act, apprehending him was no simple matter. Caminada was fortunate in that he was able to follow his quarry from the course. In every racing crowd there were swindlers, sharpers and a host of others with no sympathy for the police. It was easy for those being arrested to stir up latent antipathy to the police and organise a rush to rescue the miscreants. The actual thief was often a boy but he needed others to jostle the victim and receive the booty. A common ploy was for four thieves to converge on the target, two from behind and two from the front. If the victim kept his hands in his pockets, one of those behind him tipped his hat forward, forcing him to remove his hands in order to right it. They then pressed against him, preventing him from lowering his arms. Those who operated in this way were known as 'bloke-buzzers'.

Whatever his modus operandi, any pickpocket worth his salt would expect to earn at least five to ten shillings at a fair. Often, he made a great deal more, especially if he lifted a fat wallet. To facilitate this, many of the most successful pickpockets produced specialised tools. A wire device with three hooks and a spring that enabled it to snap shut around a wallet was particularly effective. But even the most sophisticated devices were no substitute for the audacity and coolness that marked out the pickpocket from lesser thieves. Failed dippers gravitated to crimes that afforded none of the aura surrounding the swell mob. In fact, even among the criminal fraternity, most street criminals had little standing.

Dragsmen

Among these were sneak thieves. Some specialised in trying the doors of houses in respectable areas. Mid-morning was their preferred time as servants were often busy making the beds. Clothing, umbrellas or ornaments left on occasional tables in the hall were readily saleable. Even at this level of crime the thief always worked with an accomplice. The golden rule for all thieves was to get rid of the proceeds as soon as possible. To be caught with stolen goods meant certain conviction.

Others were more diverse in their choice of a victim. These were the ones who roamed the streets looking for unfastened basement grids, back doors left unlocked, easily accessible sheds and any other opportunity that might present itself. As many shops in working class areas displayed their wares outside, the opportunist thief often merged into the shoplifter. Railway stations were a magnet for street thieves hoping to find unattended luggage or careless hauliers. These 'dragsmen' also hung about the roads leading to stations. A lax cabby might leave a fare's Gladstone bag or a portmanteau where it could be snatched and spirited away in an instant. One notorious street thief went a step further. Harry Mountfield dressed as a railwayman and helped himself to parcels. Alice Matthews also liked playing a part. She posed as a sickly woman, calling on the surgery in need of the doctor's help. As soon as the housekeeper left she stole anything of value.

Harry Lancashire matched Alice's audacity. Adopting the persona of a wealthy businessman about to make an enticing offer for a pub, he asked the landlord to show him round. No sooner had Harry left to make arrangements for the purchase than the landlord discovered valuables were missing. Harry Burke loved a surprise – none more than the ones he got when he opened a letter and found paper money or postal orders enclosed. Of course, none of the letters was addressed to him. He'd fished them out of letterboxes with a piece of wire and some birdlime. Alfred Noakes hovered in church graveyards. A posy in his hands, he hunched over a fresh grave. After a suitable time he called into the church, not to say a prayer for the dearly departed, but to prise open the offertory box.

George Nevin also had a religious bent. His clerical attire disarmed his victims. After he'd left, the goods the perplexed shopkeeper missed were concealed under Nevin's cassock.

Thomas Pickford also targeted shops. Posing as a detective investigating the passing of forged banknotes, he asked to see those in the till and, issuing a receipt, left to have them examined at the station. Likewise, John William Marsland never left the undertaker without both his sympathy and his cash – borrowed so he could remove the body of his dear wife prior to interment. Elizabeth Hodgson's interest was based not on a sorrowful past but the happy future she guaranteed all who took her advice. She was one of the many fortune-tellers of the 1870s who, by squeezing money from gullible clients, gave her profession a bad name. Similarly, Cockney Jim gave some an aversion to wedding rings.

The Wedding Ring Scam

One of the failsafe scams of the nineteenth century worked by crooks the length and breadth of the country was the ring scam. Cockney Jim was the most renowned of its Manchester exponents. Like all the best scams, it was very simple. It depended on the ability of the con man to convince the victim of his good faith. The key was to appear naïve, even simple, and to convince the victim that he was the one who was taking advantage of another's folly. The only prop was a fake gold ring, complete with a bogus hallmark, worth only a few coppers. The crooks operated in pairs, both respectably dressed, usually in the style of petty clerks.

They went to a prosperous part of town where one of them made a great display of finding a gold ring on the footpath. He then hailed the victim, who had witnessed this stroke of good fortune, and asked his opinion of the ring's value. At this stage the accomplice, posing as a curious passer-by, appeared on the scene, announcing that the ring was worth between £10 and £20 and offering to buy it. The sharp agreed, but when it emerged that his accomplice did not have the ready cash, he reluctantly offered it to the victim for less. Cockney Jim invariably got a bite.

A woman who was clearly pregnant worked a clever variation on the ring scam. She approached a respectable person in the street, or ideally a group of domestics on their afternoon off. With tears running down her pale face, she told them of a faithless husband, hungry children at home and another on the way. Nothing, she said, stands between them and the street except her one possession – a wedding ring she would gladly sell for a fraction of its worth. The dupe who fell for this immediately made his way to the nearest pawnshop to convert his good fortune into money.

Uncle's Pop Shop

Today's Britain, we are told, is drowning in a sea of debt. A flimsy raft of credit cards, overdrafts, hire purchase agreements, deferred repayments and secured loans sustains our continental holidays and luxury cars. Debt allows us all to enjoy what none of us can afford. In fact debt is less important today than it was in Manchester during the second half of the nineteenth century. Today it means extravagant leisure. Then it meant people could eat. And in place of today's elaborate financial arrangements there was, every couple of streets, a shop – 'uncle's', 'the pop shop', 'the pawn' – and a constant stream of customers, entering with newspaper-wrapped parcels under their arms and downcast eyes.

The pawnbroker, who has made a comeback in recent years, is a moneylender and in the nineteenth century he enabled the poor to keep a roof over their heads, feed their children and put clothes on their backs. In 1874 there were almost 300 pawnshops in Manchester and Salford and the poorer the area the greater their density. Charter Street, for instance, had three, Lombard Street four and Angel Street two. The poor, who made up a substantial proportion of the population, lived their lives on the verge of destitution. In good times they could pay the rent, feed themselves and clothe their children. In bad, they faced hunger, eviction and the workhouse.

In our day of high wages and ready credit, when every post brings offers of store cards and cheap money, it is impossible to appreciate the pawnbroker's importance. He was the poor man's banker. In times of crisis he was a godsend, the only source of ready money. Without the pawn a large section of the population would not have survived.

What's more, the pawn would take virtually anything as security on a loan. Valuables, such as rings and watches, were often unknown to the poor. But when a working man bought a major item of clothing, such as boots or an overcoat, he used up all his available cash. In the event of a financial crisis he pawned these prize possessions. Even if he had nothing as valuable as a decent item of clothing he could pawn pots and pans.

Later, when he got paid, he redeemed his valuables by repaying the loan and the interest on it. Poor families often pawned their best items of clothing early in the week and redeemed them on pay day for Sunday wear. The longer an item remained in the pawn, the greater the interest on the loan secured on it. Eventually, when the pawnbroker despaired of being repaid, he recouped his losses by selling the item.

For many homes this to-ing and fro-ing of the family's valuables underpinned the whole domestic economy. Yet, the nineteenth century pawnbroker has a poor reputation, similar in many ways to that of the present-day moneylender. This negative image, however, does not stand scrutiny. Just as today the moneylender's rates are often less than those charged by more reputable financial institutions, so it was with the much-maligned pawnbroker. He charged less than the tallyman, who sold clothes and household goods on hire purchase while some pawnbrokers advanced as much as two-thirds of the value of the pledge.

Unlike others', the pawnbrokers' rates were regulated. There were, of course, ways of side-stepping these regulations but there was also a limit to the amount of fancy footwork a pawnbroker might practise. He could not operate without a licence and the authorities would not renew it if he repeatedly breached its conditions. This is why many experienced policemen, like James Bent, maintained that the vast majority of pawned goods were not stolen.

Bent was a staunch defender of pawnbrokers. He claimed that in his long experience they often gave invaluable help to the police and were particularly useful in securing larceny convictions. He never knew one who did not give all possible help to the police and on countless occasions they reported their suspicions even when they had no evidence of crime. Even Bent, however, accepted there were dishonest pawnbrokers. But he also realised that without their help the police would have had no idea where to look for stolen goods. Most pawnbrokers were willing to help the police. After all, they were the most obvious outlets for stolen goods and any who got a reputation for dishonesty was totally at the police's mercy. Besides, a relatively small number of professional criminals controlled the market in receiving stolen goods. Only amateurs resorted to the pawn and their business was generally more trouble than it was worth. This is what made the pawnbroker such a danger to the thief with stolen goods he wanted to convert to cash. He had to know his pawnbroker.

In reality, pawnbrokers were on both sides of the law as shown by the events of 1878. A deputation from the Manchester and Salford Association of Pawnbrokers complained to the Chief Constable of a scam that was undermining public confidence in the integrity of its members. The moving force behind the scam was Diamond Sam, whose nickname had nothing to do with ostentatious displays of expensive jewellery. In fact Sam was never seen in possession of a diamond. What he was never without, however, were pawn tickets purporting to relate to diamonds of great value, which he sold for a fraction of their putative value. For the purposes of this particular scam, however, he was offering the tickets as security for loans. To allay his victims' suspicions he enlisted the help of several pawnbrokers who undertook to assure the wary victim that the tickets they were about to accept were indeed of great value. The Chief Constable, Captain Palin, put Caminada on the case. As usual, he adopted a direct approach: he answered the newspaper advertisement and thereby met the principal rogues and three of the pawnbrokers. He promptly arrested all six. Among those swindled was a civil engineer, a man of sixty-five, who lost over £176 – worth today about £23,000.

Of those arrested, the courts convicted five. One got off lightly with eighteen months but the others got five years' penal servitude.

Besides the genuine pawnshops, there were also many 'putty shops' or marine stores, which served the same function as pawnbrokers. The difference was they were less scrupulous about what they took and many readily dealt in stolen goods. They did not have the status or offer the security of the pawn and of course they charged higher interest on their loans. Their customers were the poorest of the poor and the possessions on which they hoped to raise a few shillings were too threadbare for even the poorest pawnbroker. The interest on a shilling was 2d or 3d a week, that is between seventeen and twenty-five per cent and no legal framework governed these transactions. The dolly shops, the hundreds of second-hand clothes dealers and the army of rag and bone men who trundled through the streets of the city, all provided means of disposing of stolen goods. Their customers were tramps, beggars and sneak thieves, the dregs of the criminal world.

Prostitutes, who were invariably thieves, also played a key role in disposing of stolen goods. They, like most petty thieves, preferred to sell their ill-gotten goods to members of the public, always offering them as 'special bargains'. The appeal of selling goods this way was that even though the thief received only a fraction of their value, he or she got more than from a fence. And there was nowhere better to meet potential buyers, all the more amenable for a few pints, than in one of the city's many pubs.

6

Pubs

An Oasis in a Brick Desert

Its amber lights softened the chill. Hovering in the misty dankness, it floated like an ocean liner, the hum of conversation like the purr of engines. Then the door opened, splashing light on the paving flags and exhaling the aroma of beer and tobacco, the musk of warm bodies, the bray of laughter and the promise of women.

The pub and the gin palace were the perfect antidote to the dark and dreary slums. Any man looking for brightness and splendour to lift his spirits above the squalor of his home, who craved extravagance and luxury to counter the grim pragmatism of the industrial town, found them all there. With the warm glow of gaslight, an elaborately carved bar of sumptuous mahogany, high ceilings, an illuminated clock, plate glass windows and elaborate plaster cornices and friezes, it was a palace. Only a remarkable man could resist the lure of the pub.

Jerome Caminada, no liberal apologist for criminals and certainly fully aware of the pub's role in crime, nevertheless said, 'Drink is responsible for many people making their appearance in gaol; but, surrounded as they are by a vast desert of bricks and mortar, with nothing except the public house in their midst to enliven them, or to arouse pleasurable emotions, is it to be wondered that women become drunken and untidy and that men desert their homes for the public house?'

To understand the importance of pubs in working class life at this time it is necessary to go back to the situation in the 1820s, when the chattering classes were agog with stories of a sodden nation adrift on a sea of cheap spirits. The purpose of the 1830 Beer Act was to encourage people to forsake spirits in favour of beer by making the healthier drink readily available. The Act allowed anyone to open a beerhouse and sell from 4am until 10pm, without the need for a justice's licence. Most of those who took advantage of this change in the law merely turned their house into a bar – the barrel stood in the corner and people sat around in a room hardly distinguishable from their own front room. It wasn't long before many commentators were deploring the effects of the Act, just as they had once deplored the previous situation. One complained that beer was now sold 'at every baker's and chandler's shop; regular drinking places opened in cellars and back premises in every alley in the town slums.' The result was an inevitable increase in drunkenness. By the 1840s, Manchester had a reputation for depravity, which all assumed was the result of its renown as the home of prodigious drinkers. Part of this insatiable capacity for drink was due to the poor quality of the city's drinking water.

Commenting on the situation in the 1840s, Friedrich Engels, who could drink and womanise with the best, was nevertheless shocked by Manchester streets on a Saturday night. 'Intemperance may be seen in all its brutality.' These scenes were repeated on Sunday night – though, Engels had to admit, with slightly less noise.

In the early Victorian period the alehouse or beerhouse sold only beer. It had neither cellar nor bar – the casks lined the wall. Customers drank at simple tables, sitting on benches or forms. Larger pubs might have a 'parlour' with chairs and pictures for the discerning customer who wanted surroundings infinitely plusher than his home. As Queen Victoria's reign progressed, pubs became more impressive and more alluring to those who lived in the dingy houses surrounding them. The saloon and the public bar – the vault – replaced the taproom. The bar appeared, replacing the serving hatch. In many Manchester pubs a number of small rooms branched off a narrow corridor.

By the 1860s these places offered food. The normal fare was fried fish and bread, sometimes supplemented by the pie-seller's offerings. Even those workmen who could not afford these small luxuries brought in their lunch to be cooked. Spartan as this sounds, it exercised a great pull, especially for those right at the bottom of the social scale. For tramps and beggars it was somewhere out of the cold when they had a few coppers. For most of the nineteenth century beer remained remarkably cheap at about fourpence a quart. For navvies and those who couldn't afford to rent or live in digs it was the only alternative to the squalor of the lodging house. For the off-duty domestic it was a place where she could meet her own. For migrant workers it was a source of information about jobs and places to stay. For street vendors and stallholders it was somewhere to take the weight off their feet.

For the ordinary working man too there was nothing to rival the appeal of the pub. That first pint on pay day was an unparalleled luxury, a well-deserved respite from numbing grind. And very often it was bought with coppers straight from a fresh pay packet, for although a law of 1883 outlawed the practice of paying men in the pub, it nevertheless remained common. Even those who received their pay elsewhere generally made it their first port of call. It was the working man's club, as exclusive in its own way as the capital's gentleman's clubs in Mayfair and Knightsbridge. As the statistician G.R. Porter noted in 1851, 'no person above the rank of labouring man or artisan would venture to go into a public house'.

The pub meant far more than drink to the working man. Many of the middle class reformers made the error of thinking that pubs were no more than places where the poor man drank himself into oblivion. But it was far more than that. It was where he met his mates and discussed the events of the day, football and their other shared concerns. It was the centre of trade union and political activity. The wise landlord was happy to extend the free use of an upstairs room to a political party or union meeting, knowing full well that talking was a thirsty business.

It often served as the workers' bank. Many pubs ran savings

clubs for clothes and boots. Others saved for an annual 'picnic' which might be a trip to a race meeting, the seaside or the countryside. Mates who spent time together developed a strong sense of community and the need for mutual support. The 'whip-round' for the unfortunate man who had lost his job or whose family was suffering illness, accident or bereavement was an established part of pub life.

The publican was often one of very few people in a working class area who had ready cash. Therefore he sometimes acted as an unofficial pawnbroker and moneylender, but only as a favour to valued customers. The pub was very much at the centre of working life because it was also an unofficial labour exchange. It was the unemployed man's first resort, the place where he was most likely to find out about available work. This was particularly the case for tramping artisans. It was common practice for a union to issue a 'blank' or a 'clearance' to any member in search of work. This entitled him to supper and lodgings and, if he failed to get work, enough money to get to the next 'house of call'. The most highly unionised workers – such as printers, builders and engineers, compositors and stonemasons – practised this 'tramping' in search of work. Having found work through 'the local' and settled in the area, the craftsman returned to the pub for much of his social life. Dog-fanciers, pigeon racers, brass bands, choirs, darts, football and cricket teams, allotment societies, angling clubs and clog-dancing troupes were only some of the groups who made the pub the focal point of their activities.

Furthermore, drink was locked into every significant working class social occasion. From wetting the baby's head to funerals, and every major event in between – the start and finish of an apprenticeship, a betrothal, a wedding, a change of job, the wakes holidays – all provided occasions for a celebratory drink. The man who didn't drink could never fully participate in community life. Is it any wonder people regarded the teetotaller as unsociable and odd?

Prejudices and urban myths reinforced the compulsion to drink. It was part of accepted working class lore that drink was good for you. Who could doubt that a man who spent all day sweating in front of a furnace needed to replace his body's lost fluids? Everybody knew that a drink kept out the cold, put an edge on the appetite, induced restful sleep and kept the bowels regular. A man's capacity for drink was a measure of his masculinity. A decent bloke 'stood his corner' and kept his mates by including them in his round. Throughout Britain, but, as the crime statistics prove, especially in Manchester, heavy drinking permeated every crevice of working class life. Like dirt on a miner's skin, it penetrated every pore.

Industry figures show that in 1876 the average consumption of beer was 34.5 gallons and 1.3 gallons for spirits. This is a staggering amount as an average which includes every man, woman and child in the country. Given the large number of teetotal Nonconformists and respectable women whose consumption consisted of a small sherry at a funeral breakfast, these figures are amazing. Their reality is best appreciated by looking at the number of pubs in Manchester and Salford at the time. Between 1850 and 1870, in a single working class area, Chorlton-on-Medlock, there were 325 pubs. (In the 1980s only twenty-four remained.) And Chorlton was nowhere near the top of the pub league. Hulme, with over 600, had almost twice as many. One of the reasons for the number of pubs in this area was the cavalry barracks opposite St. George's Church, just off Chester Road, which housed over 300 men and their non-commissioned officers. As always, the deeper the poverty, the denser the pubs. In 1892, after years of frenzied activity by the local authority in closing undesirable pubs and beerhouses, Manchester still had 3,031 licensed premises.

As late as 1896, when London had one pub for every 393 people, Liverpool one for every 279 and Sheffield one for every 176, Manchester gloried in her position as top of the table for the number of pubs per head of population. There was one for every 167 Mancunians, so many that if an invader had destroyed every dwelling house in the city, but left the pubs intact, no one would have been without a roof over his head. Salford was similarly well served. In 1861, Manchester's sister city had 387 beerhouses and

111 pubs. Ten years before, Clifton alone had fifty beerhouses and pubs. Salford too was a garrison town with an infantry barracks on Regent Road housing over 700 men and their officers.

Even this, however, does not tell the full story of the extent to which drink permeated every crevice of the city. To understand this we have to look at the illicit distillers. In no country in the world was the illicit distillation of spirits so deeply embedded in peasant culture as in Ireland. Delight in defying the excise man was many layered. Drink provided a cheap pleasure in a country where pleasures were few and it tasted all the better because it involved cocking a snook at the British authorities.

In Manchester the police fought a war of attrition against the distillers, mostly Irish. The typical moonshiner did not produce a few bottles for personal consumption. When police arrested Ellen Broadhurst while she sweated over her still, they found forty gallons of whiskey in her bedroom. In a single year Manchester coroners attributed the deaths of 200 people directly to drink. This does not include the countless thousands who died as a result of the long-term effects of alcohol in undermining their health. When the United Kingdom Alliance, an organisation campaigning for a legal ban on alcohol, decided to site its headquarters where the need was greatest, it plumped for Manchester.

What's more, there is a great deal of evidence that drunkenness among women was increasing at this time. The 1871 figures show a five-fold increase over ten years. And the evidence is that the drinking habits of the poor were changing for the worse and their liking for spirits was increasing.

As the century wore on, porter gave way to the thinner mild as the poor man's most popular tipple. This 'four ale', sold in a public or 'four ale' bar, was available at fourpence a quart. In the saloon bar, whose patrons were a few notches higher up the social ladder, most preferred bitter at three pence or even fourpence a pint. On a special occasion gin, or from the 1860s the more popular Irish whiskey, was a treat. From the 1880s Scotch took the place of Irish, though many women still preferred gin or port. Brandy, at twice the price of other spirits, was the toffs' drink and that of the man who had enjoyed a big win on the horses.

Toffs, of course, were not immune to the allure of drink. News-papers often gave the impression that drinking to excess was an exclusively working class weakness. This is because the middle class drunk did not usually end up in court; a constable was more likely to send him home in a cab. Yet there is plenty of anecdotal evidence to suggest that many reputable businessmen regularly partook of a good lunch. To the middle classes, one working man was indistinguishable from another. But differences in status be-tween working men were as great as those between the urchin and the earl. The independent artisans – skilled craftsmen, like carpenters and plumbers – were far above unskilled labourers, such as carters and navvies. A respectable pub attracted a lot of artisans and the better class of labourers, those in regular employ-ment. A good licensee was jealous of his pub's reputation and knew that in order to maintain it he had to bar beggars, criminals, prostitutes and noisy drunks and keep profanities and coarseness within the limits of decency. Most of all, gambling was a problem for the good landlord. A quiet game of whist or a board game was acceptable, but gambling led to fighting and attracted the wrong sort of customers.

Some pubs weren't respectable for other reasons. The graphi-cally nicknamed 'Blood Tub' – the Royal Oak, on Higher Cam-bridge Street – was renowned for its nightly violence. For young men in the area, drinking there was a rite of passage, proof that one was hard, a real man. As for the regulars, they were suspicious of newcomers and demanded they fight or slink back to their own neighbourhood.

The Devil's Brew

Not one nineteenth century commentator questioned the link between drink and crime. It's not only its capacity to provoke vio-lence that makes drink the author of crime. For many, especially those motivated by religious fervour, drink was the cause of all forms of crime and removing drink from working class life was the only way to put an end to it. Others argued the connection was more complex. Whatever the nature of the link, all agree that the extent of drunkenness at this time was prodigious. You have only to look at the pages of any Manchester or Salford newspaper to find accounts of drunken brawling and beer-fuelled assaults on the police.

What is most remarkable about many of these incidents, however, is the indulgent attitude of the courts. The case tried on 15 August 1885 is typical. PC Robinson told the city's Police Court that the previous night he attended the New Clavenden Inn, where the accused, Thomas Riley, was systematically smashing all the glasses in the pub. The constable's presence did nothing to deter Riley, who promptly smashed a glass over the policeman's head. Riley, a thirty-year-old clerk, pleaded guilty as charged and offered no explanation, beyond saying that he was drunk. The magistrate seemed to accept this as mitigation as he merely fined him ten shillings with costs.

Understandably the police resented this lenient approach, which they felt did nothing to stem the rising tide of drink-fuelled violence. The English crime figures for 1865 to 1866 paint a grim picture of a country awash with drink and alcohol-driven crime. During that year justices dealt with 94,000 cases of drunkenness and drunk and disorderly behaviour, or 250 for every day of the year. About one in five of these were women. Of these they convicted 63,000, including 10,000 women, the majority of whom they fined; 7,000, however, ended up in prison. By 1870, the situation was even worse as Manchester police made 11,083 arrests for drunkenness, nearly half the total for all offences.

Drunks were capable of every form of violence. There was no savagery unknown to the readers of the *Manchester Evening News* during this period. To take just a few of countless examples, the incident that took place outside Blunt's beerhouse in Gorton is particularly interesting. The accused, Joseph Smith, who appeared respectable and well-dressed, for some reason took offence at something the labourer Patrick Moran said and proceeded to bite off the lower part of his ear. A disconsolate Smith could offer no explanation for his behaviour.

James Bent recounts how he was travelling from Croft's Bank to Barton when he spotted a drunk lying spread-eagled on top of a cart of coals. The man was sliding down and about to fall under the wheels of the wagon when Bent rushed over and caught him. Rather than showering Bent with gratitude, the drunkard instead aimed a running kick at him, his heavy boot breaking the third finger on the policeman's hand. Much to Bent's annoyance his assailant got off with a five shillings fine – yet another example of the bench's indulgent attitude to assaults on the police. Nor were women much better than men. They frequently appeared in court after drunken brawls. Usually the magistrate admonished them and sent them away bound over to keep the peace. Even when magistrates imposed the usual penalty, a fine of 'five bob', this was no deterrent. It was only in 1872 that a graded scale of fines for drunkenness was introduced, from ten shillings for a first offence to forty shillings for a third.

No one disputed the effect of drink on family life. The drunken husband who beat his unfortunate wife and starving children was a standard of temperance literature. His children were starving because he drank his wages or lost his job because of his addiction. Once he reached these depths he often resorted to stealing so that he could buy drink. Meanwhile, his neglected children, growing up without proper paternal guidance, drifted into crime. The drunkard, however, was also a victim. Official Manchester police figures show that in the middle of the nineteenth century over half the victims of violent robbery had been drinking. In most cases the perpetrator was a woman – usually a prostitute – or a woman with an accomplice.

Lord of All He Surveys

Yet, though opponents of drink frequently proclaimed its evils, their efforts had no impact on levels of drinking. Even less did they diminish the number of people who wanted to spend their lives behind the bar. Running a pub, either as a tenant or licensee, was an extremely attractive proposition. For both men and women it was often their only hope of escaping the endless drudgery of the factory or domestic service.

Because beer was cheap and rent and rates low it required little initial capital. Yet a pub conferred independence and status. Landlords had standing in the local community and there is no doubt a good landlord could stamp his character on a pub. Though people of all types dreamt of having their name above the door of their own little pub, those who achieved it tended to be of a certain type. Many were the children of publicans, former shopkeepers or travelling salesmen. Many speculative builders put money into a pub, hoping to accumulate a nest egg. Former domestic servants, with their experience in household management, found running a pub very appealing. Ex-servicemen and retired policemen fancied they had the authority to keep an orderly house. Minor music hall and circus stars and former sportsmen – particularly jockeys and boxers – hoping to trade on their celebrity, often took a pub. But most of them didn't own the bar they tended. Brewery policy in Manchester was to install managers. This ensured that every facet of the industry, from brewing to placing the foaming pint on the bar, was under the brewers' control and with it the opportunity to maximise profits.

A pub was also very attractive to those who prospered in that twilight realm between legitimate commerce and dishonesty. Former sportsmen involved in gambling and fences, in particular, found a pub very attractive. It gave the fence a perfect cover for contacting his suppliers without arousing suspicion. The frequency with which police reports mention that certain pubs were the haunts of thieves suggests they played a major role in the disposal of stolen goods. It isn't surprising, therefore, that many were dangerous for strangers. Nor is it surprising that the authorities were unable to enforce the proper running of pubs and waged a fruitless battle against breaches of the licensing laws.

In the 1850s members of the Committee of the Manchester and Salford Temperance Society visited 1,437 drinking establishments. They saw little evidence of any regard for the alcohol regulations. Instead a culture of vice and violence flourished, especially in the poorer areas. Worst of all was Angel Meadow, where they saw filthy spectres clad in rags drinking and gambling in the street.

In reality there were few enforceable regulations. Those that existed required the landlord merely to prevent violence and not allow his premises to become the haunt of criminals. It was only in the 1870s that it became general practice not to serve those under the age of sixteen. Yet even these requirements proved too demanding for many landlords. In 1871 alone, for instance, Salford magistrates summoned a tenth of all landlords and beer sellers for offences ranging from being drunk to running a disorderly house. The Chief Constable, however, had no illusions that this would change anything as the penalties available were ineffective. 'The beer sellers,' he said in his annual report, 'have been exceedingly neglectful and no amount of fines seem to have the desired effect of preventing them breaking regulations.'

Nor does this mean that the remaining ninety per cent of landlords, who were not summoned, attracted a clientele consisting entirely of tip-top moral specimens. It simply means the summoned landlords were making no effort to dissuade blatantly criminal elements from using their premises to conduct their nefarious affairs. That being so, the landlord was likely to be actively involved in crime, either as a fence or a pimp. A decade later nothing had changed. A visitor to Oldham Road described the pubs and gin shops as 'roaring full'. In every pub and street rows and fights were taking place – the indifference of the landlords suggesting they were the norm. 'The whole street rang with shouting, screaming and swearing, mingled with the jarring music of half a dozen bands.'

Yet it was not until 1869 that magistrates regained control of beerhouses. The Wine and Beerhouse Act of that year signalled the beginning of a new, stricter era in the control of drinking establishments. At that year's licensing session, Manchester's mayor, John Grave, condemned the practice of indiscriminately granting beerhouse licenses to all who met the minimum rateable value qualification and could pay the two guinea fee. The result of this lax policy was that over 2,000 beerhouses, most of a 'very inferior class', choked the streets of Manchester. Nearly all were in the poorer areas of the city and the new legislation enabled the magistrates to close 200 that year. These were the worst of the worst – the haunts of thieves, fences and the lowest prostitutes. Yet drunkenness remained a major problem.

And it was by no means only low beerhouses that concerned the city authorities. Upper Moss Lane had in the Star of Denmark and Bentley's Hotel two of the city's most disreputable pubs which lost their licences in the 1890s, as did the Shoulder of Mutton in Jackson Street. All three were disorderly houses. The licensee of the Moulder's Arms in Owen Street found himself in a worse position in 1897. The court convicted him of keeping a brothel.

He was by no means the only one. Many pubs were attached to dance halls where prostitutes trawled for clients. It was quite common for the licensee to run the nearby brothel, thereby controlling the full gambit of reprehensible pleasures. Police returns for the 1870s state that there were seventy-four pubs and 121 beerhouses in Manchester 'frequented by persons of bad character'. In most cases this meant blatant prostitutes. Some Nonconformist reformers advocated nothing less than closing all such places but they were up against one of the most powerful vested interests in Victorian Britain – the brewers.

The Canterbury Hall on Chapel Street was typical of many of the bigger pubs of the time in offering a range of attractions. In 1861 Mr George Fox was advertising 'Fox's Victoria Music Hall'. Seventeen years later it was the venue for another working-class pastime – billiards – when it hosted a match between the champion, W. Cook and the former champion, John Roberts. Such a contest attracted a large crowd, a wager on the outcome sharpening the interest of many spectators. Sporting gentlemen who liked a bet featured large among the Canterbury Hall's customers and this eventually led to its demise. In 1893, when police opposed its licence, they cited the landlord's record of running illegal lotteries. They also claimed that the pub was 'not required', as in that area there was one public house for every 106 residents, a generous ratio even by Manchester standards.

Billiards also played a big part in the appeal of the White House, the oldest pub on Stretford Road. Its licensee in 1871 was James Platford, who made enough money to build a hotel in front of the pub. That year his employees included five domestic servants and a groom, all living in. Additionally, his boarder was a Mr S.W. Digges, who gloried in the title of professor of billiards.

The Railway in Greengate was one of Salford's first beerhouses. The landlord in 1869, Bill Brown, was a prizefighting enthusiast. He and another Salford landlord, Jack Miller of the Pink Tavern, fought for a purse of £50. Unfortunately for them, magistrates summoned both men, imposed fines and warned them as to their future behaviour.

Last Man Standing

During this period prizefighting remained one of the underworld's sources of income. It was an attraction that brought all classes together and had the bully rubbing shoulders with the barrister, the toff talking with the scavenger.

Deansgate was the focal point of the city's prizefighting in the 1870s. Hundreds of pounds changed hands. By the time Victoria came to the throne in 1837, however, prizefighting was already in decline and was subsequently outlawed by a series of legal judgements. Yet this mix of bare-knuckle fighting and wrestling, with few rules, still attracted vast crowds and stirred intense emotions. If the fighters sometimes lacked finesse, there was no doubting their courage and durability. Fights often ran to 100 rounds, in the days when a round ended when one man was knocked from his feet, and lasted up to three hours. Provided a fighter could get to his feet within thirty seconds there was no limit to the number of knockdowns he might survive. On each occasion he hit the ground his seconds dragged him to his corner and spent the permitted time reviving him. The crowd felt cheated if a man conceded before being beaten senseless.

It was during the years of decline that rules standardising prize-fighting came into force. The Rules of the Prize Ring introduced in 1838 specified the size of the ring, the role of seconds and umpires and banned head butting. In 1886 the Pugilists' Benevolent Association adopted the Marquess of Queensberry's rules, stipulating that contests last no longer than twenty three-minute rounds with a one-minute break between each. Now fighters wore gloves, no longer wrestled and enjoyed the luxury of a ten-second breather when knocked down.

Far more important, however, was the introduction of the points system. Prior to this the victor was the fighter who was not lying unconscious. Now they won points for both strikes and defensive parries. Further, the contest was no longer a fight to the finish: the referee stopped it if he deemed either contestant 'unfit to continue'. Displays of raw courage and the capacity to endure punishment were no longer commonplace, with the inevitable result that fighting lost a great deal of its popular appeal. No amount of finesse could match the appeal of naked brutality and dogged endurance, which ensured the sport survived underground.

After the 1860s fights continued as a niche attraction but attracted little publicity. Those who organised bouts were never full-time promoters. They were duckers and divers, men who made a living by doing a 'bit of this and a bit of that' – the 'this' was often running a pub, the 'that' gambling or prostitution. At the bottom end of the sport, some pubs had resident bruisers. Many of these declining pugilists made a living as brothel bouncers or prostitutes' bullies. Anyone who fancied his chances could hire gloves for a few coppers and take him on. Often, as at The Railway and The Pink Tavern singing and comic turns separated the bouts.

Good Enough for a Drunk

Fights were by no means the only pub entertainment available. Attractions came in an amazing variety of forms but the emphasis was very much on popular participation. People liked to provide their own entertainment, to such an extent that the distinction between the performer and the audience blurred.

Early in the Victorian period the 'free and easy' was all the rage. This was the nineteenth century equivalent of karaoke, with customers taking it in turns to sing, give a recitation or play a tune. Plenty of pubs provided music – mechanical organs, drums, tambourines and the Joanna. Sometimes there was a hurdy-gurdy man and a girl on a tambourine. Singing was a popular entertainment. Bawdy songs – the broader the innuendo, the louder the applause – were particularly popular. In March 1870 a *Manchester Guardian* journalist ventured into a working class Manchester beerhouse to observe the goings-on, in much the same way that he might have studied the Kalahari Bushmen at play. The area he explored was behind the Theatre Royal and the Free Trade Hall, a cluster of streets famous for drunken debauchery and fighting. Many of the punters were thieves and prostitutes. The prostitutes picked up their quarry there and took them to one of the many shops on Peter Street, which were fronts for brothels. It was the poor singing on offer in the pubs that had the biggest impact on the journalist. He quoted approvingly one patron's opinion: 'Anything is good enough for a drunken man, but this is almost too bad for that.' In the same pub a man singing an air from *Don Giovanni* had the tell-tale pallor and cropped hair of the recently released convict. His efforts, too, were little appreciated.

From this sort of entertainment it was a short step to the first music halls, which were no more than pubs providing entertainment. Even as purpose-built halls became major attractions, the penny-gaff remained a feature of working class areas. For those who preferred a little more excitement, there was plenty on offer. Cock-fighting, though banned in 1849, nevertheless remained popular. Fighting dogs, particularly bull terriers, retained a niche following. As a preliminary to competition, owners cropped their dogs' ears in 'sporting trim', to prevent the opponent from clamping them in his teeth. A less palatable aspect of training involved matching the fighting dog against a tame animal to get it used to killing. The use of dogs against rats was far more popular and for many years William Hamilton's workshop, next to his Pier Head beerhouse in Albert Street, hosted 'ratting'. The building conveniently overlooked the Irwell, with its plentiful supply of rats.

These contests between dogs and rodents filled the pubs that hosted them, especially at holiday times, when they were a traditional pastime. The arena consisted of a ring about 6ft across, its wooden walls rising to elbow height. Painted white and brilliantly lit it provided a sharp contrast to the scarlet rats' blood. On a good night there was plenty of gore, as a properly organised meeting required an enormous number of rats. One London publican, famous for the quality of his ratting, regularly used up to 700 a week and on several occasions as many as 2,000. He claimed that it took twenty families to supply him. Both sewer and water-ditch rats stank – filling the room with the reek of a hot drain.

The publican covered his costs by charging between sixpence and a shilling admission. Spectators, who had spent the early part of the evening drinking, discussing form and betting on the outcome, crowded round the pit, ale and gin in hand. Behind them others balanced on chairs and tables to get a better view. Betting was always brisk.

Rules governed all serious ratting venues. The organisers matched the dogs by weight and measured each animal's score in relation to its weight. A timekeeper operated the stopwatch and when he shouted 'Timer!' the owner lifted out his dog. Apart from the money won on bets, the best animals went away with trophies. But gambling was the heart of it. In the preliminary contests dogs killed a dozen rats while in the latter stages they tackled as many as fifty. The timekeeper, with his stopwatch and the umpire, who ruled on whether a rat was dead, controlled proceedings.

Pubs often staged more sombre business. Traditionally, they provided the venue for coroner's inquests. In May 1874, the Bull's Head, in Greengate, held an inquest. What came to light provides a clearer insight into Salford life than volumes of statistics.

The coroner was investigating the death of Robert Haslam, 52, who, for half his lifetime, eked out a living as a comic oinger and clog-dancer. At the pinnacle of his fame he performed at that Manchester institution, Ben Lang's Music Hall, but for many years Haslam was locked into a downward trajectory that saw him performing in pubs for a few drinks and a couple of shillings. The coroner found that he died of natural causes 'accelerated by want of medical attention and the proper necessities of life'. In other words, he had starved to death. The jury was so moved by the case and the condition of Robert Haslam's family that, to save them from going the same way, they raised a ten-shilling donation.

Most of the business of another Greengate pub, the Waterloo, was far different from the formalities of a coroner's proceedings. In fact, most of its business was in breach of the conditions of its licence. The landlord, Richard Gordon, admitted as much when summoned in 1869. The police had not, until then, posed a problem as lookouts ringed the pub. Dog-fighting was also illegal, though that only served to sharpen the enjoyment of the punters who gathered at the Rose and Shamrock in Chapel Street. In November 1861 the police ruined their night by swooping in great numbers, arresting fifty spectators and hauling the licensee before the magistrates, who gave him a month in Strangeways.

Neither press condemnation nor police raids could suppress popular entertainment. On Tib Street, a few doors from the corner with Whittle Street, there was the Black Boy beerhouse. In 1896, the magistrates convicted the tenant of organising a cock-fight. Such was the interest generated that in addition to the drinkers – each with money on his fancy – hordes of by-passers, many patrons of local betting shops, thronged the doorway and blocked the street in their anxiety to place a bet.

On the same street, where it met Thomas Street, stood the Manchester Arms, which was the subject of so many complaints in 1896 that the police started watching it. In the course of a single hour 200 people passed in and out. It was not the excellence of the Arms' brew that was the attraction but the opportunity for a flutter. The licensee sat at a table in the front room with lists of the runners and riders spread out around him. When the police descended on him, he was unable to offer any plausible explanation and the court subsequently imposed the enormous fine of £100. Undeterred, he immediately resumed business and though the court fined him a second time six months later, there is no reason to believe this made a significant dent in his profits. The courts did nothing to curtail the city's appetite for gambling. Despite the hefty fines imposed on most of the list shops in the area, several opponents of gambling complained to the local papers that the droves of punters thronging Thomas Street continued to make the thoroughfare impassable.

The Three Legs of Man was far worse. It stood opposite a cluster of houses known as Birtles Square. Throughout the 1870s both the pub and the area were the scene of daily violence. When the *Salford Chronicle* applauded its demolition in March 1880, it reminded its readers that for thirty years it had been a 'den of sin and infamy'. The British Queen on the corner of Queen Street, one of the most squalid areas of the city, also gloried in its notoriety. In 1869 the court sentenced its landlord, Cooper, a notorious fence, to transportation to Australia. For many years the pub had been a haven for thieves, prostitutes and every other species of Salford crook. For over thirty years the police battled to close it. That it survived into the twentieth century is amazing in view of their allegation that it was 'the most disorderly and disgraceful house in all Salford'. When the magistrates eventually refused its licence in 1904 it was because by then its only customers were prostitutes.

The Ship Inn, Deansgate was also run by a series of shady characters, each of whom tried to outdo his predecessor in infamy. Harry Snowden was a notorious receiver of stolen goods. John Northern, formerly the keeper of a beerhouse, was a thief and a fraud who specialised in card sharping. Archibald Coyles, a former boxer, was also implicated in a number of card-sharping swindles, as was Mark Hampson, who kept a beerhouse, the Brown Cow in Irwell Street. Hampson later became well known as a trainer of racing and fighting dogs. He was equally renowned as the husband of one of the city's most notorious pickpockets.

The Dog and Duck in Charter Street was for decades the watering hole of the swell mobsmen. Dressed in all their finery they set out to fleece the gentlemen of the Cotton Exchange and pass the forged money, which was their speciality. Many of the Deansgate pubs were among the most notorious in the city. As early as the 1840s, the Bull's Head on the corner of Deansgate and Wood Street was described by the police as 'the worst in town'. The licensee's convictions equalled those of most of his customers, 'thieves and prostitutes of the very worst description'. Though pubs near the market opened early in the morning on market days, the Bull's Head stayed open during the night to satisfy its clientele, none of whom had any reason to rise early. Nevertheless, it retained its licence and after a change of licensee was advertising 'gentlemen only' concerts and boasting of its shooting gallery. Together with The Bull in the first rank of infamy were the Dog and Rat, the Red White and Blue, the Old Ship, the Pat M'Carthy and the Green Man. No honest man used them as they were widely known as covens of thieves and prostitutes.

Many beerhouses had no licence and were fronts for prostitution and fencing. Others provided venues for dog-fights and ratting. Many in the Smithfield market area had their licences suspended as licensees were, in the words of the police, 'running them in a disgraceful manner'.

On Chapel Street, the Butcher's Arms was a brothel. The magistrates fined the licensee, Samuel Hancock, £5 for keeping a disorderly house. A number of the rooms were crowded with couches and cushions and three notorious prostitutes were in permanent residence. In the same area, Wood Street, Calhoun Street and Richmond Street were also infamous dens of vice. Another Chapel Street pub, the Lord Nelson, boasted some tasty customers. As William McDonald was leaving on a Saturday night in January 1875, Michael Gorman jumped him and tried to bite off his nose. Not surprisingly, McDonald took exception to this and rammed his finger into Gorman's mouth in an attempt to prise his jaws apart. Gorman, not content with biting the offending digit, then tore off a piece of McDonald's lip befo returning his powerful jaws to his nose. Satisfied at last, Gorman fled. When the police caught up with him, he was calmly cooking his supper: presumably McDonald's lip and nose weren't very filling. In court, Gorman showed no remorse. In fact, he could not stop laughing at the spectacle of McDonald's nose swathed in an enormous bandage. The judge failed to see the funny side and gave him six months.

Many outraged members of the public asked: How do these places, where violence is an everyday occurrence, keep their licences? The police, at all levels, often had an accommodating relationship with the licensees. This is understandable, as each needed the other. The peeler on the beat needed his easing spots, where he could rest his legs for a few minutes and get out of the cold; the licensee needed his help with drunks and troublemakers. Sometimes this relationship was a little too cosy. In April 1897 the Manchester Watch Committee felt it necessary to remind every licensee in the city that under the 1872 Licensing Act it was an offence to provide drink to a constable on duty. Bribery, it also reminded landlords, was an offence. There is no evidence to suggest that blatant bribery was a major concern. But it is equally clear that the practice of giving officers free drinks and perhaps a 'Christmas box' was commonplace.

The answer to the public's question was one the police would never publicly admit, though it was well understood among all those charged with controlling crime. The police view was that crime, and especially prostitution, were as inevitable as rain in Manchester. Confining them to pubs in certain areas of the city meant that the police could exercise a degree of control that would otherwise be impossible. Even so, there were many pubs that created a public outcry that forced the authorities to take action. Magistrates closed the Old Cat's Face on Market Street as most of its customers were thieves.

At the licensing session of August 1869 magistrates refused to renew the licences of the following: James Bradley, of The Church Tavern, Green Street; George Hardy, of The Dog Inn, Deansgate; Thomas Rigby, of The Railway Inn, Deansgate; Mary Abrahams, of The Soho Foundry, Ancoats; Matthias Mather, of The Victoria Tavern, Angel Street, and John Bennett, of The Grecian Head, Deansgate. In 1870, John Ashton, landlord of the Ducie Bridge Inn, Long Millgate, on the corner of Miller Street, stood accused of allowing thieves to meet and assemble in his house. This is in the area of the infamous Charter Street and Angel Street, described in the local press as a 'low area' and the haunt of prostitutes and thieves.

It is little wonder that John Clay, the influential prison chaplain, who ministered to the inmates at Preston for many years, maintained that the pubs, beerhouses and gin palaces of Manchester – and not the prisons – were the real schools of crime and vice. A great deal of the violence and theft of which Clay complained happened in city centre pubs, which were then, as now, the places to meet, especially for the young. Shudehill, the site of the famous Saturday market, provided free amusement.

Courting couples, boys and girls, alone or in clusters, pushed through the bustling crowds, usually between 15,000 and 20,000 strong. Between the gas-lit stalls a sea of faces, a great pulsing tide of humanity, ebbed and flowed. And every few yards there was a crowded pub. The Salford equivalent was between Salford Bridge and Blackfriars, a distance of no more than 150 yards, where there were ten pubs. The 600 yards of Chapel Street, from Greengate to New Bailey Street, boasted twenty-five pubs – some next-door to each other. As Salford's main shopping area it provided everything anyone could want. There were saddlers and harness makers shops, but more revealing of working class life are the butchers and fishmongers. They suggest that the diet of the poor was more varied than today. The butchers sold bacon, hams, eggs, strings of sausages, rump stakes, sirloins, mutton chops, spare ribs, apple sauce, tripe, trotters, pigs' cheek, cow heels and chitterlings. The fishmongers offered salmon, cod, flukes, flounders, sole, kippers and, one of the staples of the poor, red herrings. Lobsters, prawns, shrimps, periwinkles, whelks, oysters, mussels and cockles all glistened in the window. Yet among all this there were those who could not find a bite to eat. The nameless destitute that the landlady of Chapel Street's Unicorn found lying in her doorway in 1874 was scarcely alive. He was in such an advanced state of starvation that though she fed him with bread and beef he died a few hours later.

Dry Salvation

He was, according to supporters of the temperance movement, just one of the countless victims of drink. Like Canute, they set themselves the hopeless task of holding back the tide of drink that threatened the city. Major Ballentine, master of the Crumpsall workhouse, one of those who saw at first hand the degradation and poverty caused by drink, had strong views on temperance. He was heavily involved in the Manchester and Salford Temperance Society, the Lancashire and Cheshire Band of Hope Union, the Church of England Temperance Society and the Manchester Scottish Temperance Association. He saw in Manchester's squalor the evil hand of drink. Like many of the socially aware he believed that the greatest kindness anyone could bestow on the poor was to introduce them to the blessings of temperance.

Such was the effect of drink in Manchester that temperance societies came to regard the city as a sodden hotbed of iniquity, in greater need of abstinence than most cities and towns. By the 1860s there were three temperance societies with a total of fifty branches in Manchester and Salford. The conurbation's response was emphatic – a rapid growth in the number of beerhouses. As well as advocating that individuals make a personal commitment to total abstinence, the societies lobbied for fewer pubs and beerhouses. The pleasure gardens, in particular, aroused their disapproval.

These gardens entertained hundreds of people, offering dancing, concerts, plays, bars and restaurants. Many commentators regarded them as squalid and there is no doubt they attracted large numbers of prostitutes. Though there is little evidence that the drinkers of Manchester were in any way deterred by abstention-propaganda, the temperance movement retained a presence in working class life, much like the sandwich board proselyte proclaiming the evils of gambling to the crowds swarming past him into the Manchester races.

Drink and gambling were two of the unholy trinity that was poisoning society. The third could not be mentioned in mixed company.

7

Vice

Wretched Ruins

'What is your name, child?' asked the elderly clergyman.

'That's the only thing I won't give you,' she replied. 'I'll give you anything else,' she said with a wink.

The elderly clergyman was one of an army of Victorians who set out to save the prostitute. Their fixation with prostitution resulted in a plethora of research, statistics and opinions. This concern for what many regarded as the country's greatest social scandal went to the very pinnacle of British society. The leading politician of the era, William Gladstone, four times Prime Minister and leader of the opposition for many years, maintained a friendship with the intelligent ex-prostitute Mrs Thistlethwaite. Together they trawled the streets of London seeking prostitutes to redeem.

The Victorian attitude to prostitution was profoundly ambivalent. Though the age of the great matriarch Queen Victoria is synonymous with prudery, the droves of prostitutes – many of them children – and the openness with which they plied their trade in every city struck the visitor as an affront to a civilised nation. Yet there were as many attitudes to prostitutes as there were commentators. The reforming journalist, W. T. Stead, expressed the most kitsch attitude, predating the current official view of prostitutes as victims. Stead told his readers, 'Never do I walk the streets but I see wretched ruins of humanity, women trampled and crushed into devils by society and my heart has been wracked with anguish for these victims of our juggernaut.' This view of prostitutes as Mary Magdalene figures, waiting only for the opportunity to repent, was spread through popular art such as Dante Gabriel Rossetti's Found and William Holman Hunt's *The Awakening Conscience*.

A less sentimental attitude held that prostitutes were idle wretches who rejected honest labour and made a conscious decision to live by selling their bodies. All the evidence suggests that this view was nearer the reality. For most respectable Victorians, chastity, like pregnancy, was absolute: just as a woman was either pregnant or not pregnant, she was either chaste or impure. It followed that a woman who had surrendered to a single seducer was morally indistinguishable from a whore who slept with ten different men every night. Chastity was highly valued in all women. An impure woman could not expect to find a respectable man prepared to marry her.

For many commentators (like Josephine Butler, for instance – after Queen Victoria and Florence Nightingale the most famous woman of her age, who believed prostitution was the greatest of all social evils), the solution to all society's wrongs was to strengthen the family. Sexual immorality, she maintained, corrodes family life, the basis of a healthy society and the antidote to all social evils. Nothing is more destructive of the family than the unfaithfulness represented by prostitution. Thus nothing was more destructive of society than prostitution. It corroded true married love, virtue and every principle of morality.

But the threat of prostitution was physical as well as moral. The government was concerned to restrict the spread of venereal disease, especially among the armed forces where it was endemic. Where there were soldiers, there were prostitutes. The Providence Street area of Salford was known as the 'She Battery' because of the many prostitutes who worked the streets, most of whose clients came from the nearby barracks. Similarly Hulme barracks attracted droves of prostitutes. However, soldiers generally had little money and resorted to the so called 'park women' who came out at dusk. These women had grown old in their profession. Army regulations, which made no proper provision for families and often kept men away from home for long periods, made marr' difficult. The result was that only about six per cent of enlisted men were married. Consequently hordes of prostitutes thronged dockyards and garrison towns. It is hardly surprising that by 1860 venereal disease accounted for half the sickness among home-based soldiers and infected one in every three. The aim of the Contagious Diseases Act, 1864, was to stop the spread of venereal diseases among the armed forces by compelling prostitutes to undergo medical examination and, if diseased, undertake treatment. As a result of protests by feminist groups the authorities suspended the Act and subsequently repealed it. Yet throughout the 1880s the country remained preoccupied with the threat of venereal disease, understandably as it infected half of all outpatients of public hospitals.

Among the general population venereal disease was also widespread. An official estimate in 1868 suggests that it infected seven per cent of the sick poor. At the time medicine had little understanding of the causes of syphilis and gonorrhoea and diagnosis was frequently mistaken. Available treatments were painful, slow and uncertain. Additionally, many hospitals made little provision for sufferers. Those that did showed little sensitivity to the feelings of their patients in describing their treatment areas as 'the Foul Wards'.

Syphilis is most frequently fatal when neglect allows it to reach its tertiary stage. The build-up of deposits of bone inside the skull produces pressure on the brain, resulting in convulsions and paralysis. Occasionally the cartilage of the larynx falls in and the sufferer dies of asphyxiation. For prostitutes, disease was an occupational hazard. In 1867, 840 women died of syphilis in England and Wales. Despite this hazard, the number of prostitutes in the city was always high. In 1843 the Manchester police calculated that there were 330 brothels and 701 'common prostitutes' in the city. This figure, however, like all police estimates, is certainly on the low side as it includes only prostitutes known to them. The Chief Constable, Captain Palin states in his report for 1868 that ere were 981 convictions of prostitutes for being drunk and disrly and only ninety-two for accosting wayfarers. There were at that time 'over 800 prostitutes in the city and 325 houses of ill-fame', which almost certainly refers to houses, often lodging houses, used by prostitutes, as opposed to brothels. Nearly all of these women combined theft with selling their bodies.

Why did so many women become prostitutes? For many, prostitution was a more attractive proposition than honest labour. When social researchers questioned Manchester and Liverpool prostitutes in the 1840s they found that many of them, far from being victims of domestic cruelty, had fled caring homes. Many cited their love of drink and desire to have pretty clothes as steps on the road to prostitution. The Salvation Army, like other temperance groups in the city, was convinced that drink was the root of most prostitution. As one prostitute said: 'Drink? I should think so! Do you imagine we could lead this life without drink? The drink drowns all feelings of sorrow and shame and deadens the conscience.' Manchester prostitutes were extravagant, frittering away their money and consequently often in debt. In addition to drinking, they gambled, were partial to sweets and were famously generous to the poor – both deserving and otherwise. It is certain that drink and improvidence were what led many women into prostitution in the first place. Others explained that they could earn far more by prostitution than by working and more explained that it provided an escape from the deadening monotony of manual labour and domestic service.

The status of women in Victorian society at this time is hard to imagine. The 1861 census, for instance, showed that of 2,700,000 women employed outside the home, 2,000,000 were in domestic service. About a third of Victorian women had some experience of domestic service, which remained the biggest employer of women until the outbreak of the Second World War. Many of the women who were professional or part-time criminals were former domestics dismissed without 'a character'. Theft among domestics was common. One of the few saleable assets of an unemployed domestic was knowledge of the layout and routine of her former place of employment – which was of value to a burglar.

To understand why they went into prostitution, it is first ne essary to know something about the life of the domestic servant. Distinctions between servants were as great as the class distinction that separated the duke from the dustman. At the pinnacle of the hierarchy were those who served the landed aristocracy in their great houses. In many cases they ate the same food as their masters and enjoyed a lifestyle beyond the wildest dreams of the ordinary servant. These, however, were the fortunate few. Most domestics were 'general servants', aptly known as the 'maids of all work'.

The definitive account of the role of the domestic servant is *Mrs Beeton's Domestic Service Guide* of 1880, which provides a formidable list of her responsibilities. And the lower the status of the servant, the more onerous her tasks. Her work consisted of whatever tasks her employer chose to impose. As Mrs Beeton pointed out 'the mistress's commands are the measure of the maid-of-all-work's duties'. She adds, 'The general servant's duties are so multifarious, that unless she be quick and active, she will not be able to accomplish them.' Even in the bigger houses, the girls who worked as kitchen maids or 'between maids' – 'tweenies' – endured abject drudgery. They generally began and ended their day working by candlelight, rising in the dark to set the fires. Their labours ended only when they had safely delivered the warming pans to the master and mistress's beds.

Those housemaids who kept detailed diaries allow us to reconstruct the working day of the typical Manchester skivvy. She rose at 5.30am, blackened a six-foot cooking range, lit the fires in the servants' quarters, scrubbed the kitchen tables and floor and then prepared tea for the servants before calling them at 7am. Her employer gave her strict warning not to waken anyone in the household and, to ensure that they weren't disturbed, she was forbidden to wear her shoes around the house. Regardless of their station or the size of the establishment, domestics were responsible for keeping the house clean. It is difficult for us to appreciate what this involved. The Victorian passion for heavy drapes, clutter, ornaments and embossed frames all increased the domestic's labours at a time when there were no labour-saving devices. She had to scrub stone-flagged floors and corridors and clean carpets on hands and knees. There were few ready-made cleaning materials. A great deal of time was spent combining ingredients such as silver sand, vinegar, melted beeswax, turpentine, linseed oil, methylated spirit and white wax to produce cleaning agents. The mixture of soft soap and silver sand used to scrub bare boards, which left the maids' hands and arms red raw, was only one of the domestic's discomforts. Until the start of the twentieth century, gas, oil lamps and candles lit most houses. There were few bathrooms and central heating was rare. All this added to the domestic's labours. Hip baths and coal fires in every room were the order of the day – with all their attendant hauling of materials. Given this range of tasks, it's hardly surprising that they had only a few hours recreation each week.

To accomplish all these demanding tasks was not enough for the exacting employer. A good servant had to be more than a tireless workhorse. It was also essential for her to 'know her place'. The nineteenth century produced a vast literature on the appropriate demeanour of servants. All these authorities agreed on the essentials.

Servants had to be silent and invisible. They worked in silence, without whistling or singing. They spoke only when spoken to – and then as concisely as possible. Under no circumstances were they to address members of the family other than as Ma'am and Sir, and in the case of children, Master and Miss. Most important of all, they were to avoid any possibility of physical contact. For this reason, it was never permissible to place an object in the master or mistress's hand. Instead, the servant placed it on a convenient surface. Letters, for instance, she placed on a tray and then proffered the tray. Outside the house, servants walked some paces behind the mistress. Servants had to be totally discreet. For a servant to repeat family business outside the home was unforgivable, an instant dismissal offence. When waiting on table, she was blind and deaf to all conversation, no matter how insignificant.

Yet the Victorians also accepted that employers had responsibilities to their servants. To the modern ear contemporary views on these duties seem patronising and condescending. The good employer should treat servants as he would his children, show a 'kind interest in their affairs' and behave with 'goodness and justice'. In practice, employers were often suspicious of their servants. Victorian newspapers fostered this distrust. They abounded in stories of burglaries that were 'inside jobs'. Some servants were worse than dishonest.

Kate Webster [see Chapter 5] was the most infamous of Victorian servants. Her case received saturation coverage, newspapers regaling readers with all the gruesome details. Lucy Ellis, hanged in 1876 for the murder of her illegitimate child, also exemplified the servant's potential for evil and served as a warning to all employers. Many employers developed such distaste for their servants that they found even the sight of them uncomfortable. Elizabeth Simpson worked in a large house in Harrogate. The rule of the house, strictly enforced, was that none of the family must ever see her. If they happened to meet, she was not to speak but to curtsey and disappear as quickly as possible.

Servants' working conditions were entirely at the discretion of their employers as there was no legislation limiting working hours or providing for their health and safety. In the view of their employers, these were unnecessary. The way they saw things, it was the tendency of servants to give themselves airs and to regard certain tasks as beneath them that threatened the proper relationship between master and servant. *Punch* and other fashionable Victorian journals abound with jokes ridiculing the uppity servant. In reality, the living conditions of most servants were so dismal that they discouraged any pretensions. Male servants usually slept in the cellar and maids occupied the attic. Often their only light was from a small candle. Even when gas and electricity became available, employers often avoided the expense of installing them in the attic. Grey distempered walls, bare floorboards, lumpy flock mattresses on iron bedsteads, ill-assorted oddments of furniture discarded from the family quarters, cracked chamber pots and flaking wash-stands were the stuff of servants' quarters.

The frontier of domestic service ran perilously close to the margins of prostitution. Poverty was a major reason for this. A maidservant in a residential district earned between £12 and £18 a year, whereas a 'slavey' in a lower middle class home earned half that. Both got very little in cash – most of their income was in food, accommodation and clothes. Generally they got one day a month off and the fortunate also enjoyed two afternoons or one evening every week. There is no doubt that for some the excitement of a sexual liaison was a rare pleasure in a drab life. Making these liaisons a source of income was a common way of getting money to buy the luxuries that were otherwise beyond the means of the domestic servant.

Occasional or full-time recourse to prostitution was not confined to domestics but was also associated with women in particular luxury trades. Shop assistants, particularly girls working in gloves, leather goods, confectionery, milliners', dressmakers' and tobacconists' shops were called 'dollymops'. These girls, notoriously badly paid, were in daily contact with rich customers and commercial travellers and many found it difficult to resist the temptation to exploit their sole asset. This scenario was so common that it even appeared in a comic song of the period:

Such a nice little cigar divan
Is the Piccadilly cigar divan...
She says her name is Millicent, and
That she comes from France,
But I know she comes from Bow – they
Used to call her Nance...
To all but very wealthy men her prices would seem large,
For instance, an Havana smoke would cost you one and four;
But if Millie bit the end off she would charge a shilling more...

Many women, such as those employed in making and selling fancy goods, haberdashery, dressmaking, as milliners, furriers, hat-binders, shoe-stitchers and piecework seamstresses, were badly paid when employed and regularly unemployed during seasonal downturns. Many resorted to prostitution. Every prostitute dreamt of hooking a toff and becoming a society lady. The fortunate whore sometimes found a wealthy client and became his mistress. Sometimes he even set her up in private accommodation. But marriage to a man of social standing was as rare as the industrial town without soot. To reach the pinnacle of her profession required a rare combination of qualities apart from good looks. She had to be courteous, charming, an accomplished musician and a welcoming hostess. Even then, disease or pregnancy might destroy her career as a kept woman. The encumbrance of an unwanted child would certainly ruin her prospects.

In 1851 there were 42,000 illegitimate births in Britain, about seven per cent of the total. This represented a major increase in the century since 1750, when the figure had been far lower – certainly no more than one per cent. Illegitimacy was then, as today, associated with rank. About two-thirds of the women with an illegitimate child applying for support were former servants and a large percentage of prostitutes applying to rescues were ex-servants. Realistically, the best a prostitute could aspire to was what one writer called the 'seclusive' status. These were the prima donnas of prostitution enjoying the patronage of a few very wealthy men and thus able to live alone in a private house or a superior apartment.

The most famous Manchester example was Polly Evans, who later ran her own exclusive brothel. In her memoirs she spoke of sumptuous gentleman's club surroundings where the wealthy came to enjoy the company of beautiful women confident of their discretion. The police were perfectly aware of the nature of this establishment. Perhaps one of the reasons why they never troubled Polly was that the Manchester MP and city mayor, Sir John Potter, was her long-term companion. In a night she earned what it took a working man a month to amass. The professional whore working the toffs from the best Manchester hotels around the Piccadilly area might earn in twenty minutes what cost a labourer a day of backbreaking work. The semi-professional dollymop, plying her trade in Deansgate, might scrape a wage comparable to that of the unskilled labourer.

The third tier in the hierarchy of prostitutes, below the kept woman and the 'seclusive' was the 'board-lodger' who enjoyed the relative security of having a place in a brothel. In return for board, lodgings and, in particular, protection against disgruntled clients, she paid the mistress of the house a share of her earnings. Next came the well-dressed prostitute who walked the streets. She generally restricted herself to an established patch where the police knew and tolerated her.

The Manchester police had a live-and-let-live attitude to prostitutes and usually turned a blind eye. Unlike many social reformers, they entertained no illusions about suppressing prostitution. Their concern was to confine the most blatant prostitutes to the rookeries, prevent them from becoming a flagrant nuisance and restrict the number of robberies they committed.

Next in the pecking order came those who regarded prostitution as a stopgap measure, a means of feeding themselves when times were bad. When there was an upturn in trade they went back to making a living by honest labour. The mill girls who thronged the city centre in times of slack trade fell into this category. At the base of the pyramid was the 'low prostitute' who infested the poorest neighbourhoods and, at the weekend, the city centre. She sold herself to the first man she could entice and generally consummated the deal in a back alley or squalid lodging house. She generally had no experience of prolonged work and knew no other trade.

These women made up the great bulk of the profession and attracted the attention of police and commentators. What attracted more attention, however, were the brothels that were the basis for prostitution. The majority of houses described as brothels in police returns were lodging houses where prostitutes took their clients. Few were enclosed brothels, providing a base for full-time prostitutes and regular clients. Most catered for casual prostitutes who picked up men in pubs, music halls and pleasure gardens. The police attitude to these establishments was generally tolerant, provided they gave rise to few complaints of violence and robbery. After 1885, however, their attitude became more complex as the Criminal Law Amendment Act made every form of whore-mongering illegal. Those who ran a brothel were now liable to a fine and three months hard labour for a first and four months for each subsequent offence. The penalties for inducing girls into prostitution were far heavier.

Most streetwalkers lived with a bully or an owner who proved his worth when an irate punter returned in search of his wallet. It is from this occurrence that the common name for a brothel – a 'disorderly house' – arose. Despite a protector, the prostitute was sometimes the victim of violence, though judging from newspaper reports of the time this was unusual. When violence arose, it was usually the prostitute in the process of robbing a client who initiated it. Many prostitutes without protectors relied on the support of the whores they lived with, usually in a lodging house. These prostitutes' lodging houses were as corrupting an influence as their trade. The prostitutes slopped about during the day, squatting in front of the kitchen fire, gossiping and generally, in the opinion of one observer, eroding all decency, modesty, propriety and conscience. The one advantage was the women developed a camaraderie that often resulted in a belligerent client getting a good hiding and finding himself kicked out onto the street.

Manchester brothels run by madams were unusual. Mrs Matthews was a successful madam of the period. She ran a house used by Jane Doyle, a renowned prostitute, and thirty other women, mostly casual prostitutes. In Deansgate there were forty-six brothels. In the area between Peter Street, Great Bridgewater Street, Lower Mosley Street and Deansgate alone there were twenty-two known brothels and nine other suspected houses. In Salford at this time there were twenty-six. Shops, usually selling luxury goods, fronted some of the better class brothels. The Cheshire Cheese in Newton Street and Mrs Buckley's house in Ashley Lane, off the infamous Blakeley Street, were among the city's most wretched houses of ill repute. Few brothels were without the front of a lodging house or a pub. These pubs were typical working class dancing pubs. The brothel was above the pub or taproom. Benches ran along the walls, by tables, around a small space for dancing in the middle of the floor. At the end was a small dais, where myopic musicians played shrill, fast music on cornets and fiddles accompanying a singing comic with an array of risqué songs. The whores' faces were chalk white with livid circles of rouge on their cheeks. Their bright flaring dresses fanned out as they span round in polkas and waltzes.

Despite the attractions of the brothel, the alley was less dangerous for the punter than going back to a room in a house of ill repute where it was easier for the prostitute to rob him. Accounts of gullible clients being beaten and robbed are legion. In fact, many commentators believed that prostitutes were often primarily thieves masquerading as whores in order to get men into situations in which they could fleece them with impunity. A respectable man robbed in a house of ill repute was unlikely to draw the attention of the police to something he would prefer to shrug off as an unfortunate incident.

Robbery, however, was not the client's worst fear. Prostitutes and their bullies seldom robbed a punter without also giving him a severe beating. Country yokels, visiting the big city for the first time, often found that its reputation for wickedness was justified. They were the favourite targets of prostitutes. It was common for Manchester prostitutes to rob their clients of their clothes, sometimes leaving them in the buff and considerably adding to their embarrassment. Jerome Caminada tells of an interesting variation on this, worked by the Baron and Red Peggy operating on London Road station approach. The Baron dressed as a clergyman and Peggy in the height of fashion. The third member of the team, dressed to emphasise her physical assets, propositioned men as they left the station. Usually she took her client to a house where all three robbed him. On other occasions they blackmailed him. With very little concrete evidence – victims being understandably reluctant to bring charges – Caminada arrested all three. The judge sentenced the Baron to twelve months hard labour while his associates each had three months to contemplate the error of their ways.

Prostitutes were generally peripatetic. It was dangerous to stay in one place; clients who woke up without their valuables might return seeking vengeance. This is why they often worked in pairs, for protection and to make it easier to rob clients. Ellen Reece, a twenty-four-year-old Salford prostitute, confided in her chaplain while she was in prison in the 1850s. She confirmed the link between prostitution and robbery. 'None of the girls think so much of prostitution but it furnishes opportunities for robbing men. Most girls will rob by violence and especially drunken men... They will not go to a house if they can help it, but to some back street.' She explained that she worked with an accomplice who would rob the client as soon as he dropped his trousers.

Prostitutes also supplemented their income by shoplifting, even though this was far more hazardous than robbing punters and a great deal more likely to result in a court appearance. If successful, they took the spoils to Butterworth's and Porter's, on Newton Lane, two of the many pawnshops in the area where prostitutes could dispose of their spoils. Many prostitutes lived with criminals and got involved in their nefarious activities. Provided they looked respectable, they attracted less unwelcome attention than men. This is why they often worked as lookouts for burglars or carried their tools to a job and went away with the proceeds.

Some prostitutes adopted the flimsy disguise of a hawker, perhaps carrying a basket of fruit. During the day they went from pub to pub and in the evening worked the theatres. For the poorer prostitutes concealing their earnings was a problem. Many claimed the police robbed them and one way of proving to a court that a girl was living by prostitution was to show that she had more money than she could earn honestly. A policeman's search was not usually a problem. Prostitutes hid sovereigns in concealed pockets in undergarments, on the inside of garters or the underside of corset stays. There were also areas which decency protected and where as many as thirty sovereigns might be concealed. Manchester police matrons, however, posed an altogether greater threat. They were less restrained in carrying out a search and it was mainly to forestall their efforts that Manchester prostitutes took to swallowing the sovereigns they earned.

A Deansgate prostitute of the time said she had never heard of this harming anyone. Despite the rigours of the matron's search, the Manchester police treated prostitutes leniently. In 1866 only one in every twelve arrests was of a prostitute and then generally for robbing or assaulting a client.

As the century progressed this live-and-let-live accommodation became the norm. Prostitutes realised that if they refrained from aggressive soliciting and dressed in a clean and tidy way they were less likely to incur the attention of the police. Consequently, by the 1870s the average Manchester whore had abandoned the pestering approach. Instead she might first ask a prospective client for his arm while she crossed the road. Otherwise, she conveyed her meaning by smiles, looks and winks. Similarly she reduced the likelihood of arrest by moving from the worst parts of town to those areas where there were legitimate forms of entertainment such as pubs, music halls, pleasure gardens and dance halls.

Generally the prostitutes who ended up in court were the dregs – drunkards who assaulted and robbed their clients, loud-mouthed, dirty harridans who harassed the public and gave the police no choice but to arrest them. In other ways these were the most vulnerable. Often semi-professional whores who had neither pimp nor protector and living in lodging houses without a husband, they were at the mercy of the sadist and the sexual murderer. It was from this group that in 1888 London's Jack the Ripper chose his victims. The Ripper, however, was only the most infamous prostitute murderer. Thomas Neil Cream, having been convicted of murder in Canada, arrived in Britain in 1891 and immediately targeted prostitutes. Within a year he poisoned four of them before Lou Harvey, an intended victim, recognised him and alerted the police.

Many believed that murder at the hands of a sexual psychopath was only the greatest of the hazards facing a prostitute. It was widely assumed that such a degenerate life set a woman on a downward spiral inexorably leading to a squalid death. Many of the myriad nineteenth century experts on prostitution confirmed this view. One such, Dr Michael Ryan, maintained that the average life expectancy of a woman after she became a prostitute was four years. Evidence from the Lock Hospital in Edinburgh seems to confirm this view. Doctors there maintained that nine out of ten prostitutes disappeared by the time they reached thirty.

Yet there was plenty of evidence in Manchester to contradict this. For many decades in the second half of the century the area behind Piccadilly was infamous as the stamping ground of old, broken down prostitutes. These women, repellent and pathetic, confirmed the widely held opinion that women were far more difficult to reform than men and that female criminals were more depraved than their male equivalent. The hardened prostitute, without any sense of shame, was one of the most depressing underworld figures.

Yet some did change. There was a reformatory in Manchester, which took girls from prison, chiefly prostitutes. They learnt to read and write and later went into service.

The most forceful and influential proponent of the view that prostitutes were redeemable was William Acton, one of the foremost Victorian experts on prostitution. Acton's book *Prostitution, considered in its Moral, Social and Sanitary Aspects*, published in 1857, coincided with a surge of public interest in the subject. He contradicted the standard Victorian view of the prostitute as a fatally flawed individual whose immoral life inevitably set her on a downward spiral of ever increasing degradation, ending in a squalid death. Instead he maintained that most prostitutes were no more than temporary outcasts who re-entered society through marriage. Nor did he believe the life of a prostitute led to any physical damage. Quite the contrary, he maintained, 'If we compare the prostitute at thirty-five with her sister... a married mother of a family who has been a toiling slave for years we seldom find the constitutional ravages often thought to be the necessary consequences of prostitution exceed those attributed to the cares of a family and the heart-wearing struggles of virtuous labour.' In other words, whoring was less harmful than honest labour.

Acton believed that the small number of old prostitutes walking the streets of Manchester was proof that most women went back to normal life. He was also convinced that the number of prostitutes suffering from the most frightening effects of syphilis – the collapsed nose, the rotted palate and nodes on the shin – had declined. Yet though the number of people suffering from advanced forms of the disease was on the decline, the frequency of the disease remained steady. Acton maintained that an unwanted baby was the commonest route into prostitution. Similarly, marriage was the means by which prostitutes returned to normal life. Some did become madams but more emigrated and put their old life behind them.

It is difficult, however, to take the same sanguine view of those who became prostitutes before they were able to make a conscious decision.

White Slavery

Child prostitution was an important part of the nineteenth century criminal scene. One contemporary estimate reckoned that in Manchester in the 1870s there were 500 prostitutes under the age of thirteen. The extent of child prostitution was something that greatly troubled the Victorian conscience and appalled foreign visitors. Yet the demand for children for the purpose of sexual gratification was so great that by 1875 it was common for mature prostitutes to dress like children. Oscar Wilde, who regularly holidayed with his coterie in the Middle East so that they might abuse little boys, regarded the matter as frivolous. Speaking of the publisher Leonard Smithers, he said, 'He loves first editions, especially of women: little girls are his passion.'

Though the 1871 Royal Commission concluded, 'The traffic in children for infamous purposes is notoriously considerable in London and other large towns,' it was only in 1885 that the matter came to national prominence. W. T. Stead was a pioneering journalist and publicity addict who did as much as anyone to create the media obsession with the pseudo-event. The pseudo-event has now displaced reality as the focus of many newspapers. It is something that has no intrinsic importance other than that created by the media. To take but two common examples: 'Colleen seen shopping in Manchester' and 'Jade on Keep Fat Diet'.

When Stead ran his famous series of articles in 1885 the age of consent was thirteen, having been raised from twelve in 1875. Prostitution fascinated Stead. In particular he regarded the evils of the white slavery in children as a national disgrace and felt it his duty to expose it to a docile public. As editor of the prestigious *Pall Mall Gazette* he believed he was in a perfect position to focus the full glare of publicity on this shameful trade in innocent children. First he enlisted the support of the Archbishop of Canterbury, the Bishop of London and the Roman Catholic Cardinal Manning. On a more practical level he made contact with Rebecca Jarrett, a reformed prostitute. His strategy was to show the ease with which anyone might acquire a child virgin, transport her to Belgium – the reputed centre of child prostitution – deposit her in a brothel and thereby consign her to a life of abuse.

The plan went without a hitch. Stead got the child, Eliza Armstrong, from a Mrs Broughton for the sum of £5. His account of the transaction created a sensation and sales of the *Gazette* rocketed. However, Mrs Armstrong, the child's mother, unhappy at the hostile way Stead had depicted her, undid him. She teamed up with a rival publication which discovered that Stead had not sought permission from the child's father and had misled the mother by telling her he was placing the girl in service. Soon Stead found himself in the dock of the Old Bailey with two of his accomplices accused of fraudulently taking the child. Two of the women who helped him each got six months. Stead, glorying in the role of martyr, got three, which he spent in considerable comfort in Holloway where he continued to edit the *Gazette*. He remembered his Holloway days as the happiest time in his life. Imprisonment gave him the martyrdom and public attention he craved.

Apart from Stead's self-promotion, the incident had practical results. The Criminal Law Amendment Act of 1885 raised the age of consent to sixteen. It made the procurement of a girl for prostitution a criminal offence and the penalty for assaulting a child under thirteen either whipping or penal servitude.

Stead's instinct for publicity stayed with him to the very end. He went down with the *Titanic* in 1912. His campaign of 1885, however, struck a cord with the chattering classes, harmonising perfectly with the impulse for moral reform sweeping the country. Consequently, the Criminal Law Amendment Act made every form of whoremongering illegal. Sex with a child under sixteen was punishable by two years' imprisonment and by penal servitude for life if she was under thirteen. To further protect respectable women from the ordure of prostitution, the Slander of Women Act, 1891, made 'words which impute unchastity or adultery to any woman or girl' actionable, even where there was no proof of damage.

In the same spirit, concerned citizens – including the Quaker kings of chocolate, George and Richard Cadbury – formed the National Vigilance Association for the Repression of Criminal Vice and Immorality, to prevent the sort of behaviour that resulted in decent women being insulted. Their aims were nothing if not ambitious and included the suppression of child prostitution, the closure of houses of ill fame, an end to indecent performances in concert halls, obscene pictures on the doors of concert halls, quack advertisements and indecent literature. W. T. Stead, not to be outdone, urged his readers to thrash any man making unwelcome advances to a lady.

There is no evidence that any of this affected life in Manchester's rookeries. Nor did it impinge on the music hall, where stories of sexual advances were staple fare and the chief delight of audiences.

With a Goose Under His Arm

Those worried about the moral welfare of the poor bemoaned the baleful influence of the pub. The music hall, they believed, was even more harmful to decency and propriety. And the more respectable people denounced its pernicious influence, the more clergymen castigated its smutty comics, the more reformers denounced its moral corruption – the more popular it became until it assumed its position as the working man's entertainment, second only to the pub.

In the 1840s what was to become the distinctive life of the city was emerging as the new Mancunians created their popular culture. It had two major components – music and drink – and the music hall brought both together. The halls emerged from the many pubs with music. They gradually developed into music halls as the entertainment provided became as important as the drink and owners started to charge for it. Music halls were the most popular form of entertainment for working people in the second half of the nineteenth century. By the 1870s enterprising businessmen all over the country were building song and supper rooms onto pubs.

The penny gaff was the forerunner of the music hall. It was a sort of theatrical underworld, free of the decency restrictions imposed on the theatre. Many of the Manchester gaffs in working class areas were large, gutted shops fitted with a primitive stage and rows of benches, crammed together to hold the maximum number of customers. Singing and dancing were the staples. Sopranos in their early teens and comic singers, often wearing battered hats and gigantic bowed cravats, the attraction of whose acts depended entirely on a risqué phrase in the chorus, were universally popular. Audience participation was at the heart of the entertainment. Men stamped their feet, girls shrieked in delight and wide-boys heckled. And everyone sang along.

The penny gaff became fashionable in the 1860s. Open from 6pm-11pm it attracted the full spectrum of working class people: housewives with babes in arms, adolescents, cab drivers, dustmen, coachmen, sailors, prostitutes and a smattering of respectable people. The entertainers were often not the most respectable. 'Actress' was still sometimes used as a euphemism for prostitute. Many respectable people still assumed that all actresses were disreputable. One of the earliest big venues in Manchester was Ben Lang's in Victoria Street, almost opposite the Cathedral by Victoria Bridge. During the 1840s it became the city's most popular working class attraction, regularly drawing audiences of over 2,000 people. The 'turns' tell us a lot about a working-class night out. Singers of ballads, opera, sentimental and risqué ditties were always popular. Comics and freaks appeared between magicians and jugglers. Sack races across the stage and prizes for comic singers from the audience were a part of every show. To add to the spectacle those brave enough to go on stage had to perform with a wild goose under one arm. For this array of delights, they paid 2d for the galleries, 3d for the pit. Alcohol was available from the attached beerhouse and thirsty punters drank as fast as an army of waiters could ferry it.

For years it was a goldmine. Then, on 31 July 1868, it became a charnel house. When a small fire started a panic, the crowds rushed for the inadequate exits, crushing each other on the narrow stairs. The press showed little interest in the incident and less sympathy for the twenty-three victims, most of whom were young people, describing them as 'street Arabs'. Local newspapers intimated that the hall was full of prostitutes and criminals, though subsequently it became clear that the majority of victims were employed. What is sure is that they were among the poorest in the city and the press was inured to their misfortunes. Despite this tragedy, music halls remained more popular in Manchester, where pubs offering music and singing were a key part of entertainment in working class areas from early in the nineteenth century, than anywhere else.

Consequently it was not long before farsighted entrepreneurs saw the potential for purpose-built halls, serving food and drink, with a chairman, who introduced the acts and kept order. Soon an array of stars and supporting acts circulated around the country entertaining the hordes who thronged to the twice-nightly shows. It is wrong to think that only working people went to the music halls. They attracted all sections of society. But they were particularly popular among young, employed, unmarried adults.

The acts appealed to working class people and consequently reflected their outlook and values. Most of all, they provided people with the opportunity to take part, if only by singing the choruses. The audiences were never passive recipients of pre-packaged entertainment. A music hall show was what we would call today an interactive experience. The songs, which were the staples of every show, provided a shared experience, as the audience joined in heartily. Halls such as The Star, in Pollard Street, Ancoats, were so important to the social life of the area that one observer described it in the 1880s as 'the sole bright spot in a place of terrible gloom'. The acts had no need to ask the manager how they were doing. The audience left them in no doubt. They sang, cheered, whistled, clapped, barracked, booed, stamped their feet and pelted the stage as they felt appropriate. This was an essential part of the experience and created a sense of community that most of us today encounter only when we're part of a religious congregation or a large and partisan football crowd.

There were, of course, different types of halls, each with a unique audience. The better halls were spacious. The typical audience at the Wolverhampton, one of the larger Manchester venues, consisted of smartly dressed mechanics, commercial travellers, clerks, warehousemen and shop workers. One observer remarked that among the audience in the 1870s were 'steady, sober-looking men, with their wives, sometimes their children'. Refreshment tables lined the stalls of the Wolverhampton and waiters formed a conveyor belt bringing drinks from the bars. The balcony provided the cheapest seats. In effect, segregation operated. The more affluent members of the community – shopkeepers and publicans – sat in the orchestra stalls and the dress circle. Craftsmen and those in regular work sat in the pit stalls, while, in a reversal of social status, the poorest patrons were on the 'top shelf', the balcony. But most of Manchester's music halls were not the spacious, gaudy mock-grand palaces of the purpose-built halls. In fact, they were little more than pubs with music licences, packing in about fifty people. By 1891 they numbered 400.

The biggest halls appeared at the end of the period, such as the Hippodrome on Oxford Street and the Ardwick Empire, at Ardwick Green. The latter entertained an audience of 3,000 at a Saturday matinee and twice nightly. One of Manchester's earliest halls was the People's Music Hall, which opened in 1853 and ran until 1897, when it made way for another city landmark, the Midland Hotel. Other large halls were the Folly on Peter Street, renamed the Trivoli in 1897 and the London in Bridge Street, purpose built in 1862 and later renamed the Queen's.

Performers who appeared regularly in Manchester included the Preston Handbell Ringers, the Milton Brothers, 'the best song and dance artists in Lancashire', and Mr Fred Edwards, the comic vocalist. A typical programme included a quartet of comic singers, child gymnasts and a tenor singing arias from Verdi's operas. The price ranged from sixpence in the balconies to six shillings for a private box. Prices were as low as threepence in some halls. Many packed people in without any regard for health and safety regulations. The inevitable result was the sort of thing that happened in Ben Lang's.

The Free Weekend

A long way behind the halls, but nevertheless one of the city's great attractions, was the amusement park at Bellevue. The zoo opened in 1830 and after that the site was constantly expanding until eventually it offered exotic gardens, concert halls, rides and roller coasters to the growing number of workers anxious to enjoy their precious free time. Manchester workers were the first to enjoy some respite from the endless toil that made up the lives of working people.

It was in Manchester that employers first acquiesced to the novelty of a 'free weekend' – usually Saturday afternoon and Sunday. It became the norm in Lancashire during the 1840s and spread to London during the next decade and created a craving for pastimes. The opening of the first Boys' Club, in Hulme in 1886, showed the demand for active recreation. When Lex Devine opened the doors of the disused factory in Mulberry Street, the road was heaving with 2,000 boys pushing and shoving to get in. No incident from this period better demonstrates the insatiable appetite for something to do during this newly won leisure time.

For most of these children the street was their only playground. The street has always been important to working class people. Looking back on his Salford childhood, folk singer Ewan Mc-Coll, the author of the city's anthem, Dirty Old Town, remembered the street as his stage, his racetrack, his gym, his jungle, his prairie and his ocean. To those accustomed to the life of the slums, the result of this vivid street life was boisterous, harmless noise – the shrieks of those who won a game of pitch and toss, the squeals of girls being teased, the whoops of a goal scorer. But to those from more sedate neighbourhoods it was a menacing chaos that threatened good order.

A walk around the markets on a Saturday night was another Manchester institution. The strolling families and couples mingled with beggars and drunks. The roads around Oldham Street and Shudehill seethed with tightly packed humanity, oozing along the footpaths. Each stall had its spieler, enticing those who lingered to buy and filling the air with cries and patter, importuning and cajoling, appealing to common sense and an eye for a bargain. As midnight approached, the price of foodstuffs fell. The stallholders were anxious to get rid of anything that would spoil before Monday. By this time the pubs were emptying. Those who had spent their money and those who, compelled by some vague instinct, staggered for home, were out on the streets. Everywhere supine forms snared the gutters, some vomiting, some comatose, some sitting bewildered.

Among them, as among every gathering, were the beggars. Women, children, disabled men – they took every imaginable form and employed every conceivable method of evoking sympathy. Like the blackened buildings and the busy streets they were everywhere in the city.

8

Down and Out

Promoting the Sale of Gin

Beggars attracted as much debate as prostitutes in the nineteenth century. They ranked with prostitutes as a major social problem. All those who studied the problem concluded there was no such thing as a deserving beggar. Among those who took this view were many experienced policemen. Manchester's Jerome Caminada, for instance, was emphatic: 'No respectable person ever went begging on the street.'

'A serious nuisance' and 'a national disgrace' are just two of the ways in which contemporaries expressed their disapproval. Whatever terms they used they were united in their hostility to begging and beggars. Beggars were at the bottom of the criminal hierarchy, professional scroungers whose occupation was importuning, not men brought to desperation by sudden misfortune. They regarded begging as a craft and sought to improve their income by sharpening their skills. They had no intention of ever working and even when their income provided them with more than their needs, they continued to beg.

This is why Caminada regarded all beggars as criminals seeking to exploit the generosity of kindly people in order to avoid working for a living. Those who gave money to street beggars were 'merely promoting the sale of gin'. This attitude may seem unduly harsh but one of the things that sustained it was the large number of professional beggars and the variety of ruses they employed to extort charity from the kind hearted. The pestering of professional beggars was more than a minor annoyance. Successive chief constables of Manchester regarded it as a major problem, so great that Jerome Caminada was deputed to tackle it.

This unanimity of condemnation is striking. Even the most compassionate philanthropists stress the viciousness and dishonesty of beggars. The deserving poor, they maintained – echoing Caminada – never resorted to begging, which was exclusively the vocation of idle rogues and vagabonds who abused Christian charity and discredited the worthy poor. Victorian Mancunians were vocal in their condemnation of beggars. If professional beggars benefited from charity, they reasoned, idleness and deceit were rewarded and the whole moral order perverted. Only those who were poor through no fault of their own deserved charity and even that was conditional. They had to earn it by their labour. If not, what incentive was there for the poor to work?

'Cadging' was the first resort of the criminal poor but it could be hard work. Such was the competition for the charity of the gullible that standing about with an open hand was not enough. Every beggar hoped for some accessory to give him an edge and the ingenuity of those who lived by duping others was equal to the creativity of the greatest minds of the time. The returned missionary was one of the more elaborate scams. The genius of this was that it exploited the public's insatiable fascination with darkest Africa, missionaries and the exploration of Britain's empire. The professional prater or bogus preacher needed a group of helpers to create the sort of heady atmosphere in which generosity overwhelmed prudence. Four or five enthusiastic helpers formed the nucleus of the audience, generated interest and together with a few banners and a couple of musicians soon attracted a large crowd. Then it was up to the prater to work his magic.

For the best effect a converted African would display his enthusiasm for Christianity by spitting on a pagan idol before leading the assembled throng in a stirring rendition of Onward Christian Soldiers. Almost as an afterthought, the preacher took a collection. The crowd dispersed, happy in the knowledge they were helping to shed the light of the Gospel on benighted pagans.

These gatherings and their legitimate counterparts attracted the fit-thrower and his accomplice, the Samaritan doctor. This scam was a variation on the fit-thrower, but it required two people working together. One, shabbily but respectably dressed, collapsed in the middle of a busy thoroughfare and immediately a crowd gathered round. His partner pushed his way through the crowd, claiming to be a doctor. After a cursory examination he announced that the man was suffering from starvation and pushed a few coins into his hand. As he left, clearly moved by the plight of the unfortunate, he announced that only a good meal could save the man from serious illness. Invariably several members of the crowd followed the medical man's example and pressed money on the fainter. To work this scam successfully, respectable clothing was essential. A genuine destitute would not have been able to convince his audience that he was a doctor.

In fact the most successful beggars depended on a mien of respectability. This was particularly so for the writers of begging letters. Literate and capable of the research necessary to ensure that they targeted those likely to be most responsive, the letter writers were the aristocrats of begging. Many plagued prominent figures – renowned philanthropists, clergymen, public figures and lottery winners were all favoured targets. Charles Dickens was only one of the many celebrities they pestered on a daily basis. Like others in the same position, this assault on his sympathy made him cautious in distributing charity.

The more perceptive beggars, however, chose local philanthropists and those prominent in charitable organisations. Each presented a carefully developed persona. One was a distressed gentlewoman, another an officer's widow. The shipwrecked mariner, the disabled miner – unable to work after an explosion at the coal face – and the impoverished gardener in winter, were standard characters. The more audacious followed up their letter with a visit. Many were so brazen that every refusal to give money resulted in tears, hysterics and tantrums calculated to create such embarrassment that the victim was willing to pay just to get rid of the beggar.

More despicable were those who targeted the recently bereaved.

By trawling the obituary notices they found a suitable target, often a respectable woman who had recently lost her husband. The writer purported to be a former lover supported by the deceased. Implicit in the letter was a threat to make the matter public. In the majority of cases the family was glad to pay up in order to avoid scandal.

Many beggars accosted passers-by with letters of recommendation, usually from a notable public figure or clergyman. These testified to the bearer's good character and commended him to the public's charity. Such testimonials were much in demand and their production provided discredited lawyers and alcoholic clerks with a meagre income. Far subtler was the beggar who used neither the written nor the spoken word. He dressed in clothes that spoke of threadbare respectability. He entered a pub in a good working class area and, looking suitably doleful, made an inept attempt to sell something of little worth – a box of matches or some tobacco – maintaining it was his only hope of raising a few coppers. As soon as someone talked to him, he recounted his heart-rending tale of cruel misfortune. The astute practitioner of this ruse found it worked best on a Saturday evening when the pub was full of women having a drink after shopping. Generally they still had a few shillings left in their purses and were feeling, for the only occasion in the week, quite well off. This feeling of wellbeing was likely to overflow into generosity.

Another group of beggars held that a heart-rending appearance was far more effective than any testimonial. Disabled beggars did well but the most effective were the disfigured – the more shocking the wound, the greater the impact. Simulating wounds was an art as valuable as any trade or practical skill. A thick layer of soap plastered onto the arm or thigh needed only an application of vinegar to ensure that it blistered and gave the appearance of a running wound. Similarly, a piece of raw meat tied under a clotted dressing invariably melted the hardest heart. Healed amputations guaranteed a regular income. Soap, strong vinegar and blood squeezed from raw meat and applied to the stump created such a realistic weeping sore that most passers-by averted their eyes when dropping coins into the begging bowl. A brisk massage with gunpowder gave the skin the colour of decaying, inflamed flesh and was a great bonus to anyone whose living depended on arousing sympathy.

In fact, Victorian beggars showed keen insight. They knew that respectable people attached great importance to wearing sufficient clothing: apart from considerations of decency, many Victorians believed insufficient clothing was a major cause of ill health. One group of beggars sought to exploit this by calling door to door, while half-naked, asking for food and clothing. They realised people were more likely to give them old clothes – easily converted into cash – than money. Most of these beggars lived in Manchester and worked one prosperous suburb after another. Occasionally, they varied their approach, sometimes posing as travelling workmen who had the promise of a job but would not be taken on in rags.

But the most productive door-to-door beggars were women, ideally accompanied by respectably dressed children. Little lisping girls guaranteed a good haul. Beggars in the Strangeways area used little girls in a more sinister way for many years. The child accosted an adult and asked for money. Almost immediately the child's irate parent appeared and began berating the victim for using foul language to the child. Soon the allegation was stepped up and the adult demanded a pound in return for not reporting the matter to the police.

Against all this competition, the static beggar, without something to make him particularly deserving, was unlikely to succeed. Consequently many carried a hawker's tray, selling needles or matches, as a pretext for aggressive begging. A placard, setting out the heartbreaking circumstances under which the wearer suffered crippling injuries, was another favoured prop. A white stick rarely failed. Blindness was quite common among the poor, the result of industrial accidents, smallpox and untreated gonorrhoea. The obedient dog, lying by his master, was a common sight all over Manchester. But a far better prop was a child acting as a guide.

Feigning a medical condition allowed beggars to use their acting talents. Most of those with dramatic tendencies went in for fit-throwing. Some alcoholics feigned collapse near a pub in the hope that a compassionate soul would fetch 6d worth of brandy. The beggar who went in for fit-throwing was altogether more calculating. He was neat and clean and convincingly respectable in every way. Furthermore, he chose his time and location carefully. Outside a church just as the congregation was leaving was ideal. By the time he told his sad story – often supported by a written testimonial from a clergyman – his concerned helpers were pressing on him the proceeds of an impromptu collection.

Beggars of this sort were well informed as they often used events in the news to give their sorry tale a veneer of credibility. So, a man crippled in a recent pit disaster or bereft of his family and possessions in a much-publicised shipwreck was sure to get sympathy.

Despite all appearances to the contrary, beggars were far from the pathetic, isolated individuals they presented to the public. The professional beggar was part of a fellowship that shared best practice. It is no coincidence that accounts of beggars in different parts of the country are remarkably similar. The same characters appear in Manchester and Newcastle as in London and Bristol, always applying tried and tested methods. With such ingenuity in their ranks, it is hardly surprising that beggars seemed to clog all Manchester's major thoroughfares. The extent of begging was such in 1818 that concerned citizens established the Society for the Suppression of Mendacity. Though later characterised as hardhearted and callous, its members were invariably active in charitable work and the Society itself provided much help for the genuinely needy.

Its view was that those who gave to beggars had no way of distinguishing the genuine from the bogus. As most beggars were professional scroungers, giving money did nothing for the deserving and rewarded idleness and dishonesty. 'If you wish to relieve genuine poverty,' it told the public, 'you will find the means through the clergyman, the Little Sisters of the Poor or the relieving officer. In the streets you will find nothing but the professional toll takers, levying dues on personal weakness.' The Society encouraged the public to issue street beggars with tickets, which they were to present at its offices. There the deserving got aid in the form of money, blankets and clothing. They also claimed to offer suitable employment to every able-bodied beggar. Yet even if the Society had eradicated adult beggars, there would still have been a grave problem.

Child beggars outnumbered adults. They enjoyed a degree of impunity not shared by adults. The police were loath to arrest them, as the magistrates were often at a loss how to treat them and usually sent them away with a warning, knowing full well that they would immediately resume begging. If a child's parents were imprisoned for sending him begging, then the court sent the child to the workhouse. But the workhouse master was reluctant to take young children and had the magistrates committed every beggar to his care they would have swamped the poor law system.

The commonest form of begging in Manchester at this time involved a woman latching onto a victim and wailing a pitiable tale. So persistent was she that her actions amounted to blackmail. This aggressive begging was a major problem when Caminada tackled it. Shortly before eleven at night, the city's most famous detective was walking along Oxford Street, when he encountered Mary Ann, universally known as 'Soldier' because of her legion tales of being abandoned by a faithless soldier, who appeared to be comforting a child swathed in her shawl. Unaware of Caminada, she latched onto a couple emerging from the Prince's Theatre and immediately launched into her patter. She recounted the pitiful tale of a deserted wife who had walked all the way from Liverpool to find her wayward husband and now had no means of feeding or sheltering her hungry child. At this point Caminada intervened. The baby turned out to be a boy – and immediately took to his heels. His parents hired him out as a heart-rending prop for three pence a night. Mary Ann had so many previous convictions that the judge sentenced her to twelve months hard labour.

Mary Ann deserves more detailed consideration, as she is typical of many of Manchester's habitual criminals of the period. She was a woman of many aliases. This, of course, was common among criminals of all sorts, who hoped to avoid the heavier penalties imposed on habitual offenders by changing their names. Mary Ann's real name was Ann Ryan. Her offences included theft. When threatened with arrest she often resorted to violent resistance. On one occasion, when arrested for stealing corsets, she tried to fight off the police. Between 1873 and 1889 she accumulated convictions for begging, drunkenness, breach of the peace and being drunk and disorderly. One of the many professional beggars who hired children as a prop, she was in every respect the typical street beggar of the time.

James Bent, a policeman rightly renowned for his work for the poor, tells of a professional beggar operating in Davyhulme. He pretended to be a mute miner. The magistrate sentenced him to three months imprisonment. Another professional beggar posed as an invalid – he wore shoes on his hands and dragged himself along on his hands and knees. His punishment was six weeks. When Bent first started working in Pendleton he was amazed at the great number of beggars, many going from door to door. In middle class areas a servant invariably opened the door and usually offered food and drink.

Many beggars combined importuning with hawking or street entertainment as a pretext for hanging about while looking for the opportunity to steal from a passing cart or a shop's footpath display. A great deal of this sort of petty crime was the work of beggars. The police estimated that two-thirds of all crime was down to vagrants.

In fact, many of these so-called vagrants were not homeless wanderers with no fixed abode. They lived and operated from one of the city's countless lodging houses.

Flash Houses

The boy lay across a bench. Dirt smeared his face, exposed above the coat that covered him. The face of the girl who slept beside him stuck out from a bundle of rags. Upstairs, four beds completely filled one room. Couples occupied three of them and two criminals the fourth. Above them, clothes, like dead bats, hung from a line, choking the space above the sleepers. Damp had eaten the plaster from the walls, exposing the laths like a skeleton's ribs, and patches of mildew blackened the ceiling.

In another room, fourteen people were sleeping on 'filthy beds, heaped-up rags and mattress stuffing', alive with horrors. 'Pestilential vapours' poisoned the room.

This is what Joseph Johnson found when he ventured into one of Manchester's lodging houses. What was more appalling than the squalor, however, was the degeneracy of those who wallowed in such filth. When Johnson's guide shone a torch on the sleepers, they opened their eyes to reveal 'that snake-glitter, that oblique evidence of cunning' that marks out the prostitutes, the convicts, the thieves and even 'the children of tender years, old in crime'. And among all these were working men and women, people of good character. And their children.

Many of those who were not respectable sought to appear so. Prostitutes, for instance, claimed to be factory girls and dressed in what was almost a uniform – a blue Chambery gown, a red print jacket and a loose slip. The police called them 'gow-girls'. Invariably they slept with their 'fellows' and often brought drunken swells back to the lodging house.

The convicts, according to Johnson, were 'ticket of leave' men, released early from penal servitude. According to Manchester's Chief Constable, Palin, Manchester was a magnet for these criminals who were responsible for a great deal of the city's crime.

All the commentators agreed: 'low lodging houses', as the newspapers liked to call them, or 'flash houses' as the public called them, generated crime. In our age of owner-occupiers, it is difficult to grasp the importance of the lodging house in the life of the city. The statistics for 1870 emphasise their role in working-class life. Manchester, with a population of 173,000 and Salford, with 83,000, had 214 lodging houses. At this time about one in every fourteen people living in the rookeries lived in a lodging house. Their number had declined from 472 in the previous decade as the authorities closed the worst.

At this time the council carried out a detailed survey of streets that made up a part of the Deansgate area, bordered by Peter Street, Deansgate, Great Bridgewater Street and Lower Mosley Street. An area of nineteen acres, this rectangle contained 853 houses, 713 of which were occupied. In sixty-eight of these houses, families lived in the cellars.

Of the families living there, one in three lived in a single room, sometimes home to seven people. The whole area was liberally sprinkled with lodging houses. Fleet Street and Lombard Street, in the centre, thronged with prostitutes during all the hours after dark and for a good part of the day. One of these streets housed 142 families, only thirty-six of which were classified as 'clean'.

Yet amid all this squalor and defeat, there were decent people struggling to live honest and productive lives. In Swan Court, Wood's Buildings, Walker's Court, Cooper's Row, Hamilton Place, Clay Street, McGinn's Court, Hall's Buildings and Allport Street almost all the families were clean and respectable. This is a testimony to all those whose everyday courage allowed them to live unremarkable lives in the most difficult of circumstances without ever coming to the notice of the authorities.

The situation was similar in Salford, though generally conditions there were better. There were, of course, black spots every bit as bad as the worst parts of Manchester. At one house in Silk Street, for instance, ten people lived in a cellar room. At a hovel in Barrow Court, eighteen people of various ages shared two beds. The focus of the house, as of all lodging houses, was the kitchen, where people cooked, warmed themselves and gossiped. A bench and a few tables were the only furniture.

Often children, many coaxing a mean existence from begging and street trading, shared these houses with hardened adult criminals and prostitutes. When they had money, they drank and gambled with the adults. In many cases they shared their beds with girls of their own age, who were their mistresses.

By the middle of the nineteenth century the lodging house was a symbol of everything that threatened respectability. It was a seedbed of crime, sin and disorder. It embodied the breakdown of the stable family, composed as it was of rootless individuals often living in defiance of every accepted standard of decency and morality.

It is impossible to exaggerate its importance in maintaining and driving crime in Manchester. It was the criminal's abode, his labour exchange and the place where he converted his goods into cash. It acted as gang headquarters, a resort for wandering criminals, where they could be sure of a welcome, companionship, information about local conditions and help when released from prison.

All this was common knowledge with the result that complaints about the failure of the police to close lodging houses are standard fare in the letters pages of the city's newspapers. The police response was twofold: they denied that they were failing to control these places and they tried to explain to the public that they were valuable sources of information.

Neither argument was convincing. Many informed members of the public still complained that the police were 'tolerating' these places, which were no less than academies of vice. Perhaps it was true the police did occasionally seize thieves there – but for every one it yielded, it trained 100. As early as 1851 the Common Lodging House Act tried to bring them under control. The police henceforward had powers of inspection and the authority to close those that fell below basic standards of decency and cleanliness. In Macclesfield alone the police closed 150.

In the euphoria that followed the Act the police turned out the occupants of many lodgings, dumping them on the city streets and immediately overwhelming the poor law authorities. The result was more people sleeping rough and an immediate change of police policy.

During the nineteenth century the ragbag of people who could not afford weekly rent – poor families, solitary women, abandoned children, and those too old to work – inevitably drifted to the lodging house. They were just one step above the workhouse. The unemployed labourers, the sacked domestics, beggars, jailbirds and tarts represented the full spectrum of this rainbow of misfortune. They were the abodes of the occasionally homeless, but also the rootless, the wanderers, the unattached, those without responsibilities or ties and those with nothing to lose.

Though in many ways conditions in the lodging house were more Spartan than in the workhouse, lodgers were free to come and go as they liked and behave more or less as they chose. The atmosphere was open and frank and the kitchen fire warm and gossipy. Yet it's doubtful if the 1851 Act did much to improve the standard of the common lodging house. Accounts by journalists and social reformers in the 1870s and 1880s are almost identical to those before 1851. An investigation by the *Manchester Evening News* in the 1870s found that most of the poor still rented rooms in slums or lived in common lodging houses and that criminals of all sort, especially fences, still infested the latter. Fences ran many of these houses simply because they provided a perfect cover for the comings and goings of thieves. Lodging houses were the most important means of disposing of stolen goods – especially clothes and household goods – far more important than pubs or pawnshops. Though the individual items fenced may have been of little value, their aggregate value was considerable. Despite the obsession of the local press with the evils of these houses, the police were often loath to close them, as they were valuable sources of information. As many a hoary detective explained, at least with the boarding houses they knew exactly where to find their criminals.

The houses that remained after 1851 had to increase their prices to attain the new standards. Those who could not afford the new charges drifted to the casual wards in the workhouse or the refuges operated by charities, where the atmosphere was harsh with discipline and cold, improving air. Yet the great attraction of the lodging house remained: it was so cheap that all but the destitute could afford it. In the 1870s they charged no more than a penny a night and as late as 1900 it was possible to get a bed for 4d.

Not surprisingly many of the meanest lodgings remained no more than doss houses, where the beds were let for the night and residents enjoyed neither comfort nor decency. Usually the charge depended on how many shared a bed. Reliable accounts tell of houses in Manchester where up to six shared a bed. Others slept on the floor – shelter from wind and rain their only comfort. Buckets and a pump in the yard provided the only sanitation. The worst houses were in rookeries and the worst of these in Angel Meadow and Deansgate. There men, women and children slept in the same room. In many, people slept in the corridors. A survey of 1858 classified seventy per cent of them as 'filthy' and half of them had neither toilets nor water. The Irish ran many of them together with their linked pubs and brothels. The prostitutes who used them collected their clients in the pub and worked under the protection of the publican.

Germans and other foreigners tended to gather in a few lodgings where they could spend time with their countrymen. By all accounts their houses, and the ones favoured by Italian organ grinders, were far cleaner and altogether better than the norm. When Joseph Johnson, a local journalist, described the horrors of the city's lodging houses, he excepted the one used by Germans, describing it as clean, homely and 'full of good-natured foreigners'. The Italian house in Edge Street was also excellent. But these were the exception. Though few of the rest were as good as the workhouse, many of those who could not afford a lodging house refused to go 'on the parish'. Instead they slept on one of the many brick-fields that littered the outskirts of the city where tramps and destitutes too sodden or broken for anything else lay their heads.

The respectable, however, swallowed their pride and entered the workhouse. In so doing they temporarily abandoned respectability – while keeping it within reach.

The Pauper Palace

'The rooms are well lighted,' one reporter stated, 'well ventilated, and airy, while every modern appliance has been taken advantage of that would add to the comfort of the inmates.' In fact some members of the public believed it was extravagantly sumptuous. Among these was one Mr James Cheetham, who used the letters page of the *Manchester Guardian* to protest at the drain on the public purse. He accused the Board of imprudent spending, claiming that the cost of maintaining one resident was twenty times the amount an honest, sober, industrious labourer earned.

Mr Cheetham was not the only one who was angry. The letters page of the *Manchester City News* also bristled with the indignation of incensed ratepayers. What was the reason for this outrage, these accusations of extravagance? Were the city fathers investing in accommodation for civic dignitaries or squandering money on pampered employees? Neither. It was the opening of the Prestwich workhouse that sparked such fury. It was not for nothing that people referred to such places as Pauper Palaces. Virtually every aspect of life within the workhouse – 'the House' – was better than a working man could ever hope to enjoy. In fact, by 1880 its 'internal conveniences' – heating, toilets, bathrooms and running water – were better than those of many middle class homes. The old image of the workhouse as a harsh and degrading institution was no longer relevant.

The Manchester Guardians, who were responsible for the city's provision for the poor, were keen to build a workhouse nothing less than magnificent. There are many examples of the central board refusing to sanction such embellishments as encaustic tile paving in the entrance halls and a moulded Portland stone staircase to the chapel. This desire to impress is evident in the surviving workhouses, many of which – like that in Chorlton-cum-Hardy – later became hospitals. You have only to look at the pictures and surviving accounts of the splendours of the Swinton Industrial Schools to realise that Manchester's poor law managers were anything but grubby penny-pinchers doing everything on the cheap.

The workhouse was the means by which the community provided for those who were unable to maintain themselves and their families. From 1834 parishes came together to form Poor Law Unions which built and maintained workhouses. In theory, only by entering the workhouse could a pauper receive support. The regime there was intended to keep out all but those who had no other means of supporting themselves. This was essential if it was to force down the cost of poor relief, which had been increasing rapidly. In practice, this did not happen. Manchester and Salford Poor Law Unions found it neither practical nor humane at this time to deny 'outdoor relief' to certain groups and many people continued to receive help in this way. Besides, to deny help to those in need would have contradicted the powerful Victorian philanthropic impulse. The poor were a highly visible part of society and for those who were only slightly better off, they afforded an opportunity to exercise Christian charity. The generosity of the many was an essential part of the life of the poor.

Charity was a major preoccupation of the Victorians. It was their Christian duty to help the unfortunate. The hordes of beggars who clogged the street of every city and town depended on this instinctive kindliness for their livelihood. In times of general hardship – such as the cotton famine of the 1860s, when private donations amounted to over a million pounds – public generosity was magnificent. Nor was parish provision for the poor stingy. The workhouse was never as bad as its reputation. The local Boards of Guardians who ran the institutions seldom consisted of heartless bankers and industrialists concerned only to keep down rates. There is no evidence the Salford or Manchester Guardians wanted to humiliate the old and disabled or any of the deserving poor. Quite the contrary. For instance, until 1875 outdoor relief not only continued but remained the principal means of help for the poor. In fact, the generosity of the Manchester poor law unions made the city a magnet for beggars and scroungers of all sorts.

It is not, however, true to say that entering the workhouse was a matter of indifference. It shattered the self-image of the respectable poor. The head of the household could no longer pretend he was fulfilling his role as a provider. Charity shattered the ideal of self-sufficiency as it was a public admission of failure. Worse still, the workhouse separated families – men and women lived apart – and imposed rules that controlled every aspect of life. They were supposed to eat their meals in silence. Restriction made visits difficult. Respectable people fallen on hard times lived with imbeciles, consumptives, syphilitics, single pregnant women and abandoned mothers.

This applied to all of Manchester's four workhouses – New Bridge Street, Crumpsall, Chorlton-cum-Hardy and Prestwich – and indeed all workhouses, as a nationally determined set of rules designed to control every aspect of life regulated them.

We know a great deal about life in the Manchester workhouses. This is because of Major Robert Ballentine who, for the twenty-six years from 1878 to 1904, was the master of the Crumpsall workhouse. During this period he made it the best workhouse in Britain, the model towards which all others strived. Ballentine was the only workhouse master to give evidence to the Royal Commission on the aged poor in 1894, by which time Crumpsall workhouse and infirmary, with 3,000 inmates, was the largest in the country. Long before Ballentine's era the Manchester Board of Guardians was at the forefront of the campaign after 1870 to reduce the amount of outdoor relief. In 1875 they introduced the so-called 'Manchester Rules' by which single people, widows with one child, deserted wives with or without families and the wives of prisoners and soldiers could no longer claim outdoor relief. This was a severe blow to the city's criminals who detested the rigorous regime of the workhouse. All those seeking outdoor relief in times of high unemployment had to take a 'labour test'. In order to qualify for relief women had to do washing and scrubbing at the New Bridge workhouse and men had to dig in the grounds of the Crumpsall workhouse. Both received half their relief in kind. Those in furnished lodgings, with less than six months residence in the Union and those whose destitution was deemed to be their own fault, were not entitled to relief. Instead, they were set to work in the parish stone yard.

The Bridge Street building had workshops for joiners, tailors, shoemakers, hemp workers and weavers. The Crumpsall site opened in 1858 and was designed for 1,660 inmates. It was to hold 745 able-bodied men and women; 152 women with infants; 238 idiots, imbeciles and epileptics; 255 children under the age of sixteen; sixty probationers and 200 sick. This provision proved totally inadequate during the 'cotton famine' of 1861 to 1865. The American Civil War choked off the raw cotton that fed Lancashire's mills. Closures and layoffs reduced 2,000,000 cotton workers to abject poverty. Yet as far as possible the able-bodied worked for their living and received payment in kind. It was essential, the Guardians believed, that assistance did not become an absolute right and that the distinction between deserving and undeserving poor be maintained.

To achieve this, the Manchester Poor Law Guardians combined with their Chorlton counterparts to construct a purpose-built institution, the only place where the undeserving poor could get relief. The Tame Street Able-bodied Test Workhouse opened in 1897. What's more, the Guardians made every effort to make the workhouse self-sufficient. The paupers grew vegetables and kept pigs to feed the inmates. They worked as joiners, shoemakers and tailors and wove hemp ropes and sacks. Women worked in the kitchens, laundry and sewing room and after the infirmary opened in 1876 they provided the cleaning and most of the nursing staff. These 'scrubbers', as they were known, were penniless women, often mothers of illegitimate children. Even today 'scrubber' is a derogatory Manchester term for a woman of loose morals.

In 1880, thirty-three of the imbeciles and epileptics worked as farm labourers while many more cleaned the wards. Three were responsible for the ash pits, three made mats and one had the task of replacing the straw mattresses. Though enlightened and humane, the workhouse managers were adamant that inmates should work for their keep. The idea that the parish should keep someone who was not prepared to work was regarded as blatant insanity. Sometimes, however, managers carried this to extremes.

In 1882 an inspector complained that a patient recovering on the surgical ward had to pick oakum. The chairman of the Guardians was not prepared to meekly accept such criticism. 'The patients referred to,' he explained, 'were recovering but obliged to lie in bed. It was thought it would be much more agreeable to them to find them a little something to do, than that they should idle their time away entirely.'

Nor was illness sufficient reason to relax the visiting regulations. From 1879 regulations restricted visits for the sick and infirm to one hour on the first Sunday of the month. It was this rigidity of the workhouse regime that made it intolerable to criminals of all types. The tolling bell announced breakfast, as it did every event in the life of the workhouse. And the rules governing behaviour covered every eventuality that might arise, allocating a designated penalty to each. Most offences rendered an inmate 'disorderly'. More serious misdemeanours, or repeated 'disorderly' offences, rendered him 'refractory'. Common disorderly offences included making noise during periods of prescribed silence, using obscene or profane language, insulting other inmates, neglecting work, disobeying a workhouse official and misbehaving on the way to or from church.

Refractory offences included insulting officials, repeatedly disobeying instructions, striking anyone, damaging the institution's property, being drunk and behaving in an indecent manner.

The master generally punished disorderly behaviour by withholding privileges or by withholding the normal dinner for two days and substituting eight ounces of bread, a pound of potatoes or a pound of rice. Refractory inmates might suffer both these and in addition be locked in isolation for twenty-four hours. We know about this punishment because, unlike lesser sanctions, the master recorded it in the minute book.

Inmates' clothing illustrates the drive for uniformity. Paupers wore a uniform. Men wore a corduroy suit with a waistcoat and belt, a red spotted handkerchief and hobnailed boots. When working in the rain they wrapped a sack around their shoulders. The women's uniform was a white blouse with leg of mutton sleeves, a long dark skirt and a large white apron of unbleached calico. Children's uniforms were similar to the adults' and they wore their hair cropped. Imbeciles wore calico suits.

Down and Out

Detailed regulations controlled the paupers' diet and each inmate's food matched his particular needs. The aged and infirm, for instance, enjoyed a diet far better than they could afford outside. It was certainly better balanced and healthier than that of the average British adult in the affluent twenty-first century. Those on a special diet, including the old and sick, breakfasted on bread and porridge with treacle. On Sundays they ate bread, margarine and coffee.

They took their main meal at midday. On Sunday it consisted of bread with potatoes, vegetables and boiled bacon; Monday and Thursday, boiled beef instead of bacon, with lentil soup in winter and barley soup in summer. On other days they ate Irish stew, potato pie or meat stew. The aged and infirm did not get the Tuesday treat of roly-poly pudding in winter or bread pudding in summer, which was allowed to able-bodied men, women and children from the age of three to sixteen. Supper consisted of bread and gruel on weekdays and bread, margarine and tea on Sundays. In addition, the able bodied got plain cake on Sunday as did the children on Thursday. Children also got milk, cocoa made with half milk, or tea, with seed cake on Tuesdays, syrup on Saturdays and jam on Sundays. The doctor prescribed the customary diet for the sick. Generally he ordered fewer potatoes and more rice pudding, bread and milk. If the doctor prescribed a fluid diet, it consisted of milk variously thickened and flavoured with rice, arrowroot and sago, believed to strengthen the sickly.

In theory the workhouse was to provide a life not better than that enjoyed by the poorest working man. In reality it was a good deal better. By the turn of the century, in 1906, conditions were undeniably good. Nevertheless, the Guardians were against keeping the young in the workhouse. They were convinced that the constant example of shiftless and hopeless adults was bound to harm them. Instead they stressed the importance of 'moral and physical training that would eradicate the ill effects of their early experiences'. For this reason they built the Swinton Poor Law Industrial Schools, completed in 1844 and much admired by Charles Dickens when he visited in 1850. Among the things that impressed him were the pristine cleanliness of the well-ventilated rooms and the tasteful gardens, play areas and sports fields in the schools' extensive grounds. Scholars ate fresh vegetables from the schools' own gardens where older scholars received training and employment.

The school catered for 700 children: ninety-nine orphans, 281 without a father, thirty-three without a mother, 153 deserted and 134 whose parent or parents were in the workhouse.

Asphyxiation

The Swinton Industrial Schools represented the best of poor law provision, its merits lauded by national celebrities such as Charles Dickens and the envy of every union in the country. It is equally clear, however, that events in the Crumpsall Workhouse fuelled the myth of the workhouse as a brutal institution of oppression, the torturer of the poor and unfortunate. The Crumpsall Workhouse outrage took place right at the end of our period. It aroused a great deal of interest, especially among the city's poor and provoked outrage, indignation and anger. For many the events of that night in October 1900 showed the precariousness of the lives of the poor.

When Francis Southgate, a patient in the workhouse imbecile ward, died in the early hours of October 3, no one was concerned. Certainly, the workhouse doctor, Dr Muir, attached no significance to the matter and scribbled out a death certificate without even looking at the body, attributing death to 'cardiac syncope and paralysis of the insane'. That same day, however, two inmate helpers who were working on the ward when Southgate died told a different story. They maintained that George Prescott, a night attendant, had wrapped a towel around Southgate's throat and, using a poker as a tourniquet, strangled him. Once the inmates made this allegation, Dr Muir and an outside doctor examined the corpse. They agreed: the cause of death was 'asphyxiation due to strangulation', consistent with the inmates' account of what they had seen. A subsequent inquiry confirmed their story. It also found that the local lunatic asylum was full. That's why Francis Southgate and so many others ended up in the workhouse without adequate facilities or trained staff to care for them. Muir resigned his post as resident medical officer.

The case confirmed the worst fears of the city's poor. Yet for others the real problem with the workhouse was that it was so lax and indulgent that it became a den of vice. These critics maintained that the system served only to ease the movement of professional vagrants around the country and provide training grounds for criminals. Technically, the master could refuse no one admission and therefore there was nothing to stop bad characters mixing with good. The 'casuals' were the main problem. One of the principal objectives of the new system was to ensure the free movement of labour and consequently the workhouse provided for those ostensibly searching for work. Casuals were troublesome. Often they refused to do the work required as payment for their accommodation and the masters, fearing violence, were glad to see the back of them. Some masters refused to admit them while others were selective.

Any workhouse master who got a reputation as a soft touch became a magnet for paupers from all over the region. Manchester workhouses had such a reputation. This is why they changed their policy in the 1870s. All masters, not just those in Manchester, regarded the 'regular moocher' – the professional vagrant – as the most troublesome. Many were young, fit and capable of work and therefore undeserving of charity. What's more, they were generally filthy pilferers and opportunists who undermined the good order of the workhouse. Their begging was often thinly disguised intimidation and many of them terrorised people living in isolated cottages.

But their wandering life was possible only in summer. In winter they found their way to the slums and rookeries of Manchester and Salford where many found a corner in one of the many lodging houses or spent the cold months in a cell. Others ended up in the workhouse. The advantage of Manchester and Salford was that even after the tightening up of the 1870s, they were lax in restricting aid to those with 'settlement' rights. To prevent casuals from contaminating the other residents, the master accommodated them in a separate building near the perimeter wall, generally for only one night. He searched them on admission and confiscated any money, as only the destitute had a right to food and a bed. Their accommodation was a cell off a long corridor, just big enough for a truckle bed. The master unlocked the cell in the morning and took the tramp to a cell opposite, where he had to break a pile of stones into pieces small enough to pass through the perforations in a grill built into the wall. Only then was he entitled to his breakfast.

The poor Irish, many arriving in Manchester after walking from Liverpool, were less squeamish about the workhouse. By the time they reached the city their hunger had generally consumed any qualms they might once have entertained. For those who found the workhouse intolerable there were private charities, such as the Wood Street mission in the heart of the infamous Deansgate rookery. It provided food and shelter for all who called at its doors, deserving and undeserving alike. This, of course, was not in keeping with the thinking of the Poor Law Guardians. They claimed that the mission, by feeding and sheltering the undeserving, was making the city a haven for the feckless who enjoyed all the benefits of support without having to work or accept an ordered life.

What was worse, according to these critics of indiscriminate charity, it attracted not only the idle and feckless but also the dangerous and violent.

An Epidemic of Wife-beating

Thieves, no matter how devious or prolific, were not the major cause of public concern. That position, then as now, belonged to the violent criminal. And there was an extraordinary amount of violent crime in nineteenth century Manchester. Prostitutes were invariably thieves. In fact, many thieves posed as prostitutes in order to rob their amorous victims. But neither violent crime nor violence was confined to prostitutes.

Violent sports were common. There was no recreation more popular among Lancashire miners than purring, a game that consisted of opponents kicking each other's shins until one fell to the ground. On several occasions during the 1870s colliers, carried away by the euphoria of success, kicked opponents to death.

Despite this and other examples of the indigenous population's capacity for violence, many blamed the Irish. This was partly anti-Irish prejudice, partly because the Irish lived in the poorer parts of the city where violence was common. Naturally, people associated the Irish with violence. Certainly, Miller Street, in the centre of Angel's Meadow, one of the areas where the Irish lived in great numbers, had an appalling reputation for violence. It was there in 1869 that Benjamin Crowshaw and his wife fell on each other in a drunken heap. Crowshaw beat her to death. This case was an exception only in the degree of violence used and the tragic outcome. Drunken brawls between man and wife were common – so much so that the Manchester papers of 1874 talked of an epidemic of wife-beating. In virtually every case drink was a factor.

Angel's Meadow was by no means the only violent part of the city – simply the most notorious. Violence scarred all the city's rookeries but certain areas – Long Millgate and Shudehill – were particularly notorious. Yet, given the general prevalence of violence it is surprising that its victims have changed so little in the last 140 years. Those who think that modern criminals and particularly junkies are uniquely degenerate in robbing the elderly and disabled are sadly mistaken. Manchester newspapers of the 1870s differ little from today's *Manchester Evening News* in their appalled reporting of crimes against the most vulnerable. Most vulnerable of all were drunks, stumbling home along dark streets. They were most frequently victims. Yet they received little sympathy from the public, who felt that anyone who got himself into such a state was asking for trouble.

Attitudes were very different in the 1860s, however, when it seemed that criminals were targeting the most respectable and sober elements of Manchester society.

Striking Terror

For most of the public, most of the time, crime is no more than a background irritant, a dull ache like an arthritic knee. Only when a person becomes a victim does it reach the level of a searing pain. Occasionally, however, the media creates an intermediate state, a scare so widespread, intense and prolonged that everyone feels a murderer is standing at his shoulder. The most famous example of this was the Jack the Ripper scare when for a short time women in the East End went in dread of their lives.

Before that, however, between 1861 and 1864 a garrotting scare swept the country. Suddenly the media was obsessed with street robbers who strangled or choked their victims. The press so inflamed the imagination of the public that a wave of hysteria swept the country. It first hit the headlines in1862 when it started in London. Three years later hysteria gripped the country. There had been an outbreak in Manchester in 1851 but the big scare hit the city in 1865. Such was the fear of garrotting that anti-garrotting societies sprang up around the country. In 1862 the *Weekly Despatch* told a nation avid for details of the latest throttling, 'The manner in which anti-garrotters armed to the teeth proceed along the streets at night... is calculated to strike terror into the breasts of others as well as the great enemy.'

One garrotter obligingly explained his working practices to the readers of *The Penny Magazine*. He operated with two others. The 'back stall' acted as a lookout, the 'front stall' approached the victim and occupied his attention while the 'nasty-man' crept up behind and throttled him. In reality, many reputed victims of garrotters were nothing of the sort. Seeking to exploit the national obsession with this crime, newspapers often reported attacks in which victims were not choked as if they were examples of garrotting. Their assailants coshed or beat them with knuckle-dusters or pipes, as nineteenth century 'muggers' always had. But the garrotting panic made such good press that journalists were loath to ease public fears. At one stage there were so many reported attacks in the city that Mancunians would not venture out at night other than in the best-lit and busiest streets. Even then, they lived in constant fear that at any moment the arm of the garrotter might lock around their neck.

With uncharacteristic decisiveness the courts responded vigorously. In 1865 they hanged more criminals than in any year since the end of the Bloody Code. The Bloody Code was the name given to the English legal system of the late eighteenth and early nineteenth century. At that time there were no less than 225 offences that carried the death penalty, including stealing goods worth more than a shilling. After 1837, however, execution as a punishment was virtually eliminated except for murder. The Manchester courts also played their part in crushing those who terrorised the city. In July that year, when the worst of the scare was over, James Bent saw several garrotters collapse in court as the judge sentenced them to corporal punishment. The judge in this case, Justice Lush, took full advantage of the 1865 Garrotters' Act which punished violent street robberies with prison and whipping: twenty-nine strokes of the cat-o-nine-tails for juveniles and fifty strokes of the birch for adults. At the Manchester Assizes that year, Justice Lush sentenced all twenty-three accused to both penal servitude and the cat. Some of the worst he had flogged three times at the beginning of their sentences and others twice. The judge felt, as did many commentators, that prison was no deterrent as many of the convicted had served several prison sentences. Others had returned from transportation.

All the convicted blanched at the prospect of the birch. James Bent believed the decisive action of the courts brought the garrotting outbreak to a sudden end. If so, it was a rare victory for law and order.

The garrotter was among the most detested criminals of the period. He was, however, not the most despicable. Surely that accolade must go to men who did no violence and seemed to be the model of respectability.

9

Conmen

Bloodsuckers

His skeletal features, his corpse-white flesh, his eyes, bright with hunger, were those of a man only one laboured breath away from death. Yet he had no illness. He was simply a victim of one of the many quacks who preyed on Manchester's neurotics.

Anyone who has ever glanced through an old newspaper from pre-NHS days will immediately notice the many advertisements for patent medicines. Readers sought remedies for ailments affecting every part of the human anatomy, from a flaky scalp to sweaty feet and all points in between. For every ailment there were a dozen potions, pills and embrocations not only guaranteed to ensure an instant return to robust good health but also claiming to bring about a total transformation of the patient's life. All, of course, at a price.

Until the 1860s the medical miracle worker was largely confined to rural fairs. He declaimed his promises from a podium, in the middle of which sat an old lady who was deaf, blind and lame. During the course of his demonstration he restored her health and vigour. Reputable manufacturers offered some products that were effective and safe by the standards of their day. But many were nothing but harmless placebos. Their only damaging effect was to deprive the credulous buyer of a few shillings.

By the 1870s, however, this scam was more elaborate and involved far more money. It was also more sinister. Con men now sought out the desperate and the vulnerable and squeezed them dry. In some cases they did not stop there. Many of these charlatans flourished unimpeded for so long that they came to believe their own claims. They behaved as if they really were respectable physicians of unimpeachable character. They spent enormous amounts on advertising – it was impossible for anyone to walk along Manchester's main thoroughfares without being accosted by someone passing out handbills advertising the services of a fraudulent physician.

Jerome Caminada despised those who preyed on the sick and deluded. He describes them as the 'bloodsuckers of the human race', a greater threat than the garrotter and the burglar. In particular he loathed them because the bulk of their victims were the poor. Yet the profits they made were enormous, amounting to many thousands of pounds.

Caminada recounts a case so poignant that it fully explains his contempt for swindlers of this type. It began one Saturday when a friendly pawnbroker called the detective to his premises on the corner of Deansgate and Gregson Street. He was suspicious of a young man of striking appearance who was pawning prints. The prints, it turned out, belonged to the young man's employer. Even as Caminada arrested him, he was appalled by his appearance. In an age when death from tuberculosis was common, this man was frighteningly sickly in appearance. Like a spectre, with 'cheeks hollow, shrivelled and cadaverous, eyes large and unnaturally bright, his form was shrunken and bent'. The reason was soon apparent. Caminada found 153 bottles of medicine in his home. Immediately he knew the root of the problem – he had fallen under the thrall of a quack.

A typical hypochondriac, the young man had in fact been in perfect health when he first consulted a quack doctor. The doctor, of course, played on the victim's morbid imagination and convinced him he had a life-threatening illness, which he alone could cure. But only with a lengthy programme of treatment. First he fleeced his victim. Then he directed him to a loan shark. In order to repay his debts, the young man sold two houses he owned. Then the quack, having convinced him that he was at a critical stage of his treatment, induced him to steal.

Without looking very far, Caminada was able to summon twelve such quacks to prove they were doctors. Many did a side-line in pornography and he also summoned seven of them to explain why the police should not destroy obscene books found on their premises. The first of these defendants was John Lewis, who had premises at Booth Street, Chorlton-on-Medlock. Mr Lewis, despite having no medical qualifications, was evidently prospering as a doctor, as he also maintained addresses in Leeds and Liverpool. He also did a brisk trade in dirty books and police found no less than twelve-hundredweight of them at his Manchester premises. The loss of this reading material was a far more severe penalty than the £20 fine he received. This is another instance of the courts' inexplicable leniency in dealing with such criminals.

A slight variation on this scam enjoyed popularity in 1877. A number of advertisements appeared in religious publications making claims for the Reverend E. J. Silverton's 'Food of Foods'. According to this man of the cloth, his patent food was a guaranteed remedy for deafness. When Caminada responded to one of the advertisements, the Reverend asked for a fee. When the detective went to the address in the advertisement, he found it empty. But he did not forget what he had discovered of the way in which this particular fraud operated. Sure enough, the Reverend was at it again in 1884, this time advertising more extensively than ever. On this occasion he hired the Free Trade Hall, where he offered his services free. Yet when Caminada consulted him, he found that the Reverend's immense skills extended beyond curing the hard of hearing. When the detective complained of a sore foot, the doctor, without any examination, charged him for a guaranteed remedy. Other detectives had similar experiences. Once the newspapers covered the Reverend's arrest, many of his victims came forward. Several were incurably ill. One woman had sold everything for her son's treatment. Many explained how the Reverend's pamphlets, liberally sprinkled with Biblical quotations, had fooled them.

A well-dressed gentleman who went from door to door worked

a low-level variation on this scam. Armed with testimonials from prestigious hospitals extolling the wonders of his potion, he made an excellent living for many years. A more despicable and brazen variation was that of the 'official hospital agent' who invited people to make a small donation towards the building of a new ward. Polite, respectable and unassuming, the collector seldom attracted unwanted attention and by moving from area to area lived better than any honest working man.

In an age when class distinctions permeated every area of life, when men of the cloth and those in the professions commanded deference, few working men would challenge an apparently respectable gentleman. This, more than anything else, allowed these con men to operate with impunity – even when the bait they dangled was the implausible promise of an unearned fortune.

Equal to the National Debt

No con man ever failed to make money because he overestimated others' greed. The avarice of the Manchester public flourished when J. S. Rogers offered them unearned fortunes, theirs for the taking.

In May 1882, Jerome Caminada went to impressive offices, sumptuously furnished, at 72 Piccadilly. Outside, restrained by two flustered peelers, an irate crowd of 100 people surged forward, demanding to speak to the proprietor, Mr J. S. Rogers, Attorney. Rogers had duped the bemused office junior just as he had his irate customers.

The next of kin fraud that Rogers operated with such spectacular success was, like all the best deceptions, very simple. It played on people's greed, their desire to get something for nothing and their natural tendency to trust members of the educated middle class, especially when they have impressive offices and are associated with the law.

Rogers advertised in local newspapers offering to help anyone who thought he might have claim to a bequest. This advertisement came immediately after local and national coverage he received courtesy of an accommodating journalist. This story claimed that through the efforts of the Next of Kin Agency a local man had secured a bequest of £200,000 – worth about £27 million today. While this story was still reverberating around pubs and music halls, the tricksters struck. They hired Stockport Theatre for a public lecture entitled 'The Unclaimed Property of Next of Kin Lying in the Hands of the Government'. The speaker maintained the sum involved was equal to the national debt. A large and rapt audience hung on his every word and afterwards many stayed behind to arrange a private interview.

First Rogers promised to discover if his client had a claim to money or property left in a contested will. Invariably he was delighted to announce that this was, in fact, the case and the client was about to become the beneficiary of a large inheritance. All he had to do was cover Rogers' trifling expenses while the Attorney expedited the process. Having hooked his prey, Rogers showed great skill at exploiting the expectation of immediate wealth to bleed his client of every penny. Upon investigation, Caminada found that Rogers was in the process of reeling in 270 dupes. Perhaps the most pathetic of these were two elderly ladies who, in order to pay the fake attorney's fees, sold the entire contents of their home and then borrowed money they could not repay. All that kept them from the workhouse was the sixteen shillings a week their children gave them.

Rogers' squalid career had begun as a moneylender. He fancied himself as an impresario, leasing a theatre, which he later abandoned owing money to everyone associated with the enterprise. His next venture – an exclusive club – ended in like fashion. In operating other ventures he used the aliases the Reverend J. S. Rogers and J. S. Rogers, BA, Next-of-Kin and Foreign Law Officer. Nor was he alone in operating this fraud. Its extent was so great that he ran offices all over the country and employed three fellow conspirators.

Rogers' modus operandi was always the same. First he induced his victim to sign an agreement granting him ten per cent of all money received, together with all out-of-pocket expenses. For this he charged £1.12s 6d – a week's wages for a working man. Then he drew up a power of attorney, for which he charged as much as he felt prudent. Next he charged for 'declaration', followed by a charge of between £10 and £20 for 'administration', which also required a trip to the London courts and further unavoidable expenses. The number of these trips to London depended on the client's gullibility.

Then, of course, there was the cost of taking counsel's opinion, which he sought on several occasions. When a client pressed for results, Rogers was quite prepared to provide proof of progress. He even took one dupe down to Somerset House where she met a bogus commissioner who assured her that the case was progressing well. That same day he took her to view the Old Red Cap Hotel, which, Rogers assured her, was part of the inheritance coming her way. All she had to do was pay the fee of £575 to cover the legal technicalities. This particular victim travelled to London with Rogers on a further two occasions. She was not the only one whose reservations he soothed in this way.

When Rogers eventually appeared in court in July 1882 the case attracted blanket coverage. A large, indignant crowd packed the public gallery. They had no time to take refreshment while the jury was deliberating – the twelve men returned their guilty verdict without leaving the court. Rogers received the remarkably lenient sentence of two years' hard labour and his associates got lesser terms of imprisonment. At least one of them, McKenzie, was undeterred. Five years after his release he was back in court, this time the Old Bailey, to receive a ten-year sentence for frauds similar to those he carried out in Manchester.

Despite the publicity surrounding the case, the British public remained as gullible as ever and men like Rogers lost none of their faith in the power of avarice to distort a man's judgement.

Handsome Charlie and George the Greek

The ignorance of those who live outside the business world blinds them to its pitfalls. The uninitiated believe anyone can make money. Loan swindlers exploited this naivety. Surprisingly, the victims of these scams were not the poor or those who are often deceived into paying exorbitant interest on tiny loans. These particular sharks were after more substantial fish. Their victims were usually gentlemen anxious to make a quick return on their disposable income. Most had no business experience but had saved money through thrift and self-denial. They now hoped to reap the benefits of their frugality.

The con men put advertisements in the local newspapers inviting interested parties to lend £50. As security they offered jewellery worth far more than the loan. Not only that, but they offered to repay interest at the extremely generous rate of £10 per calendar month. To the unwary this was an attractive proposition with no risk. A Manchester crook who delighted in the sobriquet of 'Handsome Charlie' operated this scam until complaints led Caminada to answer one of his advertisements. Another practitioner was 'George the Greek'. Both got six months hard labour.

A similar scam came to light in 1886, when two men newly arrived in Manchester from Liverpool, Samuel Bush and Thomas Holliday, placed an advertisement in a local newspaper. It read: 'Money. £25. A gentleman requires this amount for a month. Will give £5 interest and deposit his railway bonds for £200. Strictly private.' Bush and Holliday were practised frauds. Holliday had lived at Stoke Newington, where he described himself as a merchant and financial agent. In fact, his activities consisted of operating a version of the long-firm scam, a perennial favourite with professional criminals and practised by both the Krays and the Richardsons in the 1960s. Holliday's version of the long-firm scam was beautiful in its simplicity. He set himself up with a valid bank account and used it to build up a record of prompt payment for small consignments of goods, which he sold abroad. Once he had established his creditworthiness, he placed large orders with many Birmingham suppliers and sold the goods to Italy. When his Birmingham creditors began to close in, he simply disappeared.

He next washed up in Liverpool, where he set up as an endorser of bills of exchange, working on commission. It was while there that he came across bogus railway bonds for the non-existent Iowa Pacific Railway Company, nominally worth $1,000, and promising a half-yearly yield of six per cent. Having successfully operated the loan scam in Liverpool, he and Bush tried their luck in Manchester. They had not been in the city long before the police arrested them. Holliday got eighteen months with hard labour and Bush twelve.

This, however, did nothing to deter others operating the same scam. James Melville and George Beck were in many ways more interesting characters. These incorrigible rogues had total confidence in their ability to charm their way out of any situation. It never occurred to either man that the people they duped would ever do anything so disagreeable as to involve the police. James Melville called himself a 'commission agent' and resided at a variety of addresses in Manchester's respectable suburbs. He was, in fact, a cashier in a bank and active in a Manchester chapel, where he often spoke from the pulpit. Despite this Melville was no ordinary member of the city's solid commercial class. He had at least one previous conviction for embezzling from his employers. His colleague, George Beck, lived in the less fashionable Leamington Avenue, Chorlton-on-Medlock. He appeared to be what he had once been – the owner of a large ironworks near Manchester, before gambling on the stock market reduced him to penury.

Melville placed an advertisement in the local papers: 'Wanted £16 for two months. £2 interest will be paid; good security. No loan co. need apply.' Attracted by the generous rate of interest, many people responded. Having met Melville, any reservations they may have had evaporated. The epitome of the substantial businessman, he seemed a model of integrity and was also witty, charming and patently honest. Besides, he was offering excellent security – a warrant on a case of cigars deposited with a bonded warehouse in Salford. Beck's involvement came later, when the disgruntled lender, having been repeatedly fobbed off, finally sought to realise his security. At this point Beck offered to buy the warrant. This, of course, was merely a delaying tactic, which ended when the lender was totally entangled in a web of warrants, promissory notes and solemn undertakings that never materialised. Beck seems to have convinced himself that he could string along his victims indefinitely. When one called upon him, embarrassed at having to ask for his money, Beck greeted him like an old friend. Clasping his hand in both his, he smiled and joked, asked about the family and soon had the victim feeling thoroughly ashamed of himself.

Eventually though even their charm ceased to work. They stood in the dock, unlikely looking criminals, charged with conspiracy to defraud. Beck had orders against him going back over a decade and had never paid a single penny. This time they both paid with two years' hard labour.

Just as Melville and Beck depended on charm, Reynor & Co. relied on effrontery. When Caminada investigated them, in response to the complaints of unpaid clients, it was immediately apparent they were operating a variation of the long-firm scam. They rented offices all over the city in different names. Each office provided another with references, on the basis of which they opened bank accounts. At their Watling Street office they received goods from Italy – oil, leather strapping, lace and fancy goods – for which they never paid. When their creditors began to close in, they abandoned this office, moved to another and continued the scam from there.

When Caminada visited one of their many offices, he met only affronted innocence – quickly followed by a solicitor's letter informing him that he had no right to harass his clients. This solicitor was in fact one of the team operating the scam. But it wasn't only their suppliers they didn't pay. When a disgruntled landlord tried to evict them from their prestigious offices in Silver Street, off Portland Street, they barricaded the doors against him. Later they forestalled the bailiffs by the same means. This method did not work against Inspector Caminada, nor did it prevent him from gathering sufficient evidence to convict them at Manchester Assizes on 28 February 1890. The judge sentenced each of those involved to fifteen months' hard labour.

Conmen

After a long period of trouble-free swindling, they thought they were fireproof. It was as if they believed they really were operating a legitimate business. Yet these were not the most so-phisticated of Manchester's white-collar crooks. That accolade belongs to card sharps.

The Magsman

Many of the magsman frauds sound totally unconvincing. We find it difficult to believe that anyone but an imbecile would fall for them. This is because no account can convey the key element common to all of these scams – the psychological subtlety that draws the victim into a relationship of trust with the man who is about to fleece him.

Central to this is the con man's approval of his victim, expressed in an ingenuous smile, a pat on the back or a word of praise as the dupe wins during the build-up to his inevitable ruin. When the venue is a pub, the trickster buys all the drink, insisting his new friend must not put his hand in his pocket. How could anyone distrust such a generous, friendly person? Besides, the dupe owes it to this man to try his luck – it's the least he can do. What harm is there in a friendly bet? he reasons. Things are going well and he is winning. It wouldn't be sporting to stop while ahead and walk away with his winnings without giving his friend a chance to win back some of his money. Later, when he is losing, the trickster offers the dupe such favourable opportunities to get back all he has lost that he cannot resist. After all, he surmises, with double-or-quits odds he can't possibly lose indefinitely.

But he does.

More difficult to spot were the sharpers who operated a variety of racecourse scams. One of the most common involved a team of three or four, one posing as an unofficial bookie – offering better odds than the legitimate bookies – the others as punters. They usually latched onto their dupe at the bar. At first he wins. Then, of course, he suffers a major setback and the bookie and the punters turn nasty. The magsman's skill is not so much in his sleight of hand but in his disarming smile, the inept way he shuffles the cards, his ponderous movements, his generosity, the little confidences he shares, the way he makes his victim feel a shrewd man of the world whose company and opinions he values. He operated wherever there was a crowd to work. A race meeting, fair or carnival guaranteed a large number of punters in a frivolous mood and game for a wager.

At its most basic this scam required only a folding table, three thimbles and a dried pea, which the magsman was able to pick up under his thumbnail. The three-card trick and loaded dice are variations. A second man, working with the magsman, betting heavily and winning, adds greatly to the credibility. Ideally, however, the sharps work in a group of four. One throws a blanket down on the footpath and his two companions, posing as bypassers, attract attention to the game. Another accomplice, pretending not to know the others, draws the dupe into the game. In one case Caminada recounts the dupe lost his gold watch and the magsman told him he could get it back for £20. He gave the Millstone Hotel on Thomas Street as his address. The dupe went to the police and Caminada watched the hotel from the cellar of an unoccupied house opposite. It wasn't long before he spotted characters who had been involved in this sort of fraud before. Eventually, having established they were the villains, Caminada swooped and after a struggle arrested all four.

The subsequent court case made it clear why the four fought so fiercely against arrest. The Manchester Assize Court took a dim view of what was a widespread type of fraud and sentenced each man to five years' penal servitude. Their previous convictions amounted to what the court regarded as damning form. They had served time for conspiring together to defraud a gentleman of his gold watch and chain guard worth £30. For this they each got five years' penal servitude. Individually, one had eight previous convictions, two others seven, and the fourth four, all for similar forms of dishonesty.

Does the number of their convictions suggest that they were inept? Or was it that the proceeds were so great in Manchester that they could not resist staying too long? Either way they came to regret the time they spent in the city, unlike those who operated a more lucrative scam and escaped unscathed.

Gizza Job

Most of us have reluctant admiration for rogues. While not approving of what they do, we can't help but admire their skill and audacity. However, those who worked the employment scam don't enjoy this indulgent attitude. Theirs was a particularly despicable racket because it exploited people who were seeking work and prepared to spend the little money they had to find it. The victims in this 1887 case were domestic servants, many young country girls, away from home for the first time.

This scam robbed both the domestic in search of work and the prospective employer. Like so many of these ruses, it started with an advert in a local newspaper.

Replies went to a prestigious address in Piccadilly, where two outwardly respectable ladies carried on their business with a combination of effrontery and blind optimism. Despite mounting complaints as they failed to arrange any employment, they carried on taking fees. Caminada's enquiries showed that these demure ladies had fooled at least 100 people, extorting from each a £1 registration fee – a month's wages for a domestic. Each served four months' hard labour.

A similar scam used a house in Chorlton-on-Medlock to which respondents sent 5s to prove they were genuinely interested in a position as a farm bailiff. After a number of complaints the police watched the house and eventually arrested a woman who called twice daily to collect the post. When arrested she had £11 in letters on her. The organiser, however, got away with £700.

The lottery scam is similar to the employment scam in that it takes advantage of people's implicit trust in anything that appears in a newspaper and uses the post as a means of distancing the swindler from his victims. Lots of shops ran lotteries which promised substantial prizes, often as much as £100. Many were fraudulent and the only winner was the organiser, who often made vast sums.

After receiving a number of complaints about one particular lottery, Caminada traced the organisers to a postal address in Toxteth Park, Liverpool. He hid in the house for three days and when eventually someone came to collect the post he followed him to his home, a sumptuous residence, proof that the owner was living in what Caminada describes as 'magnificent style'. It subsequently came to light that the occupier, a clerk on a weekly wage of £1.10s, had recently spent over £3,000 furnishing his home. The large prizes promised to punters were bogus – he gave a few small ones to shops that were doing well.

As despicable as the operator of an employment scam was Walter Hamilton, another exploiter of those decent poor people anxious to improve their lot by spending their hard-earned coppers. When it comes to unprincipled dishonesty, Hamilton is right up there among the worst scoundrels who ever trod the streets of Manchester. During 1884 he delivered a number of public lectures, advocating emigration as a guaranteed way for the poor to improve their lot. He placed advertisements for the British Employment, Emigration and Aid Society, an organisation which, he claimed, provided all its subscribers with employment or the means to emigrate and set themselves up in business. It operated from an impressive address on Princess Street. To verify its bona fides the Society claimed testimonials from prominent clergymen, including the Bishop of Manchester. Of course, none of this was true. What is true, however, is that emigration was in vogue at this time and many legitimate societies did help poor people to make a better life abroad. All sorts of organisations supported emigrants – even trade unions helped to pay their members' costs. It is understandable that Hamilton's scam deceived many people. He even interviewed and appointed a number of agents who went about the city recruiting members and collecting subscriptions. He paid none of them and while they were busy taking money from the unsuspecting, Hamilton simultaneously ran three other scams, posing as an employment agent, an insurance agent and an investment consultant. In the former capacity he targeted vulnerable women, promising marriage. None of these romantic entanglements, however, prevented him from absconding with his landlady's daughter and setting up home with her in lodgings on Denmark Road, Moss Side.

When Caminada investigated complaints about Hamilton he soon discovered the charming philanderer and compulsive liar had appeared in court on similar charges in 1883. On that occasion he escaped conviction, even though he had an 1882 conviction for obtaining money by false pretences. In 1884, however, his luck ran out. Manchester October Assizes gave him five years' penal servitude and three years' police supervision.

No sooner had he served this sentence than he resumed his career as a financial adviser with a special interest in his female clients. On this occasion, however, it was not his financial dishonesty that proved his undoing. When he began a sentence of six years' penal servitude in 1894 it was for bigamy.

Ironically, Hamilton, one of the most repugnant of Manchester scoundrels, remained irresistible to the women he duped.

Kiss and Tell

Not that women were always the victims of criminal deception. A number of Manchester ladies were as bad as any of their male counterparts.

As with their male equivalents, it is difficult for us to feel anything but contempt for them as they happily destroyed men's lives in order to line their own pockets. A young man complained to Bent of a woman extorting money from him. He'd had a liaison with the wife of a sea captain who was away from home for between three and six months at a time. When the relationship ended the man married. Now the captain's wife – currently shacked up with a released prisoner – claimed the young man had fathered her child. She demanded maintenance, threatening to reveal all to his new bride.

Bent came across many varieties of this scam. Any young man who made a good marriage was vulnerable – even when the allegations were totally false. One woman made an excellent living out of it. She usually waited until a man was about to marry. Many men, though totally blameless, nevertheless made payments for many years.

Bumpkin Scam

Some criminals were so prolific that they constituted their own crime wave. One such was Jimmy Gayner from Failsworth, who in a long and unsuccessful career served 100 prison sentences. Though a failure, no one could accuse him of lacking originality. In one scam he operated he swindled a Herefordshire farmer out of three Ayrshire cows – without leaving Manchester.

Posing as a big landowner he wrote to the farmer, claiming his bailiff assured him that a large quantity of grass on his estate would benefit from the farmer's Ayrshires grazing on it. Each animal was worth £30. The gullible farmer supplied the cattle, only later realising his mistake. When he sought Bent's help, the policeman gave him advice, which was hardly legal even in the 1870s: he told him to break into the thief's barn and retrieve his cattle.

The Herefordshire farmer was not the only countryman to discover Manchester was full of crooks and no place for an honest person. Many like him concluded there wasn't an honest man in the city. In March 1884 a Cheshire farmer, having just arrived by train, was walking down Market Street, when someone asked him for directions.

'No matter,' said the inquirer, when the farmer explained he was a stranger in the city. 'It's my first time here, too.'

The two repaired to the nearest bar, where they fell into conversation with a third man, who mentioned that his father, recently dead, had left £400 for distribution among the poor of his native Cheshire. Before long, the recently bereaved son asks a favour: would his two new friends be prepared to distribute the money for him? He would be greatly indebted if each of them would distribute £200 to Cheshire's deserving poor. He would, of course, recompense them for their trouble. Would £20 each be acceptable?

It went without saying that he would require securities, but that was a mere formality they could sort out later. They agreed to meet the following day in a pub on Oxford Road.

The next day the farmer arrived with his security – two Bank of England £100 notes in an envelope. The benefactor examined them, deftly switching them for two sheets of paper and then repaired to the toilet. After ten minutes his accomplice went to check what was amiss. By the time the farmer had realised what had happened the sharpers had cashed one of the notes for gold and smaller notes. Unfortunately for them, as was normal practice then, the cashier recorded the serial numbers of the notes and was able to give a good description of the men. One of them had signed his name Henry Johnson on the back of the note and Caminada recognised him from the cashier's description. Though the Manchester police searched all Johnson's haunts, they found no trace of him. Later some of the money turned up in London and detectives traced the second £100 note to a notorious fence based in Boulogne whose clients were English and French railway and steamboat thieves.

Some time later, Caminada spotted Johnson in Manchester. Wisely the con man had changed his appearance, in particular shaving off his distinctive whiskers. This presented a major problem, as the detective feared the witnesses might not identify him. He decided to wait and watch.

His opportunity came in an unexpected fashion. Caminada was in Oak Street, near Smithfield Market close to the Old Fleece Inn, a haunt of thieves. A fight broke out and when the detective intervened, Johnson, now looking more like his old self, fled. Caminada chased and caught him. Subsequently witnesses identified him and despite his forceful denials the Assize Court sentenced him to ten years' penal servitude. Johnson deserved his fate. How much more deserving of prison were those who systematically robbed the kindly and the generous?

Helping the Ragged School

Whereas there is something distasteful about cheating the gullible, cheating the charitable is despicable. Criminals, however, exploit every situation in which their victim is likely to be off guard. Who is more worthy of our trust than someone who devotes himself to helping those in need? How could anyone doubt the purity of his intentions?

Bogus charities were a rich source of income for swindlers. In an age when Christian generosity was an esteemed quality, when those not in need felt a moral obligation to help the poor, when many wealthy people actively sought worthy outlets for their charitable impulses, the callous swindler had access to untold riches. By the standards of our cynical world, late nineteenth century people seem naïve. But there was no government regulation of charities then and the only safeguard against malpractice was the integrity of the organisers. When this was absent there was endless scope for abuse.

One particularly despicable case of 1888 illustrates this. James W. Barlow's (real name Chadwick) request for subscriptions to a ragged school and mission in Canning Street resulted in many generous subscriptions. One family gave £30. Caminada traced Chadwick to his correspondence address only to find he had fled. An informant then told the detective he was in Fallowfield. When Caminada swooped, he captured not only his quarry but also incriminating documents. Chadwick had prepared an elaborate account of the mission's activities for distribution to current and prospective donors. He was also in the process of compiling the charity's balance sheet. In the Manchester Assize Court it came out that Chadwick had lived very comfortably for many years on the proceeds of charity. To lend the scam further credibility he had even persuaded one of its most prominent benefactors to accept the position of honorary president. Without having seen the school, he agreed.

Chadwick got nine months with hard labour. There is no doubt the courts treated him and his like with remarkable leniency. Anyone convicted of producing counterfeit money, however, could expect a long sentence.

Coining

By the 1850s coining was a growing underworld industry. No longer a capital offence, its appeal was greater than ever. Coining was seldom a full-time job, usually just one of many strings to the resourceful crook's bow.

The coiner seldom tried anything as adventurous as making gold sovereigns as they were valuable enough to attract scrutiny and would pass muster only if they contained a high percentage of gold. The production of silver coins, however, was something of a cottage industry in the rookeries. Sensible coiners used women to pass their wares in city centre shops while they peddled their handiwork at fairs, race meetings, markets and above all pubs in the slums.

In 1869 there was a spate of arrests in Manchester for passing base coins. The police sent Caminada in search of the coiner. At this stage all the detective knew was that a shadowy character, Brocky Dave, was keeping company with a renowned coiner. Caminada followed his normal procedure – shadowing the suspect to discover his associates. What he discovered seemed to confirm his suspicions. However, in order to secure a conviction for coining it was usually necessary to capture the suspect either in the act or on premises with the means of producing the counterfeit. This is exactly what he did when he arrested Brocky Dave, Raggey Burke and Scotch Jimmy. All three appeared before the Manchester Assizes on 15 January 1870 and were duly convicted. As always the court took a dim view of anything that might undermine confidence in the currency. Jimmy's sentence of seven years' penal servitude seemed moderate in comparison with the fourteen years dished out to his partners.

Brocky was an incorrigible counterfeiter, with convictions going back over twenty years. Raggey, too, was no stranger to the treadmill. His previous sentences included both a four- and a ten-year stretch, during one of which he orchestrated a riot in Dartmoor. His punishment on that occasion was a flogging.

Far more ambitious, however, were those who produced paper money. Forgery was in fashion in the 1880s and Manchester was at the centre of it.

Big Jim

Note forgers were at the very top of their profession and generally went for the £5 and £10 notes. Yet even with these smaller denominations few attained the degree of competence needed to produce facsimiles good enough to deceive a bank. The major problem was the watermark. Even the best forgeries were not proof against a drop of water, which dissolved the fake watermark. Besides, the smallest denomination in circulation was the £5 note, sufficiently uncommon to attract scrutiny.

Large-scale production of notes required machinery weighing over a ton and almost impossible to install and operate secretly. For this reason most of the best notes were the work of small businesses that also produced legitimate printing. Most of those who made a success of this were based in London and Birmingham. In 1861 they went a long way towards swamping the country with forged notes. They managed to get a considerable amount of paper from the Laverstoke Paper Mill, the supplier of paper to the Bank of England since the mid-eighteenth century. The moving force behind the conspiracy was James Griffiths, a master forger who had made a very comfortable living from his craft for seventeen years. Just as he was in a position to make himself fabulously rich, the police swooped. The court dished out sentences of twenty and twenty-five years to William Burnett. The severest penalty they reserved for Griffiths – penal servitude for life.

In 1887 Caminada dealt with a case of banknote forgery, which is worth recounting because it tells us a great deal about the characters who peopled the Manchester underworld, how they operated and their links with other parts of the country. Reports of forged notes reached Manchester from all over the country. A number of banks offered large rewards for the arrest of those responsible.

At the time Johnny the Lawyer, known for the legal advice he gave fellow criminals, was in Manchester, often in the company of Big Jim. Jim had a rich and singularly unsuccessful criminal past which had taken him all over the country to many of Britain's prisons. He paid for a Christmas hamper swindle he ran in Birmingham with five years' penal servitude. Later he served ten years for forgery and two months for receiving stolen goods. None of this deterred him for he subsequently served five years for obtaining £5,000 by means of a forged letter of credit. Once more at liberty, he was ostensibly making a living as a shopkeeper. He and Johnny the Lawyer spent a great deal of time in the company of another shopkeeper, a man who had served fourteen years' penal servitude.

Reading between the lines of Caminada's account and the newspaper reports, it is obvious that the detective knew, through his informants, that the trio was responsible for forged notes currently in circulation. Proving it, however, was an entirely different matter. Even when a man matching Big Jim's description passed a forged cheque at a Manchester bank, Caminada was unable to hold him for lack of evidence. The detective was reduced to impotent fuming. Passing forged cheques was a highly specialised field. No scruffy thug with a cauliflower ear and a nasal mumble could hope to pull it off. It needed a presentable fraud who exuded integrity. It also required careful planning.

At this time cheques were in the form of blank sheets and it was impossible to work this fraud without the details of someone with an active and substantial bank account. The easiest way to get this was to engage an attorney to recover a small debt. The attorney invariably passed on the money to his client in the form of a cheque, thereby providing the forger with a sample of his signature and details of his account.

One of Caminada's more successful drives against forgers occurred on another occasion when he heard that Johnny the Lawyer, Bottle Wilson, Charlie the Barman, Jack the Carpenter and Starve were drinking together in Harpurhey. All had convictions for serious commercial scams. Their common interest on this occasion, however, was forged notes, many of which were surfacing in the Wakefield area. This time when Caminada swooped, he found the necessary evidence to sentence Johnny to seven years, the Barman to ten and Bottle to fourteen. His disappointment that Jack and Starve went free was tempered by the two rewards he received.

A more direct way to get money from a bank is to walk in and rob it, a crime for which the USA is famous.

Dithering Yanks

Queen Victoria's Golden Jubilee in 1887 attracted many American and continental con men who saw in the British mood of celebration an opportunity. Manchester, as one of the country's great commercial centres and host to a celebratory exhibition, attracted more than its fair share.

Two New York gangsters, both with convictions for robbery and burglary, robbed banks in London and Liverpool before arriving in Manchester. They fixed on the King Street branch of the Manchester and Liverpool District Bank as their next target. Despite their wide-ranging criminal experience, they proved singularly inept bank robbers. They spent so much time dithering near the bank and aroused so much suspicion that before they got round to robbing it the manager summoned Caminada who promptly arrested them. As with many criminals, looking suspicious proved the downfall of the American bank robbers. A small number of crooks, however, depended for their success on looking seedy. Among these were the phantom pornographers.

The street trade in pornography was a common scam in the Manchester of the 1870s. A sealed envelope and the promise of salacious pleasure for only 6d was difficult to resist. The more reluctant the buyer, the greater the depravity promised. When the purchaser returned home and with trembling hands tore open the envelope, he found only a missionary tract or the pages of an old newspaper. This only worked when the goods were sold in the street, where the buyer was too ashamed to open them and check the nature of the contents.

Ringing the Changes

In any scam effrontery is everything. This was particularly so with the 'ringing the changes' fiddle, the beauty of which was its simplicity. Audacity was all that was required. Working as a team, two men went into a shop where one bought something for less than a shilling and proffered a sovereign in payment. On receiving the change, his companion said, 'Give him that back. Take it out of this,' offering a half sovereign to the shop assistant. As the assistant gave the second man his change, the first said, 'Here, I have a shilling. Give him back his half sovereign and take it out of this.' In most cases the assistant returns both the sovereign and the half sovereign without claiming the change for either.

Simple as this sounds, this scam invariably succeeded when worked by skilled operators. One team of particularly slick swindlers pulled it off forty times in a single week in 1884, often six times in a single day. They were a perfect team, both well-dressed gentlemen outwardly respectable. One was slow talking and easygoing. The other claimed to be a dealer in antiquities. Both got nine months.

The same quality of respectability was essential for the 'knife grinder' scam. The thief waited until he saw the mistress leaving the house then reported to the servant that the lady of the house had sent him to grind the best carving set. A similar ruse involved a boy calling at the house on the pretext that the master had sent him to get a suit of clothes as he had been soaked rescuing a child from a canal. Unsuspecting servants invariably supplied clothes and shoes which were promptly sold. This scam required a great deal of brazen effrontery, whereas the snoozer needed above all a strong nerve and an easy manner.

Snoozers

As one of the country's major commercial centres, Manchester boasted many splendid hotels, catering for a vast population of businessmen. It was an ideal environment for the snoozer. A snoozer was a well-dressed, inconspicuous gentleman who specialised in stealing from prestigious hotels. He was a criminal aristocrat, a man with a cool head and quick hands. Usually he carried a range of skeleton keys and a few select burglars' tools – but his greatest asset was his plausibility. Highly respectable and unobtrusive he blended into his surroundings. He looked perfectly at home in the hotel lounge and dining room, a patron no member of staff would ever challenge.

Before the credit card era, when relatively few people carried chequebooks and hotel accommodation was quite expensive, most travellers relished the security of a wad of paper money or a purse of sovereigns. The snoozer invariably booked in and then dined in the hotel. Apparently self-absorbed he watched and listened intently to his fellow guests, deciding which were likely to provide the richest pickings. That evening he arranged to check out early the following morning. That night he entered as many rooms as possible, hoping ideally for cash but also prepared to risk taking watches and jewellery. The next morning he left before any of his victims realised their loss.

When the thefts came to light, most hotels were concerned to preserve their reputation by avoiding unfavourable publicity. Indignant guests found management anxious to placate them and unwilling to involve the police. The wiser hotel managers, however, referred the matter directly to a particular detective, a man whose renown spread far beyond Manchester and gave him a national reputation.

10

The Good, the Bad and the Dangerous

The Master Detective

'He can't be,' said the cabbie. 'Let me see,' he said, shouldering the peeler out of the cab doorway. A string of spittle hung from the corner of the old man's mouth. His head lolled on his chest.

'Come on, sir,' said the cabbie, shaking him by the top of his arm, 'you have to wake up.' The spittle formed a viscous pearl on his lapel.

'I told you,' said the peeler. 'Nowt'll wake him till the Last Judgement.'

The death of a wealthy businessman in a cab on a dank Tuesday night in February 1889 began a chain of events that made a Manchester detective a national figure and sparked a furious debate in legal and medical circles. In an age when immigrants – especially the Irish – were blamed for a great deal of the nation's crime, Jerome Caminada was an unlikely master detective. The son of an Italian father and Irish mother, he was anathema to the Manchester underworld and gained a reputation that extended far beyond the city. He was the Manchester Sherlock Holmes.

But he also had a pronounced streak of the Clint Eastwood cop. Caminada employed Holmes-like logic to solve crimes, but he was not a detached intellectual happy to leave the unpleasantness to others. He relished a good scrap and delighted in thrashing any criminal who resorted to violence. Like most men who excel in their chosen profession, he had no sense of proportion. He was relentless in pursuit of his quarry, regarding crime, no matter how petty, as a personal affront. Pragmatic and dogged, he regularly rendezvoused with informers in the back pews of the Hidden Gem, the church of St. Mary's, Mulberry Street, secreted between Manchester's warehouses and mills. There, he bowed his head like a man in prayer while a fellow penitent whispered in his ear.

The most important of his assets, however, was his intimate knowledge of the city and its people. He knew its streets and courts, its rookeries and lodging houses, as only one who has grown up in the city can. The pulse of the city beat in his veins. If something was amiss in a crowded street or a thronging market, he spotted it. He had a nose for criminals and was as observant as the sharpest pickpocket looking for a likely victim. He was also a master of disguise.

In 1868 he began three years walking the beat in parts of the city where all peelers were fair game. His very presence in some areas was dangerous. On several occasions locals jumped and beat him for no reason. Caminada had no intention of becoming a punch-bag. It wasn't long before he was thrashing assailants and had a reputation as a tough and effective peeler.

But it was as a detective that he achieved acclaim. He frequently won gifts and rewards – not only from the victims of robberies, grateful for the return of their valuables, but even from the Watch Committee, which on his retirement in 1899, granted him a special pension of £210 a year. At a time when his salary was about £250 a year, he frequently won rewards of £100, the grateful gift of a bank or business saved from forgery or fraud. Famously, he cracked a case in which a fraud obtained £2,200 by forgery. A group of local businessmen were so grateful to him for the deterrent effect this had on others that they presented him with a cheque for £300.

But the highlight of his career was undoubtedly the Manchester cab murder of February 1889 when Caminada secured a conviction and a death sentence within three weeks of the murder. It began with what could have been a scene from Fergus Hume's *The Mystery of a Hansom Cab*, a popular thriller of the day. On a dank winter evening, at about 7pm, as mist snaked around the gargoyles of the cathedral, a stocky young man hailed a growler – a four-wheel horse-drawn cab.

'The Three Arrows, Deansgate,' he said, leaping in, while his older companion, steadying himself against the doorframe, levered himself into the cab. It struck the cabbie that the Three Arrows was not the older man's sort of place. He looked prosperous, not the sort to drink in such a dive. Told to wait, the cabbie drew a horsehair rug around his legs, hunched his shoulders against the dampness and pummelled his gloves. Then he heard the roar of a lion.

Pivoting in his seat, he saw first the man on stilts, like a jerky compass, and then the ringmaster in front of him. The clowns, tumblers and acrobats followed, waving with mechanical jollity. When the odd pair emerged and ordered the cab to Stretford Road, the older man was swaying. The circus procession snarled the traffic and the cab moved at a walking pace towards Cambridge Street. Just as the growler reached the railway bridge on Whitworth Street, a labourer shouted from the pavement, 'Your door's open, pal.'

The cabbie sighed and peeled the rug from his stiff legs. Inside the cab, the old man sat wedged in the corner of the seat furthest from the open door. The young man was gone. Without the disappearing passenger, the death might have attracted no attention. The body bore no signs of violence and the doctor's initial diagnosis was that the man had died of heart failure after drinking too much. However, someone had interfered with the victim's clothes and he had neither watch nor money. The autopsy detected a lethal dose of chloral hydrate.

The dead man was fifty-five-year-old John Fletcher, senior partner in a long-established Lancashire paper-manufacturing company, a member of the county council and a Justice of the Peace. His nephew revealed that when he left his Cannon Street office at 1pm on February 26, the day he died, he was wearing a watch worth £120, gold-rimmed spectacles and had at least £5 in cash. In fact he was carrying a much greater sum. Watch, glasses and money were missing.

Caminada soon discovered that Fletcher liked a tipple and that drink made him careless of his welfare. He had business premises in the city, though he lived in Birkdale near Southport, and was in Manchester that day to attend the sale of a mill at the Mitre Hotel. In his account of the case, Caminada says cryptically that he 'avoided contact with the dead man's family'. At no stage does Caminada discuss the obvious question: what was Fletcher doing in a dive like the Three Arrows with a much younger man of an entirely different social class?

No doubt Caminada asked himself this question. Presumably that is why he kept clear of Fletcher's family. Instead, he relied entirely on his greatest strength – meticulous police work. His first task confirmed what he already suspected: the address on Stretford Road was a ruse, intended only to get the young man away from the city centre. It turned out to be the home of an entirely respectable tailor who had no link with either Fletcher or any dubious characters. Fletcher, it seemed, left the Mitre in the late afternoon, saying he was going to Sinclair's Oyster Room. Caminada hoped that by trawling the city's bars and the prostitutes' stalking grounds he would uncover details of his movements up to the time of his death.

He gleaned information here and there and eventually felt sure he was onto something. Edward Lait ran a dried fish and game stall near Sinclair's. He knew Fletcher and remembered seeing him that day with a young man. Fletcher looked as if he had been drinking. The landlady of the Three Arrows confirmed that two men answering the description of Fletcher and his young companion were drinking there at 7pm on the evening of the twenty-sixth. In several other pubs he discovered that in the days after the twenty-sixth a young man matching the cabbie's description had been spending money freely. What's more, he was wearing a very distinctive watch, its chain adorned with dangling seals – exactly like that taken from Fletcher's body.

Caminada questioned every cabbie operating in the centre of the city and eventually struck gold. One recognised the description of the young man with the distinctive watch chain and remembered taking him to The Locomotive. Caminada knew all about the infamous pub. The Locomotive Inn, New Cross, Old-ham Road, known as Jack Rooks, was a notorious haunt of fight-ers, a meeting place for boxers, trainers and the touts who clus-tered around the sport. The chloral hydrate that killed Fletcher now fell into place. Fight fixers used it to dope boxers. In particu-lar, Pig Jack Parton used it for this purpose by putting it in op-ponents' mouthwash. In his youth Parton had been a good light heavyweight bare-knuckle fighter before becoming a promoter. He always bet heavily on the matches he arranged and liked to give himself a little edge.

Later as a landlord he used chloral hydrate to rob customers he then dumped in alleys. However, Pig did not fit the cabbie's description – but his son Charlie, though taller than the five foot three the cabbie estimated, did. Charlie too was no stranger to the police. Though only twenty, he had crammed many things into his short life. Work, however, wasn't one of them – his only experience of honest labour was the few months he'd run messag-es for a Manchester hotel. He was, however, a promising fighter and spent some time in America advancing his career. No sooner was he home than he embarked on his criminal career – stealing from a hotel in Market Harborough and defrauding a railway company.

Caminada's suspicions were further confirmed when press reports brought forward two men claiming that Charlie had drugged and robbed them. It was time to arrest him. Charlie an-ticipated this and fled. A few days later the police caught up with him and the cabbie made a positive identification. Nevertheless, Charlie was cool and defiant. The cabbie was wrong, he said, and he could prove it. He had an alibi. He was at a coursing meet-ing in Liverpool that day and he even detailed the streets he had visited.

Once more Caminada used meticulous police work to breach a tricky impasse. He discovered that a few days before Fletcher's death someone had robbed a chemist's shop in one of the Liver-pool streets Charlie had mentioned. The description of the thief matched Charlie and the substance stolen was chloral hydrate.

The Liverpool chemist identified him. Even worse for Charlie, many of the Partons' enemies saw in the family's troubles their opportunity for revenge. They started to talk about a number of people drinking with Charlie who had suddenly become ill and later woke up in an alley penniless.

So many spectators wanted to see the trial at Liverpool Assizes that crowd control outside the court required relays of peelers. Charlie's only possible defence was mistaken identity. His counsel worked hard trying to widen into a reasonable doubt the discrepancies between the cabbie's description and his identification of Charlie. But the Liverpool chemist who confidently identified him as the man who stole the chloral hydrate undid all he achieved in this area. What confirmed Charlie's fate, however, was Caminada's meticulous research. He uncovered a witness, a respectable bookkeeper, who swore he saw Parton slipping something into Fletcher's glass in the Three Arrows. After a two-day trial the jury retired. Parton, who made a great show of his cool indifference, swaggered to his cell to enjoy a meal of turtle soup, game and French pastries, courtesy of his friends. He had just dug his teeth into the dark partridge leg when the usher summoned him. The jury had taken less than twenty minutes to reach a unanimous decision. They pronounced him guilty, though with a recommendation for mercy. The judge, however, in sentencing Charlie, warned him to prepare for death.

The case stirred up intense controversy. What had happened, many asked, to the missing witness, about whom there was so much talk in Manchester? Apparently, this man visited Charlie in prison where the boxer made a full confession. Rumour had it that this was John Whittaker, a friend of Parton's, and that Charlie told him he knew Fletcher from his days as a hotel messenger. They had met again on 26 February, fallen into conversation and agreed to share a drink. It was at this stage that Parton decided to drug and rob him.

The case also caused a stir in medical circles. No less a publication than the *British Medical Journal* published an article by a Dr Gumbert in which the Manchester doctor attacked the findings of the city's analyst, Charles Escourt. According to Gumbert the amount of chloral found in Fletcher's body was not enough to kill him or to have contributed to his death in any way. The most likely cause of Fletcher's death was, according to Gumbert, alcohol poisoning.

All this added to the doubts surrounding the verdict and fuelled the campaign for a reprieve. Several politicians supported the reprieve petition, signed by over 3,000 in Manchester and Liverpool and personally presented by Parton's solicitor, William Burton. What gave Charlie's case real hope, however, was the backing of the trial judge.

On the other hand, powerful forces opposed a reprieve. Certain sections of the press argued that to reprieve Charlie was tantamount to telling every thief intending to use drugs that he need not worry about his victim dying as he would not hang. Many felt the courts had to send a clear message to the likes of Parton.

For a while Charlie's life hung in the balance.

On appeal the court reduced his sentence to penal servitude for life. When he heard, Charlie, who throughout had made a great display of his cool detachment, burst into tears. In fact Charlie served only eleven years. After spells in Portland and Dartmoor he became the first convicted murderer released on a ticket-of-leave after less than twelve years. Later he made a career of his notoriety. He claimed that, contrary to what the police believed, he had robbed Fletcher not only of a watch and £5 but of £500 in cash. It was through his interest in horse racing that he came into contact with hardened criminals and he was with such a group of men when he met Fletcher that February night and decided to drug and rob him.

After his release Charlie travelled the world but returned to enlist on the outbreak of war in 1914. His luck held and he survived the holocaust of the Western Front. But neither trench warfare nor hard labour changed him. Shortly after the War he received a six-month sentence for stealing a bag from Euston Station. While in prison he went into a decline so alarming that he secured an early release on medical grounds. Once more he travelled the country trading on his infamy. But his criminal tendencies resulted in a string of convictions and a further ten years inside – always, in his opinion, for trivial offences.

Jerome Caminada, however, shed no tears for Parton. In his view, the fighter got away with murder. Shortly after Parton's reprieve, John Parky died after an illness of several months. He was another of Charlie's victims who never recovered from the effects of the drugs.

The case of John Parky aroused great interest though in many ways it was commonplace. Like him, many died from substances administered to them for gain.

Gangs

'Hello, sailor,' said Joseph Hillyard, jiggling the blade in his right hand. 'What say I carve you up?' As Peter McLaughlin turned to run, Hillyard drove the knife between his shoulder blades.

This was only one of the thousands of acts of gang violence played out on the streets of Manchester and Salford during the last decades of the nineteenth century. The perpetrators were happy to use belts, blades and boots to slash flesh and smash skulls – just to show they were hard. Within their subculture brutality was a quality, savagery guaranteed esteem and total disregard for one's personal safety in the pursuit of injuring others was the highest ideal. They were called the 'scuttlers'.

The scuttlers were caricatures of the working class hard man. They distorted and magnified the importance of being able to 'look after yourself' to such an extent that they sought out their rivals so that they could 'carve them up'. As vicious as the Teddy Boys, Rockers and Skins who succeeded them, they made the pubs, music halls and streets of Manchester their battleground. For many years their exploits filled the pages of the local newspapers, evoking the envy of their peers and the fear of respectable people.

Just as the cut-throat and bicycle chain distinguished Teddy

Boys, the scuttlers' weapon of choice was the belt. Thick leather, decorated with metal pins in the shape of serpents, arrow-pierced hearts, feathers, clogs, animals, stars, the owner's name or that of a girlfriend, it was both a means of identification and a fearsome weapon. Wrapped around the owner's hand, the buckle on the end of a length of leather broke bones, tore flesh and split skulls. Not that the scuttlers confined themselves to the use of belt and clogs. Among weapons the police confiscated from Manchester scuttlers were cutlasses, pokers, lengths of strap with iron bolts fixed to the end, knives and loaded sticks.

Belt apart, scuttler attire was as distinctive as that of today's Grunge and Goth and appeared every bit as bizarre. Their hairstyle was short-back-and-sides with a foppish fringe plastered across the forehead in the manner later immortalised by Hitler. With their loose white scarf, worn muffler-style and a cloth cap with the peak pulled down over the right eye, they affected a menacing slouch. Their bell-bottom or flared trousers predated the 1960s by almost a century and had to conform to rigid criteria – fourteen inches round the knee and twenty-one round the foot. Narrow-tied brass tipped clogs were *de rigueur* as part of the uniform and as lethal weapons.

The uniform, however, was a double-edged sword. Wearing it gave them the kudos of belonging to a group both feared and envied. Young men and boys looked up to the scuttler – he was hard and not to be messed with. His bravado and recklessness attracted girls. But it was an invitation to other scuttlers, defying them to attack. A scuttler who ventured into alien territory was challenging his rivals. His presence said, 'I'm in charge. What are you going to do about it? Beat me or else lose face.'

Scuttlers enjoyed far more newspaper coverage than the footballers and boxers who were the working class heroes of the day. For the last three decades of the century the local papers covered their exploits with a mixture of horror and disbelief. In working class Manchester and Salford they were the envy of the young. The more the newspapers insulted them, calling them 'slum monkeys', 'savage hooligans' and 'street blackguards', the greater the public fascination. They invested them with an aura of heroism, bestowing on them all the romance of the desperado who defied authority and damned the consequences.

They stood in the tradition of the popular heroes who took on authority and thereby evoked horror and awe. Such outlaws have always had a place in popular affections and during the nineteenth century they and the most notorious criminals captured the working class imagination. *The Penny Magazine*, the serialised novel and the Saturday newspaper glorified their exploits. Such was the public's insatiable appetite for accounts of low life that many commentators believed that the obsession with violence and squalor was poisoning the minds of the young. During the last three decades of the century the scuttlers attracted immense interest and many blamed their mindless violence on the media which inflamed their imagination and stimulated a morbid love of horror and atrocities.

The broadsheet and the penny dreadful were popular among the Manchester poor. The ballads, which sold on single sheets, touched on every aspect of Victorian life. But of all the topics they covered none was so popular as crime. The street sellers advertised the most gruesome crimes with cries of 'Horrible Murder', 'Dreadful Slaying' and 'Vile Seduction'. The titles of many of these make it clear that their appeal was pornographic and sadistic. Titles such as 'Shocking Rape and Murder of Two Lovers' guaranteed good sales. This particular title referred to the case of John Hodges, a farmer's son, who raped Jane Williams and then murdered her and her lover, William Edwards.

Almost as popular were accounts of executions. Those embellished with a gruesome woodcut showing the victim in his death throes were particularly appealing. Verses frequently accompanied them, allegedly the work of the criminal in his death cell the night before his execution. As one seller of broadsheets said, 'There's nothing beats a stunning good murder.' The Bebbingtons of Manchester and Preston's Harkness family were among the biggest producers of these broadsheets. Many commentators abhorred the popular preoccupation with 'the sensual, the violent

and the horrible'. One feared it stimulated 'the animal propensi-
ties of the young, the ardent and the sensual'. This public preoccupation with crime was most evident in the enduring popularity
of *The Newgate Calendar* and the obsession with newspaper accounts of the Jack the Ripper murders.

As if to confirm the dire effects of the media on the young,
Manchester's local papers during the summer of 1870 were full
of indignant citizens' complaints about the street urchins, mainly
youths and young men, who congregated in Oldham Street in
the evenings, particularly on Sundays. The situation had been developing for some time. Oldham Street become an established
rendezvous for young boys and girls who spent the hours between
8pm and 10pm there. Accounts of their antics bristled with indignation. 'Urchins with bare heads,' one report recounts, 'sang vile
comic songs.' The banter between the assembled throngs consisted mainly of curses and crude suggestions. Lads entertained
themselves by 'rudely jostling' girls of similar age who delighted
in the attention. Worst of all, however, were the 'fast young men'
distinguishable by the latest fashion accessory, the paper collar.
This group contained a number of Jews.

But what seems to have most worried those who complained
to police and newspapers was the number of 'respectable-looking'
young women taking part and who, instead of protesting against
this affront to their sensitivities, delighted in finding themselves
the object of such posturing. In their frenzy to get a partner,
many of the lads were oblivious to older pedestrians – either that
or they were trying to impress the girls – and drove them off the
pavement into the road.

It seems the police were little concerned by all this. Many
of their detractors complained that they took no action, simply
walking by oblivious to the 'tide of indecency'. Meanwhile, as
the evening wore on, shrieks and yells filled the air as the bands
in the bars along Oldham Street struck up. Many of the young
men, having acquired a partner, retired to these boisterous places
of entertainment. Eventually the adverse publicity prodded the
police into action. They wanted to send out a warning to those

concerned and they also wanted to show their critics that they were not ignoring the problem. Consequently on 20 August 1870 James Douglas, James MacDonald, Thomas Drury, William Rebers, Thomas Churchill and John Bater stood accused of disgraceful conduct, which the *Manchester City News* report goes on to specify as 'disrespectful treatment of respectable young ladies passing through the street', a reference to the lads amusing themselves by making suggestive remarks to any young woman who happened to pass. The magistrate was clearly incensed at this affront to decency. He fined each of the accused £2 with the alternative of a month's imprisonment.

The scuttlers, who delighted in behaviour that affronted magistrates, first made the newspapers in October 1871, with fights between Catholics and Protestant gangs in Angel Meadow. In the following months street and locality based gangs spread throughout Salford and Manchester. The history of scuttling is the history of local rivalry perverted into a grotesque antagonism against all those outside one's own patch.

In the 1890s, for instance, the Chapel Street gang and the Margaret Street boys marauded around Salford and Manchester in search of blood. They delighted in smashing up coffee stalls, pubs and cheap eating houses. They felt that staff in these places were fair game for a good hiding. They robbed and assaulted old ladies and attacked foreigners – the Italian ice-cream seller and café owner were common victims.

The Grey Mare Boys of Bradford, the Ordsall Lane Gang, the Terrace Lads, the Hope Street Gang, the Holland Street Boys, the Alum and Bengal Tigers from Ancoats, the Little Forty of Hyde Road and the Hanky Park gang from Hankinson Park in Salford were the most infamous gangs, each determined to uphold the honour of a few streets of terraced houses. The Bungall Boys from Fairfield Street area went in for full-scale pitched battles against their rivals, often prearranged and waged on open ground.

The most obvious expression of this obsession with dominating their own territory was 'holding the street', in which a gang closed off a street. The holding gang kicked and robbed anyone unwise enough to try to get through. Far more exciting than this passive display of ownership, however, was the invasion of another gang's territory. On Sunday 20 October 1890 a gang from Bradford invaded Gorton. What the police described as 'a pitched battle' ensued in which both sides used belts, knives, stones and bricks. At the resulting trial magistrates sentenced eleven youths to nine months hard labour for causing a riot.

In the same year Holland Street, Newton Heath, came to resemble a war zone. Between 500 and 600 youths grappled with opponents, using belts, bottles and iron bars and throwing bricks. Terrified shoppers fled under a hail of missiles and shopkeepers, in fear of their lives, barricaded themselves inside their shops. During 1889 and 1890 the Ordsall and Hope Street gangs carried out a series of running attacks on each other which involved the use of knives and belts and resulted in several court cases. Once attacked and bested, scuttlers felt compelled to mete out vengeance. The result was that every fight had the potential to develop into a guerrilla war.

It is wrong to think that violence of this sort was unusual. The incident in Holland Street was unusual in scale, but as James Bent pointed out, not a day passed without at least one person being carried into Manchester Royal Infirmary injured as a result of a scuttler attack. It is also wrong to think that scuttlers attacked only other scuttlers. The thrill of violence was so addictive that they frequently directed their aggression at individuals totally innocent of any gang involvement, including the elderly. Nor did the scuttlers have any rudimentary sense of honour, or any concept of a fair fight. If a gang of thirty cornered a single rival, they kicked and punched him mercilessly. The scuttlers also went in for mindless vandalism of the type that not only destroyed property but also endangered life. They placed obstacles on railway lines and wrecked shops.

From the police point of view there were no criminals worse than scuttlers. They not only attacked the police but encouraged others to do likewise, with chants of 'Boot 'em! Boot 'em!' As they operated in gangs, arresting them required both courage and strength in numbers. Attacking a 'blue bag' was the quickest way for a scuttler to win status. A court conviction was a badge of honour, the equivalent of today's ASBO on certain council estates.

The scuttlers, however, did not create working class antagonism to the police. It was already an established part of the culture in certain areas. What intensified it in the 1890s was the police campaign against street gambling, loitering and football. To many adolescents and young men this was a frontal attack on harmless recreation. This resentment often showed itself when the police tried to make an arrest in a working class area. Frequently a mob gathered and setting up a chant of 'Rescue! Rescue!' attacked the police and released anyone they had arrested. This collective action against the police was commonplace in Irish areas of the city from the early nineteenth century. These battles soon became the stuff of lore and a means of lionising those who took part. The scuttlers loved these tales and gloried in their part in them. They told and retold the stories of battles in their area with the emphasis on violent injuries and especially murders.

The growing popularity of professional football provided a perfect outlet for local chauvinism. From the formation of the Football League in 1888 crowds were large, loud and violent. Pitch invasions and fighting between fans were commonplace. The increasing number of violent incidents at matches during the last years of the century was closely linked to the presence of scuttlers in the crowd. They hadn't come to watch the action. They created it.

Most scuttlers joined a gang soon after leaving school. This was a crucial stage in their lives as they now had money of their own and were no longer under the same sort of control they experienced at school. Now they spent their time hanging around on street corners. Most lads started work between twelve and fourteen and earned about ten shillings a week. Even though they were expected to contribute to the household they nevertheless had more spending money than at any time in their lives.

Many held onto legitimate work like someone holding on to

the tailboard of a van. In particular, those who had street jobs – messengers and street traders – were said to make easy money and to be totally beyond adult authority. Many lived in the common lodging houses in the slum areas, rubbing shoulders with those on the fringes of society: tramps, drunks, drifters and beggars. There was an enormous demand for boy workers and because they were cheaper to employ bosses found them a better prospect than adults. There were also numerous street jobs. Invariably they lost these jobs when they reached their late teens.

During the 1890s the national press was full of accounts of the activities of these 'street Arabs' or hooligans marauding round Manchester terrorising the population. Local newspapers spoke of the scuttlers reducing the streets of the slums to a state of anarchy, where law-abiding citizens went in fear of their lives. There is no doubt the scuttlers got a great thrill from the fear they induced in others. They thrived on the buzz of the chase and the high of an adrenaline rush. They regarded sweethearts as their property and used them as a means to demonstrate their hardness, usually when avenging slights, often entirely imaginary.

'Who you looking at?' the scuttler says, eyeballing a passer-by.

'Nothing,' protests the pedestrian.

'You were looking at my girl,' replies the scuttler, as he knocks the passer-by to the ground.

This scene was acted out dozens of times in the city's pubs and music halls every weekend. Yet, remarkably, given the level of violence and the sinister weapons used, there were only five scuttler deaths.

One of these reveals the reality of the scuttlers. In 1892 William Willan and two other members of the Lime Street Gang murdered a member of a rival gang. They intended to kill him and spent some time working out how they would do it. When they isolated their victim, they repeatedly stabbed him in the back. As the judge donned his black cap, Willan, looking a lot younger than his years, clasped the bar, his bare feet scratching the timber of the dock. As the judge began to pronounce sentence of death, Willan's high-pitched shriek filled the courtroom.

'Oh, master, don't!' Willan cried. 'Have mercy on me, I'm only sixteen. I'm dying.'

Unlike Willan there were Manchester criminals who murdered entirely for gain. William Chadwick was one such.

A Lavish Tipper

William Chadwick came early to murder. When he was only seventeen he smashed the skull of an unfortunate clerk who tried to stop him robbing an office. Largely because of his youth he escaped with seven years' penal servitude.

Chadwick's good fortune, however, did nothing to deflect him from a life of crime. It merely taught him that violence was best avoided. Consequently, he developed a clever operation, which yielded a good living without the unpleasant necessity of having to work. He posed as a commercial traveller and spent his days travelling on the London and North Western Railway, alighting at Manchester, Preston, Carlisle and Crewe, but always returning to his home in Eccles. Equipped with a number of labels each bearing one of his many pseudonyms, he brazenly plastered one over the name of the owner of an expensive piece of luggage and then, before leaving the train, collected it from the baggage van. So confident was he in his deception that on at least one occasion he had a porter carry a stolen trunk to a nearby hotel. On arrival he announced he had lost his keys. The obliging porter fetched a locksmith.

His veneer of respectability enabled him to steal from guests at the hotels on his route. Polite and personable, a lavish tipper, he was a familiar and welcome figure along the Manchester to Carlisle line. Chadwick's mistake was that too many of his victims were from Eccles. It didn't take many days of watching the station before the police had their man.

Chadwick's house was an Aladdin's cave of stolen goods. To make matters worse he had carelessly retained pawn tickets from Liverpool, Salford, Preston and Manchester. In all he had the proceeds of thirty different robberies to the value of about

£1,000. All this was bad enough, but it did nothing to suggest that Chadwick had returned to his murderous ways. It was Chadwick himself who did that. Soon after his arrest he told a warder that he expected Bent to charge him with the Atherton murder, for which the courts had already tried and acquitted a man. Someone murdered Walter Davies on 22 July 1889. Davies worked for the pawnbroker John Lowe and on that morning he opened the Liverpool shop at 8.50am. Before nine he had his first customer of the day – a man seeking an excessive loan on some silk handkerchiefs. Other customers saw Davies bargaining with the disgruntled customer. Twenty minutes later someone found Davies dead at the foot of the cellar steps, his head swathed in blood. The murderer had stolen his watch, chain and money and then helped himself to other watches in the shop. It was these watches that put the noose around the killer's neck.

Bent traced Davies' watch to a Manchester pawnbroker, who had taken it from a customer using the name Fred Smith. There the trail went cold. Now Bent went through the goods found in Chadwick's house to see if they tied him to the Atherton murder. Bent was able to prove that silk handkerchiefs, a coat and a vest found in Chadwick's house came from Davies' shop. First a pawnbroker picked out Chadwick as the man who had pawned several of the watches from the same place. Finally, a host of witnesses put him in Atherton at the time of the murder.

This time Chadwick did not escape the hangman. After his conviction at Liverpool Assizes the trapdoor fell away under him at Kirkdale Gaol on 15 April 1890.

Chadwick had got away with a life of crime for so long because he continually altered his appearance by the use of hair dyes and cosmetics. In his day he enjoyed a brief celebrity. Far more infamous, however, was Charlie Peace, one of the most fascinating criminals of the nineteenth century.

Charlie Peace

Of all the Manchester criminals of this period none compares in notoriety with Charlie Peace. He was the talk of the country, attaining cult status in the underworld and becoming a northern folk hero. According to many he was Britain's Jesse James, John Wesley Hardin, Pretty Boy Floyd and John Dillinger. He was an expert burglar, a master of disguise and a psychopathic murderer.

Yet Peace's self-image centred on none of these. He saw himself as a sophisticated man of culture, a lover of the good life and a suave seducer, irresistible to women. The reality, of course, is at odds with all of this. Peace was a singularly unsuccessful criminal, arrested on several occasions and locked up for eighteen years before his murder conviction. He was also vicious, ruthless, vindictive and hot-headed. When his blood was up he was anything but the calculating master criminal of popular myth, but acted with all the foresight of a drunk on a stag night. He was as savage as the best gutter scrapper and regardless of the consequences he would have his revenge on those who thwarted him. And it was this lunatic rage that was his undoing.

Elements of Peace's story are so improbable they might be lifted from a comical recitation. A small, insipid man, with white hair and monkey-like features, his father was a one-legged lion tamer. Charlie was the classic slum kid, marked out for crime from the start. He was born in one of the poorest parts of Sheffield, Angel Court, and left school at twelve, the year before his father died. He went to work in a steel mill and it was there that he suffered the gruesome injury that made him instantly recognisable for the rest of his life. A red-hot metal shard shot through his thigh and came out behind his knee, shattering his kneecap. He spent eighteen months in hospital and the doctors told him he would never walk without a limp. Charlie had other ideas.

He spent months developing a walk that disguised his disability. The result was that for the rest of his life he moved on tiptoes, like a man stalking a bird. But even this remarkable achievement was not enough for Peace. He taught himself gymnastics, developed a tumbling act and made a living entertaining drinkers in pubs and gin palaces. To complement this he learnt the violin from an itinerant musician. He became a successful and versatile pub entertainer who sang, gave recitations, played the fiddle and even acted out scenes from popular melodramas. He loved being the focus of attention. This shady world of bars in the poorer areas of the city was only a short step from crime.

As an intermediate step, Charlie became a hawker – which provided plenty of opportunities for weighing up buildings he later burgled. His early criminal career was far from promising. At the age of nineteen he unwisely burgled the home of the mother of the mayor of Sheffield, John Carr, with the result that he immediately became the sole focus of police activity. As with so many novices, it was the disposal of the proceeds that led to his arrest. The police traced him through a pawnshop where he had deposited the mayor's pistol.

On release he teamed up with Emma James and Mary Neild, also professional burglars. Their relationship violated every convention of the day as all three shared the same bed. This cosy arrangement was disturbed only when the police caught them in 1854. Once more police traced him through the pawnshop he used to dispose of the proceeds of a burglary. By now the courts regarded Peace as an incorrigible criminal and sentenced him to four years' penal servitude in Wakefield gaol.

After a failed escape bid, the governor slapped him in solitary. His resolve broke. He cut his throat with a rusty nail, narrowly escaping death. Yet this brush with death did nothing to reform him. On his release in 1858 he decided to exploit the anonymity he would enjoy away from the Sheffield constabulary, who were obviously too familiar with his ways. He moved to Manchester.

Charlie's imprisonment had tested his endurance to the limit but it did nothing to diminish his appeal to women. On release he immediately moved in with a widow, Hannah Ward, and her son Willie. She was unable to wean Charlie away from his criminal ways. He teamed up with Alfred Newton and resumed his career as a burglar.

Their first target was a mansion in Rusholme. They stowed some of the proceeds in a sewer near Brighton's Green. Unfortunately, police discovered their cache and lay in wait for them. When the unsuspecting Charlie returned he revealed the vicious side of his personality. Perhaps it was the memory of his last stretch that drove him to punch and kick a policeman unconscious. Whatever the reason, his actions did him no good at his trial. Though he gave his name as George Parker and his mother obligingly provided an alibi, the judge was unimpressed. This time it was six years' penal servitude.

Charlie was no sooner out on ticket of leave in 1866, halfway through his six-year term, than police arrested him while he was burgling a house in Victoria Park – one of at least two houses he burgled that night. This time he got seven years, enough to break the most hardened jailbird. But Peace had no intention of doing his time quietly. In Portland he organised a riot for which a warder strapped his hands above his head on a timber frame and flogged him with a cat o'nine tails. Then they transported him to the penal colony on Gibraltar.

Despite his appalling record and the trouble he caused in Portland, the authorities nevertheless released him on ticket of leave in August 1872. Perhaps it was Charlie's pathetic appearance that made them take pity on him. Though only forty, his hair was white. He looked a broken man. Never was appearance so misleading. Charlie was as agile as a lizard, able to scale walls and squeeze through tiny openings. What's more, he was determined never to go back to prison.

He and Hannah, now married, opened a grocer's shop in Long Millgate but their talent was not in the retail trade. Perversely, he returned to Sheffield in 1872 with the widow and resumed his criminal career. From this time on Charlie was either luckier or more careful than previously. He now enjoyed the golden age of his career, the longest prison-free period of his criminal life. He also took the precaution of appearing to earn an honest living as a joiner, woodcarver and picture framer. At night, however, he was up to his old tricks and in the process building up a substantial nest egg. He bought a house in Darnell, where he lived in modest comfort. He became extremely friendly with his next-door neighbour, Arthur Dyson, who was fifteen inches taller than Peace. Another neighbour, seeing the two men on the street, described them as 'the organ grinder and his monkey'.

It was during these years that the Peace myth grew up. It was said he had a remarkable way with animals and could win the confidence of the most ferocious guard dog.

Unfortunately, Charlie couldn't quieten his own animal instincts. Katherine Dyson, Arthur's young wife, was a beauty and Charlie was determined to have her.

The physical disparity between the pair did nothing to cool his ardour or deflate his self-confidence. Mrs Dyson was a striking woman in every respect. She was not only attractive but also tall and statuesque, in the fashion of Victorian beauties. By contrast, Peace, according to a police description, was thin, slight, with grey hair, beard and whiskers. He had lost at least one finger from his left hand and walked like a cowboy with his legs far apart. In addition, he had a speech impediment, giving the impression that his tongue was too big for his mouth. Despite all this, he was making some progress with the stunning redhead when Arthur discovered what was going on. It was at this point that Charlie's judgement failed him. He threatened Dyson, pushing a gun up his nose.

When he heard that Dyson had complained to the police he fled to Hull. There he set up the widow in a café and continued his life of crime. The entire stock of the café came from Sheffield restaurateurs Charlie targeted during his final weeks in the city. By now he realised he stood a far better chance of staying out of prison if he moved around the country. He took another precaution to ensure he didn't go back inside: he went nowhere without a gun.

On 1 August 1876 Charlie was in Manchester. He'd spent some time watching the home of a Mr Gratrix in Whalley Range. The church clock was striking midnight as he approached the house at the junction of Chorlton Road and Seymour Grove. Unknown to Charlie, Nicholas Cock, a twenty-year-old probationary constable, a Cornishman and ex-miner, saw him passing through the gate to Gratrix's front garden. As Cock approached the house he met a colleague, James Beanland. Charlie was still inside the house when he saw the policeman's hat at the window. He froze. The hat moved away to the back of the house. Charlie drew his gun as he ran to the front door and dashed out of the house – straight into Constable Cock.

Two shots rang out.

Beanland carried his colleague to the nearby house of Doctor Dill. Cock died there. Next day Charlie killed again. This time it was premeditated.

Arthur Dyson was regretting telling the police about Peace. Almost every post brought a new threat, another promise of vengeance. What was even worse was that Arthur was convinced someone was watching him. During this period Charlie made regular trips to Sheffield where he roamed the streets in disguise. Dyson was so unnerved that he moved house in the hope of escaping from Peace. As the Dysons arrived at their new home with the removal van they spotted a tiny figure standing on the doorstep. As they drew level with the door, Charlie turned and greeted them with a malevolent smile.

The day after he murdered Constable Cock he was back in Sheffield, prowling the streets, when he ran into Arthur Dyson. Peace shot him twice in the head. Several horrified witnesses saw Charlie flee. Police issued a detailed description and launched a nationwide manhunt, making Charlie the most wanted man in the country. People claimed to see him all over the north of England. He narrowly escaped capture in Sheffield, Hull and Manchester. Yet none of this stopped him from going to the last place anyone would expect to find him. He went to see another man stand trial for the first murder he had committed. Throughout the two-day trial of the Hebron brothers at Manchester Assizes, Charlie sat in the public gallery. He had no need of a disguise – he looked like a thousand second-hand clothes dealers, an insignificant little man with a dull life. Though Cock died without regaining consciousness, the police were convinced they knew his killer. Hours before the constable met his death his evidence had convicted three brothers, the Hebrons, of drunkenness. The fiery

Irishmen had sworn vengeance. Cock took their threats seriously, reporting them to his superior, James Bent, one of Manchester's most celebrated Victorian policemen. He told Cock to take care but reassured him by saying that 'a threatened man rarely came to any harm'.

Immediately after Cock's murder police swooped on the near-by Firs Farm, where the Hebrons worked. They found all three brothers in bed and arrested them. The evidence against them, though entirely circumstantial, was nevertheless compelling. Several witnesses swore to their loud and oft-repeated promise to avenge themselves against the constable. Others swore to see-ing William Hebron priming gun cartridges in a local shop. The magistrates dismissed the case against Frank Hebron, but sent William and John to the Assizes. Several witnesses told the court of the Hebrons' threat to revenge themselves on Cock but Con-stable Beanland's description of the man he saw fleeing the house was vague enough to fit either brother.

Footprints found at the scene of the murder and leading to-wards Firs Farm also gave credence to the prosecution case. Ex-pert bootmakers claimed they matched the boots William wore on the night of the murder. During his court case William's employer told the jury that Hebron had 'the most abominable temper of any man I ever knew in my life'. Unfortunately for the brothers this echoed the popular image of the fiery Irishman, prone to outbursts of fury. What damned William, however, were the Hebrons' lies. When arrested they claimed they had been in bed since 9pm, yet inquiries revealed they had been drinking in a pub until 11pm. The pub was one that Cock had passed at about five minutes past eleven, shortly before someone murdered him.

Immediately after the shooting police put a lot of manpower into the search for the murder weapon. They searched ditches and pits in the area without success. It is likely that a navvy named Fay solved the mystery thirty years later. In 1907, while clearing a clay pit in preparation for the building of a school near Oswald Street, Chorlton-cum-Hardy, he uncovered a gun. At the time of Cock's murder the police dragged the pit without success. Against the advice of their counsel the prisoners insisted on calling a number of witnesses to provide them with an alibi. This proved disastrous as the prosecution exposed them as liars. This totally discredited the Hebrons in the eyes of the jury and was certainly one of the reasons for their conviction.

The manner in which the Hebrons had conducted themselves during their original trial – the one which led to their vow of vengeance against Cock – also contributed to the conviction in the murder trial. Prior to this trial John Hebron had threatened a number of witnesses. The police also received a number of anonymous threats, warning of dire consequences should any of the Hebrons suffer punishment. On that occasion James Bent warned the brothers that should any of the witnesses suffer harm he would hold them personally responsible.

After two-and-a-half hours the jury acquitted John Hebron. William, however, they found guilty. The judge sentenced him to death. He was eighteen. Many people believed his sentence should be commuted to life imprisonment and presented a petition to this effect to the Home Secretary. It was almost certainly William's youth that saved him from the gallows. Another section of the public, however, deplored the Home Secretary's leniency. For these, PC Cock was the focus of their sympathy. They raised a public subscription to fund the memorial headstone that stands above his grave in St. Clement's churchyard, Chorlton-cum-Hardy.

Nothing that happened in court troubled Charlie's conscience or dulled his ardour. Though the jury convicted William Hebron and the judge sentenced him to death, Peace was nevertheless able that same day to seduce Prudence Simpson, a court secretary.

Shortly after this he decamped to Nottingham, where he took refuge with a Mrs Adamson, a landlady and fence. A few days later he met Susan Bailey. From the moment he saw her she beguiled him. She responded to Charlie's improbable charms and they embarked on a nationwide tour, travelling as Mr and Mrs John Thompson.

Finally, Charlie washed up in London. The inability of the police to catch him convinced him he was fireproof. Once more he set up an unconventional household.

The fact that Hannah Ward and her son were with him didn't prevent him from immediately acquiring a new mistress, the vivacious 'Legs' Thompson. To accommodate his passion for her lovely limbs, Peace once more adopted Bohemian domestic arrangements. He relegated the widow and her son to the cellar, while he and his mistress occupied the rest of the house. Predictably, the women who vied for Charlie's affections were constantly at loggerheads. Hannah was neurotic and sour while Legs soon became a hopeless drunkard. Charlie was so worried about her that he set Hannah and Willie the task of chaperoning her wherever she went.

As relations became fractious Charlie took to beating his churlish family. On occasion he threatened them with the weapon he had used to murder Cock and Dyson.

He was only happy when he and his new friend, Henry Brion, were concocting improbable moneymaking schemes. They discussed raising sunken ships, irrigating the Sahara and devising means of walking through fire unharmed. Charlie also enjoyed making his own specialist burglary tools. His enormous overcoat had concealed pockets and his violin case contained the customised instruments of his trade.

Yet for all his Bohemian ways, Charlie craved respectability. To win over his neighbours, he hosted regular musical soirees at which he played the classics on his violin, accompanied by his wife Hannah on the piano and his stepson on the Spanish guitar. Using the alias Mr Thompson, Charlie was the image of middle-class respectability as he gave recitations before rounding off the evening with hymns. By now, 1878, Charlie was robbing mansions. Then, just as Peace seemed ready to step up a league and embark on the most profitable phase of his career, he met three policemen of remarkable bravery and tenacity.

He was burgling a splendid Blackheath residence when three policemen disturbed him. Though Peace fired five shots, one of which hit PC Edward Robinson in the arm, the other peelers disarmed him. At this point he produced a knife and tried to stab

Robinson, before they again disarmed him and hauled him to the lock-up. Though the trial ended with Charlie getting life for attempted murder, he was nevertheless relieved. The court tried him as John Ward and incredibly didn't realise he was the man wanted for the murder of Arthur Dyson. Nor did the police suspect he had anything to do with the murder of PC Cock. Peace might well have spent the rest of his days in prison had it not been for a small oversight. He had made no provision for Legs, who decided to claim the £100 reward for the arrest of Charlie Peace.

Even when exposed as a murderer Charlie was not prepared to accept his fate. Halfway between King's Cross and Leeds he wriggled free from his guards and, as the train slowed, threw himself headlong through a window. Miraculously he suffered no injuries but the handcuffs slowed his escape and his startled escort was able to grapple him to the ground. News of Charlie's desperate bid for freedom reached Leeds before him and further incensed the vast crowd waiting for him at the station.

The trial was a foregone conclusion. Mrs Dyson, who had emigrated to America after the death of her husband, returned to give damning evidence against her former suitor. One of the police officers who brought Charlie to justice described him as 'the most industrious, ingenious and ruthless villain of all time'. As the judge donned the black cap, the court secretary, Prudence Simpson, crashed to the floor.

It was at this stage, as Charlie sat in the condemned cell facing the certainty of his death, that he confessed to the murder of PC Cock. Initially, the official response was sceptical. After all, Charlie was a notorious liar who loved the limelight. With the shadow of the gallows hanging over him he had nothing to lose by confessing to a murder he hadn't committed. Quite the contrary, he stood to gain further notoriety and to boost his reputation as a criminal mastermind. Fortunately, the Home Secretary had commuted Hebron's death sentence to life imprisonment. Now he granted the young Irishman a free pardon and in what was an almost unprecedented step awarded him the enormous sum of £1,000 in compensation.

The Good, the Bad and the Dangerous

Even in death Peace added to his reputation as a courageous outlaw, able to face any ordeal without a quiver of fear. Immediately before his execution on 25 February 1879, he made a short speech in which he showed that death held no dread.

'I know where I'm going,' he said, with all the confidence of a nun on her deathbed. 'I'm going to heaven.'

Just before Marwood pulled the lever, Peace spoke a final sentence. His voice was calm and even. 'Amen, God bless you all.'

The Manchester police emerged from the Charlie Peace affair with little credit. By now many believed their inability to counter the forces of lawlessness was one of the reasons why crime in the city had reached such unprecedented levels.

11

Killers

Harrison's Vermin Killer

Poisoning was becoming so common in the 1850s that Charles Dickens warned his readers that the country was in the grip of an arsenic epidemic. Arsenic, the poison that cut a swathe through Victorian Britain, was popular with murderers because it was so difficult to detect. Symptoms mimicked those of Asiatic cholera, which periodically decimated Victorian towns and cities. Countless murders certainly went undetected.

But arsenic was not the sole problem. Many other poisons were also readily available. In the 540 recorded cases of poisoning between 1750 and the beginning of the Great War in 1914, murderers used fifty different substances.

Poisons had many legitimate uses – from controlling vermin to curing horses of parasites. Chemists sold strychnine, for instance, as a rat poison and stocked poisons on the same shelves as medicines. Strychnine's great disadvantage, however, was that its effects were so extreme that any competent physician could correctly attribute them. The telltale signs were excruciating stomach cramps followed by convulsions.

Consequently arsenic was far more popular. Besides, more than any other poison it had a range of legitimate uses. For centuries women used it to treat skin problems. Several medicines marketed as cancer cures contained it and many men took it in small doses as a tonic. It was a major constituent of treatments for anaemia, malaria and cardiac pain. But its major use was in the control of vermin – rats, mice, beetles, fleas, lice and bed bugs – against which the Victorian housewife waged a relentless struggle. Arsenic was therefore readily available in every town and city in the country.

It was also cheap. In March 1837 a penny bought one ounce of white arsenic – enough to literally kill a horse. Three grains – as much as will lie on the tip of a knife – is sufficient to kill most adults. Odourless and tasteless, it is easy to conceal in food. In almost half of the recorded poisonings during this period, arsenic was the murderer's poison of choice.

One of the most notorious cases of this era sent sisters Catherine Flanagan, aged fifty-five, and Margaret Higgins, forty-one, to the scaffold. The women lived in the Skirving Street area, one of Liverpool's most deprived areas. In the early 1880s the Liverpool duo poisoned with arsenic nine people, though recent research suggests they may have been responsible for the murder of as many as seventeen. In 1884 Liverpool Assizes finally convicted them of the murder of Margaret's husband, Thomas, and they hanged together at Kirkdale Prison. The motive in each case was greed as each victim yielded a small sum in insurance money.

A few years later Amelia Winters and her daughter, Elizabeth Frost, became even more infamous than the Liverpool poisoners. Indicted for three murders, the police discovered they had insured over twenty people, five of whom had died in suspicious circumstances between 1886 and 1889. Like the Liverpool sisters, they exploited the lax procedures of life insurance companies in order to benefit from their victims' deaths.

The new burial clubs and insurance societies gave parents a financial incentive to dispose of children they saw as a burden. During the mid-Victorian period, children under the age of five made up sixty-one per cent of all homicide victims. The high death rate among children gave murderers reasonable grounds for believing they would get away with it. The Bolton housewife Betty Eccles, however, surpassed all other child murderers. Before she went to the gallows in May 1843, she poisoned her three daughters, to make herself more attractive to a suitor. As soon as she married, she killed one of her new husband's children, a teenage boy, and her own remaining child in order to get the fifty shillings life insurance. By her own admission she was about to poison her remaining stepchildren. She also confessed to poisoning a baby boy she was nursing in order to defraud his father of seven shillings.

The case of Mary Ann Britland is in many respects typical of the poisoning epidemic that swept the country at this time. Britland moved to her new home in Ashton-under-Lyne in 1885 and quickly became popular with her new neighbours. Her husband Thomas and their daughters, Elizabeth, nineteen, and Suzannah, eighteen, were industrious, polite and extremely respectable. The family were happy in their new home. There was only one problem: mice overran the house. They ate the food, ravaged clothing and gnawed skirting boards. Britland complained bitterly to her landlord but he was dismissive.

Fortunately for Britland there was a vast array of patent vermin killers on the market and she resolved to put them to the test. One, Harrison's Vermin Killer, was such a lethal cocktail of strychnine and arsenic that she had to sign the chemist's poisons book when she bought three packets. That night her daughter Elizabeth woke with violent stomach cramps. The doctor diagnosed an upset stomach and the girl seemed to recover. Britland, however, still preoccupied with the problem of vermin, bought another packet of Harrison's Vermin Killer. Later that evening Elizabeth suddenly took a turn for the worse and began shaking and twitching uncontrollably. Then she started to fit. By 9pm she was dead. The next day Britland visited her 'club man', the agent for the Prudential Insurance Society. She collected the £10 due on her daughter. Though bemused by Elizabeth's death, the doctor had no reason to suspect foul play. His death certificate cited bilious vomiting, convulsions and spasms of the heart as the causes.

Approximately seven weeks later, Britland called on the agent again. Though the 1s 8d premium on her husband's policy was not due, she insisted on paying it in advance.

'Better safe than sorry,' she said.

Three days later she visited the chemist's again. The mice were worse than ever. That night her husband, Thomas, took ill. At first he rallied. His condition stabilised. Mrs Britland, relentless in her battle against vermin, again visited the chemist. The same evening Thomas died. The doctor who attended Thomas was not the one who treated Elizabeth. Thomas, according to his death certificate, died of epilepsy. The same day Mrs Britland collected £11 7s 0d from the Prudential agent and £8 from the Independent Order of Goodfellows. Thomas, in joining the Order, had shown himself as prescient as his wife.

Throughout this typhoon of misfortune, which swept away her husband and daughter, the support of her neighbours, the Dixons, was unwavering. Now alone in her house – her daughter, Suzannah, was in service in Oldham – with only the mice for company, the Dixons again displayed their kindness.

'Move in with us,' they said, their arms open, their eyes bright with compassion.

This arrangement, however, excited comment from the neighbours, already buzzing with rumours that something was going on between Britland and Mr Dixon. Before long, Mrs Dixon became ill and died of what the death certificate described as 'abdominal spasms'. Her husband collected £19 17s 6d from the Union Friendly Insurance Society and neither the police nor doctors saw anything amiss.

Presumably the matter would have rested there but for the indignation of a neighbour who wrote anonymously to the police. Early in their investigation, it became clear that Mr Dixon was guilty of nothing more than being extremely obtuse. The post mortem on Mrs Dixon showed her body contained lethal doses of arsenic and strychnine. The exhumed bodies of Elizabeth and Thomas were also laced with poison.

Before Monday 9 August 1886, when Britland became the first woman hanged at Strangeways, the whole story came out. She confessed her guilt to her mother and remaining daughter. What we will never know is how many Mrs Britlands went undetected. But for the indignation of Mrs Dixon's neighbours even a murderer so lacking in subtlety would have escaped. It is clear that doctors routinely wrote out death certificates entirely on information from the deceased's next of kin.

The 'club man' lifted the dread of a pauper's grave from many a respectable house. But how many did he induce to commit murder?

The Ultimate Transgression

Of all crimes, murder is the most enthralling. The murderer violates the most fundamental rule of society, desecrates the sanctity of life and usurps a power that belongs only to the state and ultimately to God. More than the cruelty or the evil, it is this monstrous arrogance of the murderer that divides him from lesser criminals. What sort of person is so arrogant as to decide if another human being should live or die? Most criminals, no matter how hardened, refuse to cross this line.

What adds to the subject's fascination is that most murderers are criminal novices. Most lead blameless lives up to the moment they commit the ultimate transgression.

Because of this they seldom take the precautions necessary to give themselves even the remotest chance of escaping the consequences of their actions. For every one like Charlie Peace – a professional criminal, who murdered a policeman without leaving anything to link him to the crime – there are ten like John Simpson, who cut the throat of his lover in a public bar and sat stolidly beside her as she bled to death. It follows that those who suffer the ultimate punishment are seldom professional criminals or part of the underworld. Habitual criminals and those who live off crime usually act in their own interests – and murder is seldom beneficial.

There are exceptions. Like Charlie Peace, John Jackson and William Chadwick were both criminals who murdered in the course of crime, while Emmanuel Hamer, though not a professional criminal, murdered to conceal his crime. In 1868, Hamer, a thirty-three-year-old house painter, was working in Salford. He noticed an old lady living alone next door and entered her house, presumably to rob her. When she confronted him he bludgeoned her to death with a lump of coal from her own scuttle. Hair, skin and blood stuck to the murder weapon.

Though Hamer murdered while committing a crime he was not a criminal. He was gainfully employed and had no previous convictions. Yet no account of the Manchester underworld would be complete without some mention of the murders of the period. Murder is a lens that reveals much about the society in which it occurs. The gangland murders of 1920s Chicago, the political murders of Ulster in the 1970s and the drug-related gun crime of present-day Manchester all highlight key features of the society that spawned them. It was as recently as 1868 that the Capital Punishment Act elevated murder to the unique position it occupied for a century as the only crime that carried the death penalty. After the Act a few unfortunates suffered the ultimate penalty for treason but the vast majority of those who ended their days at the end of a rope were murderers.

Unlike today, murder in Manchester in the second half of the nineteenth century was rare. In a typical year, such as 1868, Manchester coroners found two cases of murder and ten of manslaughter. They recorded 266 accidental deaths, twenty-six due to intoxication and twenty-eight to suicide. The number of murders is remarkably few given the general level of violence. The scuttlers of the period routinely used knives and heavy belts and their activities daily put people in hospital. Yet murder was sufficiently uncommon in Manchester for the press to make much of it. The public had an insatiable appetite for every aspect of a murder case. Local papers ran detailed, often verbatim, accounts of the court proceedings and reported any snippet of information relating to those involved, often with no attempt to verify it.

Yet an overview of the Manchester murders of this period reveals a striking similarity between many of the murderers. Very few were from the respectable working class. Instead, they were men who hovered on the periphery of the underworld. Most were unskilled labourers in precarious employment or unemployed. A great number were not married but in what was then a scandalous relationship with a woman – the sort of relationship that respectable working class people spurned. In a quarter of the cases the murderer was drunk. In almost half the cases where a man killed his wife, drink was a significant factor.

The case of 58-year-old Michael Kennedy is in many ways typical. He and his wife of thirty-six years had a volatile relationship and when, on 8 October 1872, Kennedy returned home from a day's drinking to find she had not made his dinner, he was indignant. Later, somewhat mollified, he asked her for a kiss and when she refused he shot her. The only unusual aspect of Kennedy's case is that he bought the gun some days before he shot his wife. This suggested a degree of premeditation sufficient to convict him of murder rather than manslaughter.

The case of William Flanagan is a paradigm of murder in Manchester at this time. Flanagan was a lay-about drifter sacked because, in the words of his employer, 'he was insane'. On the evening of 8 September 1876 he and his common-law wife, Margaret Dockery, returned to their lodging house from the pub and continued drinking with other lodgers. The next morning, after an argument in which Flanagan accused her of stealing from him, he cut her throat. Flanagan pleaded insanity. Investigations revealed he had made numerous suicide attempts. This defence, however, did not save him from the gallows.

James McGowan, a Salford bleach worker hanged in 1878, was much like Flanagan. While in a drunken rage he cut his wife's throat with a penknife. He then reported his crime to the Manchester police.

William Cassidy, another wife murderer, was unusual only because of the excruciating pain he inflicted on her. He told his drinking mates that he was going to kill her, went home, doused her bed in paraffin and set her alight. The case aroused fierce hatred of Cassidy. Whether maliciously or not, William Marwood, the executioner, gave Cassidy a drop of ten feet which almost tore his head from his body.

Drink was a major factor in the case of Thomas Leatherbarrow, a forty-seven-year-old unemployed labourer, who shared his Pendleton home with a Mrs Kate Quinn. One Saturday night in January 1887 they went to the pub where Mrs Quinn bought drink all night. As the night wore on Leatherbarrow became more and more belligerent and by the time they reached home his rage was such that he kicked Mrs Quinn to death. He could offer no explanation for his actions and went to the gallows without a word of protest.

The case of Walter Wood in 1887, though outwardly identical to that of many other men hanged for murdering their wives, was unique in one respect. Wood was a former school friend of his executioner, James Berry. This is why the two sat together for several hours in the condemned cell.

John Gell's case was similar to that of Leatherbarrow. Gell lodged with Mrs Mary Miller and her daughter, Isabella, in Moston. By the end of February 1888 Mary's patience was exhausted. Gell had been out of work for some time and was making no contribution to the household. On 1 March she gave him an ultimatum: find a job or get out. Gell responded by attacking the two women with an axe. Though he fled the police he later surrendered and confessed. Yet he went to the scaffold an aggrieved man. Just before Berry pulled the trapdoor lever, Gell shrieked, 'Isabella Miller, I hope you have your revenge!'

The murder charges that resulted from the Shudehill stabbing deserve a more detailed examination. They tell us a great deal about the culture of violence in one of Manchester's most infamous rookeries. On Sunday, the last day of January 1869, just before midnight, the streets around Shudehill thronged with revellers squeezing the last drop out of the weekend. Three young men – John Oldham, James McIntyre and James Burns – lounged on the corner of Copperas Street, waiting to see what the ebb and flow of the street might cast up. They didn't have long to wait. Coming down the street towards them were three Italians – John Bernadotti, Joseph Retson and Bartholomew Galgani – their arms linked, scattering pedestrians from the pavement before them. But Oldham, McIntyre and Burns were not planning to move and as the Italians approached they fixed them with the look.

'Wops!' 'Greaseballs!' 'Spics!'

There followed a flurry of fists, the flash of a blade in the street-light, blood on the grey paving flags. Women shrieked. Oldham fell to the ground, scarlet seeping between the fingers clasped to his throat. McIntryre pressed his flat hand to his side as if stopping his organs from escaping and walked like a zombie across the road. Boots scraped on the flags, men pulled and hauled. Women clasped their mouths to stifle screams. There were more shouts and scuffles.

When PC Ashton arrived on the scene by-passers had disarmed Bernadotti and Galgani. Retson had fled but helpfully left his cap behind. A passing doctor attended the wounded men and took them to the Royal Infirmary. The police caught Bernadotti and Galgani literally red-handed. PC Ashton said they looked as if they had been butchering a pig. Worse still, from their point of view, Oldham hung on to life until 19 February, by which time he had made a statement before a local magistrate in the presence of the accused, clearing Retson but identifying Bernadotti and Galgani as the men who stabbed him.

Nevertheless, the police charged all three with wilful murder. They pleaded not guilty but the jury convicted them of manslaughter. In his summing up, Chief Justice Brett concurred with the finding, accepting that there had been some degree of provocation, without which the charge would have been murder. Yet if this gave the Italians hope, the judge soon dashed it. There was far too much of this casual violence, the judge pronounced, and unless the courts made a stand against those involved some might think such behaviour acceptable. Brett gave all three twenty years' hard labour.

This was the typical crime that resulted from the hard man culture that dominated working class areas of the city. Men with no aspirations to respectability prided themselves on being hard. They could hold their own in a scrap, take and give punishment without complaint or remorse and never backed down from a challenge.

Killers

This was especially important when confronted by foreigners, like the Italian youths, who sought to assert their superiority.

Chief Justice Brett made it clear in his summing up that the use of knives in street fights was commonplace and was not restricted to 'foreigners'. Yet this case served only to reinforce British stereotypes of the period: Italians were cowardly foreigners who didn't know the meaning of a fair fistfight and resorted to knives, while English lads fought fairly and never used weapons.

The case of Michael Johnson also indicates the importance men attached to hardness. In particular, it highlights the lengths to which many went in avenging a slight, real or imaginary. Dick McDemott was hoping for a good night. It was Boxing Day 1867 and he'd hired a band. He and Patrick Nurney had moved the tables of the saloon bar against the walls, clearing a space for dancing. With any luck the Cambridge Inn on Regent Road, Salford, would soon be bouncing and the sweating dancers drinking plenty of ale to slake their thirst. Patrick was a man of many parts. The barman at the Cambridge was lively and affable, quick, alert and witty. He had a smile for every customer, a quip for every situation. He was also a gifted musician. He had only to hear a tune once before he was able to play it from memory.

It was Patrick who had organised the band, in which he took a leading part. Between dances he scurried around, collecting pots and pulling pints, calling every customer by his name, producing each man's tipple at a nod of the head. The night had hardly started when Michael Johnson lurched in. The nineteen-year-old dyer fancied himself as a hard man. He traded on a reputation he didn't really have. His stare fixed on first one and then another before settling on the landlord. Dick McDermott held Johnson's stare. Then he made a mistake.

He looked away, deciding to give him the benefit of the doubt. He served him a glass of porter.

He soon realised his error. Johnson was sizing up the dancers, pointing and jeering. McDermott asked him to leave. Johnson looked at him with incredulous scorn.

McDermott fetched the police. 'Come along now, Mickey,' said

Sergeant Toole, flanked by two constables. All eyes were on the three peelers. Patrick Nurney struck up The Star of the County Down. Johnson feigned deafness. He lifted the porter to his lips and took a slow draught. Again he lifted it to his lips and all but drained it. Then with a third slug he emptied it.

'That's a sound lad,' said Sergeant Toole. 'Go home to your bed, now, like a good man,' he added as he pointed Johnson away from the pub.

No sooner had Patrick Nurney finished the tune, than Johnson was back in the bar. This time McDermott didn't hesitate. He grabbed two handfuls of Johnson's collar and frog-marched him to the door.

'Get out to hell,' he shouted as he pushed Johnson backward through the front doors. That seemed to be the end of it. But after Nurney played four or five more tunes and was outside the bar collecting pots, Johnson reappeared.

'Come out, you bloody sod,' said Johnson. 'Come outside and fight like a man.'

'By God, I'll teach you this time,' said McDermott, reaching for a hawthorn stick he kept under the counter.

'Now,' said Nurney, extending his splayed hands as Johnson drew a knife from his jacket. 'Take a good man's advice, Michael, and go away.'

Before McDermott could lift the bar flap, Johnson lunged. Nurney leapt back, hit the bar and crumpled to the floor. The blood coursed through his shirt and spread around his body like oil from a burst engine.

It took the jury twenty-five minutes to find Johnson guilty of wilful murder. Mr Justice Brett concurred in their judgement. 'The crime of stabbing is a frequent crime in this city and this district,' he intoned. 'It is well that many in this country should know that if a man stabs another with a knife, and a man dies in consequence, the result to him who stabs is also death.'

On 29 March 1869, Johnson became the first occupant of Strangeways' condemned cell. For the first time the black flag fluttered over the prison, indicating that an execution had taken place and the victim's body was still hanging for the prescribed hour. It was seventeen days after Johnson's twentieth birthday. Johnson himself provided a link with the old days of public executions. As a Detective Williams took him into custody, the cab passed the spot where in 1867 William Calcraft had hanged the Manchester Martyrs, three Fenians, in Britain's final multiple public execution. Johnson pointed it out to Williams, recounting how he had risen early that November morning and walked across the dark city to get a good view of the execution. Johnson shared more than their fate. His final resting-place was beside the Martyrs, in the burial plot against the prison wall.

If Johnson's case illustrates one major characteristic of working class culture that has endured into the twenty-first century, the case of the Gorton abortionist highlights another that has changed. For thousands of British women today, abortion has become almost another form of contraception. Medically it is a simple routine and for many – though not all – the idea that it might have moral implications is alien to the twenty-first century British mindset. Not so in the nineteenth century. Then the public viewed the killing of an unborn child as a uniquely evil act. It struck at the base of society by introducing murder into the heart of the most intimate of human relationships, the bond between mother and child.

For a woman to abort her child was to make a decisive step beyond the world of respectability into the underworld. Some, like Margaret McKivett, never returned.

When Margaret's parents summoned the surgeon, Mr J.L. Fletcher, to their twenty-six-year-old daughter one Monday night in March 1875, they didn't tell him the truth. When he arrived at the confectionery shop at Hyde Road, he quickly realised the woman was beyond help. On his return the next morning the McKivetts told him Margaret had died at 5am. The surgeon wanted a post mortem but the couple pleaded, imploring him to spare them the ordeal. Fletcher relented and made out a death certificate, attributing death to 'derangement of a portion of the kidneys'.

The matter would have rested there but for an anonymous informant telling the police that Margaret had miscarried on the morning of her death. Police inquiries led them to Alfred Thomas Heap's chemist's shop on Gorton Lane, where the sign over the door declared the proprietor was a surgeon. Though Heap's qualifications were unknown, the man himself was no stranger to the police. They had first charged him with the murder of a woman in 1867, under circumstances very similar to those surrounding Margaret McKivett's death. In both cases his botched abortion killed a young woman. On the first occasion he was acquitted by the jury. The next year he got five years' hard labour for carrying out an abortion. Charged again with murder, Heap had little chance of escaping death. The jury at Liverpool Assizes found him guilty and the judge despatched him to Strangeways to await execution.

The case attracted nationwide publicity. As Heap sat in the condemned cell sympathisers organised petitions for his reprieve. Part of the fascination with the case was the build-up to the execution, the prospect of a reprieve heightening the tension. There was only one thing the Manchester public found more interesting than murder – execution. The reading public demanded to know every detail of the procedure that swept the convicted murderer from the bar of the court to the end of a rope.

On the Other Side

In particular, the Manchester public were fascinated by the reactions of the condemned man as he confronted his death. Once condemned the prisoner was taken to the condemned cell. In the New Bailey this was a dungeon with no natural light. The prisoner was never left alone for fear he might commit suicide and thus cheat the crowd of the spectacle of his execution. There was nothing to give him temporary respite from what awaited, not even the food. He ate normal prison fare – usually gruel and water. If he was lucky he might get meat and potatoes.

For many, the anticipation was more excruciating than death.

During the 1870s it lasted a fortnight. After that it was 'three clear Sundays', during which the prisoner hovered between irrational hope and profound despair, enduring wild shifts of emotion, lurching from the heights to grim depths and back again. It left him emotionally shredded. He was on the verge of tears and mania. Every minute he lived out his execution. Over and over he asked the same questions: Will my nerve hold? Will I break down, crying, screaming for mercy, though I know the judge's words have put an end to mercy? Will I wet myself or soil my pants?

Eventually the day arrives. He wakes after dozing a few fitful hours plagued by the loop running in his head. He has seen it a million times and now he is to act it out for real. But which version? The one where he goes to his death with a quiet dignity? Or the other one? Now events take on their own momentum. The prisoner finds it hard to engage with what is happening. It's as if he is outside himself, looking down on the scene.

He sees the chaplain enter the cell and wake him. His voice is soft, his face compassionate. He leaves when the breakfast arrives and the prisoner feels the bile churning in his guts. He eats a few bites to quell the quaking in his stomach. Then they take him out, to the holding cell. As soon as he enters by the door from the corridor, his eyes fasten on the far door. He knows what is on the other side. No one has told him but he knows with absolute certainty. His stomach churns. His pulse is racing and his limbs are screaming for him to run, flee from this. The priest returns, makes the sign of the cross over him and starts reciting from the book he holds open on the flat of his hand. The lock on the door clatters and the priest raises his voice. The executioner, a tangle of leather straps and buckles across his arm, and his assistant, enter.

A man with the face of a third-rate solicitor, the executioner, offers his hand. The prisoner touches it as if it is a gift. In a second they slip the harness around him and fasten his crossed arms, straitjacket style. Now he believes it. He really is going to plunge into the abyss. Lashing serpents take possession of his legs and intense pins and needles muffle the sensation in his feet.

They steer him to the open door and the crowded corridor. A column of men stand with their eyes to the floor. The executioner places him between two lines of four warders and the hangman and his assistant take up their position at the head of the procession. A few yards along the corridor and then a door opens. The noose hangs from a beam. They manoeuvre him under it, onto the trapdoors, on each side of which there is a plank – one for each of the warders. The hangman ties his ankles. His knees are about to buckle. The priest's constant, steady voice is stifled by the whoosh of the trapdoors and the rope snaps taut. The rope sways. The beam creaks. The body must hang for an hour.

The rope, believed to possess curative powers, is of finest Italian hemp, thirteen feet long and five-eighths of an inch thick. The man who has not cried or pleaded has passed the ultimate test of courage. He becomes the hero and role model of every scuttler, his exploits told and retold on every street corner and in every pub in the city. In dying with indifference he proves that he is hard.

A few privileged journalists witnessed the hanging. By convention their report merely recorded that the execution was carried out humanely and, where appropriate, that the condemned man died with fortitude. But infamous criminals had a capacity for generating legends about the manner in which they faced their death.

12

Police

On Twenty-five Bob a Week

In 1866, two policemen came across fourteen-year-old Edward Ward swimming in the canal in Canal Street. When he ignored their orders to get out one of them pelted him with stones, cutting and bruising him. A hostile crowd soon gathered and put the police to flight. The boy suffered a fit. Subsequently a sergeant and two constables stood in the dock, accused of assaulting Edward. This incident illustrates the problems facing the Manchester police during this period. Many peelers lacked the training and temperament essential to the efficient discharge of their duties. Their reaction to a defiant child who was larking about served only to antagonise the community.

Public attitudes also added to the difficulties of the police. In particular the alacrity with which people resorted to violence against them was underpinned by a deep-rooted antagonism that affected not only the criminals of the rookeries but also a significant section of the working class. Yet few of these problems were evident at the force's first scrutiny by the Inspectorate of Constabulary in 1857, when Lieutenant Colonel Woodford found a force composed of 522 officers and constables. He was impressed by the quality of 'a remarkably fine and effective body of men, most of them in the prime of life and health'. The force was also generously staffed, with one constable for every 540 of the population.

The new police force Woodford complimented was definitely a step forward in the fight against crime. But criminals were not standing still, they were more mobile. The professional criminal, like the craftsman in search of work, had to go on the tramp to avoid detection. This is why the workhouse and the lodging house were such an important part of the infrastructure of crime. Despite the Inspectorate's optimistic report the force was not equipped to meet the challenge of this new, mobile criminal. One reason for this was inadequate pay.

In 1851 an ordinary constable earned between 21s 6d and 25s 1d a week, while a probationary constable had to survive for the first two years on less than a pound. This rate of pay, poor as it was, nevertheless put the Manchester men in the top ten per cent of the fifty-two forces in the Northern Division. They also enjoyed other benefits not shared by their colleagues everywhere. In return for a weekly contribution of 5d they entered a superannuation scheme which entitled them to a pension after twenty years' service and one-third of their salary if invalided out of the force after fifteen years. Yet for any advantages they enjoyed over peelers in other parts of the country, their pay was barely adequate. It was only slightly better than the wage of an unskilled labourer, though it had the great advantage of being regular. Unskilled labourers were in erratic employment and had to tolerate periods of unemployment when they earned nothing. Even so the peeler's wage was little more than subsistence level and, despite lengthy negotiations with employers in 1853, they secured improved pay only after 250 constables gave notice.

This threatened mass resignation is instructive. Given the widespread disapproval of industrial action among the middle class and the press, it is remarkable that local newspapers supported their action and agreed their claim was justified. This was one of the rare occasions when a local newspaper *The Manchester Guardians* supported increasing the wages of municipal employees. Usually journalists backed the instinct of taxpayers to resist any increase in council spending.

Throughout the 1850s James Taylor, Chief Constable of Manchester, repeatedly referred to the problem of poor pay. He had great difficulty in recruiting the number of suitable candidates required to maintain the strength of the force. Salford – where pay was lower than in Manchester – had an even greater problem. The slightest upturn in trade led officers to desert for work as labourers or in mills where pay was better. But pay was not the only problem. The requirements recruits had to meet reduced the number of candidates. After 1839, candidates had to be under thirty-five years old, over 5ft 8in tall, of stout build, in good health and able to read and write. In 1865, because of the lack of recruits, the chief constable reduced the height requirement. Even then many were critical of the selection criteria. *The Manchester Examiner*, for instance, bemoaned the practice of selecting men 'for their height and bulk rather than for their handiness and acuteness'. The height requirement was often a problem in an age when many started life malnourished. It is hardly surprising that at certain times it was necessary to relax these qualifications in order to fill posts.

Even so, in 1865 the Manchester force had 272 vacancies, 128 due to the resignation of men with less than a year's service. Despite a national advertising campaign in 1875, the watch committee found it necessary to send the Chief Constable to Scotland on a recruitment mission. The situation in Salford was again even worse. By 1870 there were 151 policemen of all grades in the Salford force, that is, one for every 1,048 of the population. This was far worse than the ratio for Manchester, where the force was proportionately more than twice as big, having one officer for every 452 citizens.

Though the problem of poor pay affected the force throughout this period it was not the sole cause of dissatisfaction. Long, unsociable working hours, harsh, pseudo-military discipline – which involved a great deal of marching and drilling – and the suspicion, if not the hostility, of neighbours made the job unappealing to many. The policeman enjoyed the benefit of a free uniform and one day off a fortnight. But he did not get Sunday rest and was, of course, expected to patrol his beat in all weathers. His annual holiday quota was four days leave with pay. Promotion depended entirely on the whim of the constable's superiors. There were no clear-cut criteria for promotion. Seniority and good conduct were essential but the circumstances that brought a man to the attention of senior officers depended almost entirely on good luck. Nor was there a rising pay scale for superintendents. The holders of these posts in 1871 had all served between twenty and thirty years.

Public and press attitudes certainly deterred many prospective constables. *The Manchester City News* repeatedly complained that the rising cost of policing the city resulted in no improvement in efficiency. The paper maintained that the streets were awash with thieves and prostitutes and that robberies were constantly increasing. No man with any hope of getting skilled manual or clerical work would put up with such poor conditions. Consequently the force recruited entirely from the unskilled labouring class.

The high expectations of employers and the respectable middle classes also weighed heavy on the shoulders of many. This and the paternalistic attitude of the police authorities showed themselves in 1855 when the Manchester Watch Committee ruled that all constables must attend church or chapel regularly.

At least by 1866 a Manchester constable's weekly pay had improved a little. Over 100 of the rank and file were earning £1 1s 6d. At the top of the hierarchy a superintendent was earning almost £5, an inspector about £3, station and detective sergeants about £2 and sergeants about £1 12s. By 1870 the average Manchester peeler could expect to take home £1 10s – the minimum required for a man to support a wife and two children. His Salford counterpart, however, was still lagging behind and as late as 1875 most constables were earning only twenty-five to thirty-two 'bob' a week – slightly more than subsistence level.

There were ways in which a peeler might supplement his income. It was common for victims of theft whose goods were restored by the police to give the officer involved a monetary reward. Jerome Caminada won many such rewards. The public, however, had doubts about this system of rewards. Cynics maintained the police only sought goods for which there was a reward.

A Plasterer from Rochdale

What manner of man joined the force? Given pay, conditions and the nature of the job it is amazing there were any recruits. Most were working men, generally labourers or 'operatives', in the parlance of the day. A small number were artisans or clerks. In the 1850s most came from the poorer parts of the city, many from Ancoats. The prospect of a regular wage was for these men the major attraction. In some ways a number of them were on the periphery of society. Many were Irish – seventy-one out of 671 in 1865 – but whereas most Irish in Manchester were Catholics, many Irish peelers were Protestants.

Those who weren't outcasts when they joined the force soon found that their position in working class society was no longer that of an ordinary working man. The uniform and the exacting standards imposed by the job made them different. Within a short time they developed their own police subculture. Without this subculture few would have survived the hostility of the 1840s. For most of this decade the police adopted an aggressive strategy of harassing known offenders: a 'zero-tolerance' policy. They drove thieves and bogus beggars from the streets – but at a cost. Saturation policing and a high profile in the rookeries, especially in the notorious Deansgate area, met with hostility, not only because of its effect on criminals but because it interfered with all aspects of street life. The result was a sharp increase in assaults on the police and widespread anti-police disorder in 1843.

Not surprisingly, the next decade saw a change. The police adopted a less abrasive approach and as the number of arrests fell so did assaults. However, this policy was unpopular with the city's influential middle class. The police 'strike' of 1853 tainted relations between the police and ratepayer, who begrudged paying more for what they saw as a deteriorating service. They resented what they perceived as the new laissez-faire attitude to street nuisances and demanded a return to a muscular approach to beggars, prostitutes and drunkards, especially those of the Irish variety. The public believed that their presence, their vigilance, their oversight of an area, were deterrents to criminals and the measure of their efficiency. If they were doing their job properly, the argument went, criminals would not have the opportunity to commit crime.

Sometimes public resentment at the perceived failures of the police found expression in the columns of the local press, much to the embarrassment of the constabulary. In December 1857, William Connell of Union Street, Ancoats, complained of three houses in the area which were openly used by 'prostitutes and bad characters'. In April 1859, Mr Kawson, with a prestigious address on Ardwick Green, bemoaned police indifference to the gangs of youths who brought 'annoyance and indecency' to the area every Sunday evening. Such goings-on were proof to many that the Manchester police were idle and incompetent. This pressure from the suburbs resulted in a return to the policies of the 1840s. During the 1860s prosecutions tripled from 10,000 to almost 30,000. The emphasis was on drunks and prostitutes.

But this policy was costly. Assaults on police soared to an extent unique to Manchester. There was a city-wide crime wave. For many the cause was obvious: the Irish. The police didn't disagree. In the last three decades of the century, police activity pinpointed what they saw as a major source of crime – those who worked on the streets. The Irish were strongly represented among the hawkers, beggars, street musicians and the flotsam of the city and for many the two groups were indistinguishable.

What was different about this drive of the 1860s was the emphasis on reforming and reclaiming outcasts by removing the founts of sin. Public houses, brothels and gambling dens were the objects of police attention as much as drunks and prostitutes.

A number of crime panics, such as the nationwide garrotting panic of 1862-3, drove the purge of the 1860s. The press also stirred up hysteria about the number of 'ticket of leave' men descending on the city. The Chief Constable latched on to this and blamed it for Manchester's soaring crime figures. It is hardly a coincidence that Alfred Aspland, one of the most outspoken critics of the city police, was a prominent figure in the Discharged Prisoners' Aid Society.

Police

The 1860s were a difficult time for the police generally and not only in Manchester. National commentators questioned their honesty and the integrity of the courts. The most prominent of these critics was Serjeant William Ballantine, a senior barrister, who found expression for his concerns in papers such as the *Daily Telegraph*. He maintained the police routinely gave perjured evidence to the courts, which readily conspired with them. W.T. Stead in the *Pall Mall Gazette* and the *Review of Reviews* threw his considerable weight behind these complaints. William Morris's famous socialist journal, *The Commonweal*, regularly criticised court decisions.

Worst of all in its effect on public regard for the police was the 'Trial of the Detectives' of 1877. Three of Scotland Yard's most senior detectives stood in the Old Bailey dock accused of conspiracy to pervert the course of justice. The Court sentenced two of them – together with a corrupt solicitor – to lengthy terms of hard labour.

Cases such as this and changing public expectations increased the pressure on the police. Like every aspect of society, policing is affected by fashions. The fashion in the 1870s was for detection. The master detective, the intuitive and ingenious guardian of society, a match for any evil machinations, was the order of the day. In this, as in so much else, life mirrored art. This was the time when Arthur Conan Doyle's Sherlock Holmes was at the height of his popularity and the public's confidence in the capacity of detectives to solve crime was boundless. The detective became a key feature of law enforcement. The peeler on the beat deterred criminals. The detective uncovered the hidden criminal and brought him to justice. By the 1880s, this emphasis on detection was clear. The slow erosion of crime that continued until the end of the century had begun. Yet criticism of the Manchester police hardly abated.

No police force is without its critics. The Manchester Constabulary of this period was no exception. During 1865 the city's letter-writing citizens were outraged at the force's inactivity in response to the goings-on around Deansgate. In particular, the

Rector of St. John's complained of half-naked women cavorting around the Deansgate area, to the apparent indifference of the police. He maintained that on another occasion, when a crowd of over 100 gathered to watch two men fighting, the police did not intervene. Chief Constable Palin, with his customary vigour, refuted allegations of police inertia. In a six-week period, he said, the police arrested over 400 people in the area.

Publicans were particularly critical of the police, maintaining they were being persecuted. Their sense of being under siege was such that they formed the Publicans and Beersellers' Protection Society. At their meeting of 18 January 1866, they expressed a complaint which they were to repeat over the following decades, decrying 'the objectionable practices resorted to by detectives in entrapping beer-sellers to infringe the law'. The cases they cite seem to justify their indignation. In particular, one Manchester licensee told of how a detective dressed as a labourer, with a trowel stuck in his belt and a feigned limp, had duped him by claiming he had walked from Rochdale and implored a drink. On getting it he immediately charged the landlord with serving after hours. A more serious case against the police arose in August 1870, when Patrick Nolan, a forty-six-year-old coach painter, died in the street. Subsequently, PC George Johnston appeared in court charged with using unnecessary violence against Nolan.

There is no doubt that the force was keenly sensitive to anything that besmirched its good name. This is clearly shown by an exchange of letters in the *Manchester Guardian* during November 1871. On 4 November a correspondent signing herself 'A Young Lady' complained of the 'disgusting conversation' of a policeman while on a tram travelling down Oxford Road. 'We suppose policemen to be the guardians of decency,' she bemoaned. Clearly, the Chief Constable was of a similar opinion for a week later his letter appeared in the same newspaper assuring readers that after a full investigation he had dismissed the culprit. In a final paragraph that sent a shudder down every policeman's spine, Palin welcomed complaints and assured the public of a full investigation in all instances.

Police

The morale of the force improved during the 1860s. In 1860-61, Palin dismissed forty-one officers, whereas a decade later it was only seven. The evidence also suggests their status in the community was growing. Yet although the conduct of officers certainly improved, other problems proved intractable. Though the average length of service was six years and nine months, the majority of men were both young and inexperienced. Of 737 officers, a third had less than two years' experience.

Alfred Aspland blamed the extent of crime in the city on the weaknesses of the Manchester force. His analysis showed that a third of the men at any one time were raw recruits. On average, 150 men resigned each year – more than one in five of the total force – and eleven were dismissed. This problem was by no means confined to Manchester. At the same time one quarter of the Liverpool force resigned each year.

Despite the problems with manpower the number of arrests increased enormously, and the number of prosecutions increased by 260 per cent between 1860 and 1870. Yet Aspland maintained that conviction figures in the late 1860s were depressingly low, no more than six per cent. For the same period, the figure for Salford was seventy-eight per cent. The national figure at the time was about thirty per cent.

Aspland claimed that the number of major crimes was far greater in Manchester than Liverpool. Burglary and breaking into shops were four times more frequent in Manchester, highway robbery, larceny and forging coins three times. Manchester, with one-sixtieth of the population of England and Wales, had between a sixth and a seventh of all burglaries, a fifth of shopbreaking, a third of highway robberies and one fifth of all the cases of passing base coin. What made matters worse was that in Manchester fifteen per cent of all the crimes committed were those most dangerous to society – burglary, house breaking and highway robbery. These were only ten per cent of crime nationally.

Aspland went on to look at the percentage of crimes that resulted in committals. Again, Manchester was bottom of the table.

In Birmingham the figure was forty-eight per cent, in Leeds sixty per cent, and in Sheffield sixty-five per cent of crimes led to a committal. For Manchester the figure was just 7.8 per cent.

Aspland saw no alternative explanation other than that the Manchester force was inefficient.

His Head in the Kitchen Chair

It's impossible to examine the effectiveness of the police without looking at its organisation. As with many other forces, military thinking had a considerable impact on the running of the Manchester constabulary. Generally ex-military men filled the senior positions in the country's forces. Such experience, it was assumed, provided the necessary administrative and disciplinary expertise.

But how did the police actually police the city?

Before going on duty all officers presented themselves at the Watch Office – their station – where the duty sergeant inspected them for fitness to go on duty. They had to be sober, clean and fully equipped. Each man reported to his corporal, who issued him with a lantern, a rick (a rattle for summoning help) and a padlock and marched him to the starting point of his beat. While walking his beat he checked all doors and windows. He had to complete his assigned circuit at least twice every hour. Any officer who deserted his beat – other than to frog-march a prisoner to the lockup or to go to the assistance of another officer – committed a serious breach of discipline.

While on his beat the peeler concentrated on drunks, vagrants, prostitutes and brawlers. These were the most obvious criminals, the ones who, left unchecked, would provoke a public outcry. Their approach was standard. The police tracked 'suspicious persons' and 'known offenders', in the hope of catching them in the act. They focussed their attention on fairs, race meetings, shady pubs and the other places where criminals gathered. This was a sensible thing to do as both Manchester and Salford figures show that known thieves, prostitutes, vagrants, habitual drunkards and 'suspicious characters' accounted for the vast majority of crime. In what would today be labelled 'harassment', the police deliberately badgered known criminals by adopting a 'zero tolerance' policy, arresting them for the slightest infringement.

As today, the success of the police was then largely dependent on the support and cooperation of the public. Without their information and willingness to give evidence, and in some cases their readiness to wade in to help an officer under attack, the policeman's task would have been impossible. Many examples have been quoted to show that the majority of people were prepared to help the police, even at the risk of their own safety. True, there were many attacks on the police and certain areas of the city were hostile territory, whose residents were more likely to assault than assist a peeler. But these were not the rule. A surprising number of civilians were prepared to do even more than this. Throughout this period, members of the public handed over many wrongdoers to the police.

In the 1870s Mancunians had a strong sense of civic pride. They believed their city and the local community were worth standing up for. Just like today's courageous few who stand up against 'hoodies' and others who make life on council estates intolerable, they put themselves on the line. In many ways it was easier back then because most people had a clear sense of right and wrong and neither the press nor the courts were likely to regard criminals as victims. Respectable working people were hostile to crime and what they called 'loafers', those who lived without working, at the expense of the industrious.

But having said all this there was a hard core working class antagonism towards the police, especially among the Irish and especially among men involved in industrial disputes. They referred to the police as 'blue bottles' and 'blue bags'. This reflects something of their hostility. The clearest reflection of this, however, are the figures for assaults on the police. In the 1860s and 1870s, over 100 people appeared before the courts every year charged with assaulting a policeman. Contrary to what we would expect, the majority of these were not individuals trying to resist arrest. Most often the aggressors were in gangs with the officer severely outnumbered.

Crime City

One of countless such cases occurred one Saturday night in April 1864, on Fawcett Street, off Great Ancoats Street. The constable on his beat came across several men abusing a woman. He intervened and ordered the men on their way. One of them responded by kicking the constable and when the limping peeler tried to arrest his assailant, the man's friends, helped by a crowd of onlookers, set upon him. The arrival of several other policemen only served to incense the growing crowd who laid into the peelers with such ferocity that they were in fear of their lives. Only the intervention of two riflemen saved the lives of the police.

Yet for all the severity of the peelers' injuries the court took its customary lenient view of the incident, sentencing two men to a fine of forty shillings or one month in prison and requiring the others to find securities of £20 to keep the peace for three months. This indulgent attitude to those who assaulted the police is typical of the courts. It seems the magistrates believed peelers should accept attacks and beatings as an occupational hazard.

There is no doubt that the twenty-first century policeman's lament that courts deal inadequately with violent offenders is nothing new. His nineteenth century predecessor felt the same and perhaps with more justification.

Among the Irish, resisting arrest was a matter of honour. Many Irish families felt it was a personal disgrace to allow the police to arrest one of their neighbours without going to his assistance. This attitude was also common in many non-Irish sections of the city. Nor was resisting arrest and helping others to do so confined to adults. Among the many adolescents who sought to emulate their elders was thirteen-year-old James McCoy. In October 1870 he stood charged with assaulting PC Henry, as he was taking a prisoner to the Bridewell. Young McCoy then went to ground but Henry was not a man to forget a face and several months later his assailant appeared in court and got two months' hard labour.

In the same month, John Clancy of the Bowling Green, Salford, showed McCoy how it should be done. One Saturday night as he walked down Chapel Street, he spotted two constables on their beat. Clancy obviously saw something provocative in the way they were walking and, incensed, attacked them. James Bent tells the story of how, while he was in the process of arresting a man for beating his wife, the assailant almost bit off his thumb. Understandably, the policeman was indignant when the culprit, in Bent's words, 'got off with the reward rather than the punishment of one month's imprisonment'. On another occasion a suspect he was pursuing hit him on the thigh with a brick. He was unable to work for three months and suffered the effects of the injury to the end of his days. Once again, the culprit got off with a derisory sentence.

As for the respectable Manchester public they too posed problems. They were neither deferential nor uncritical in their attitude to the police. Both the Watch Committee and the local newspapers received almost daily complaints about policemen neglecting their duties, with the alleged result that people were living in fear of crime and faced by intolerable nuisances.

Then, as now, the police response to a complaint depended to a large extent on who was complaining. When, for instance, McConnel & Co. complained of disturbances near their mills in Ancoats, the Chief Constable himself Captain Palin ordered an immediate response. A similar complaint from the residents of Collyhurst elicited a more leisurely reaction. After all, the McConnel mills were among the city's largest employers and the owners were influential citizens whose good opinion was valuable to anyone in public office.

Nor is the current fashion for convicts, thugs and sociopaths to take legal action against the police new. Many seeking legal redress in the nineteenth century were no more deserving than their twenty-first century counterparts. Bent tells a story that shows as much. On hearing that a man in Newton Heath had knocked down his wife and was jumping on her, he went to investigate. By the time he arrived friends had rescued her and it was the husband who was in danger from several hundred neighbours who had gathered round the house ready to take retribution. Behind the bolted door, armed with a knife and a poker, the husband was loudly threatening to kill anyone who crossed the threshold. Bent, like most policemen of the time, favoured the direct approach. He kicked down the door and snatched up a kitchen chair, which he used to pin the wife-beater's head to the wall. Bent was a great believer in the effectiveness of a chair as a weapon against anyone wielding a knife or a poker and used it to good effect on many occasions.

The six months the wife-beater spent in Strangeways only served to deepen his sense of grievance. No doubt the laughter of fellow inmates when he described his arrest did little to reconcile him to his sentence. On release he appealed to the magistrates for a summons against Bent for putting his head in a chair – without success.

Nor was notoriety a bar to legal action. Many thieves demonstrated a touching confidence in the ability of the law to protect them from the consequences of their dishonesty. No one had more regard for British law than Jack, a notorious thief. According to Bent 'he was considered one of the greatest thieves ever to trouble Flixton and neighbourhood'. He specialised in stealing fowl and when Bent questioned him he immediately threatened legal action on the grounds that the police were harassing him without any justification. On that occasion the court, unimpressed by his claims of victimisation, sentenced him to six months and later, after a short interlude of freedom, to fifteen months.

Most likely to threaten action against the police were thieves with a veneer of respectability. Those of middle class origin felt socially superior to policemen. The middle class criminal assumed he was not only better educated but also more intelligent than the policeman arresting him. Those at the other end of the social spectrum, who had no social pretensions, also posed difficulties, making it hard for even the most upright policeman to keep his good name. After all, criminals were then, as today, the best source of criminal intelligence. Any detective who hoped to succeed had to maintain informants and the best informants were the ones nearest to the criminals; that is, the ones who were themselves active criminals. When a detective gets such a useful source he is loath to lose it. The problem is that there is a thin line between cultivating an informant and conspiring with a criminal to protect him from punishment. Who is to say when a detective has crossed it?

Jerome Caminada certainly nurtured his contacts. He guaranteed their anonymity, a consideration that extended long beyond their usefulness and into his retirement, even to the extent that in his memoirs he makes no mention of their existence. Sometimes the police got lucky: a man with a grievance denounced a former accomplice, or a neglected mistress, like Charlie Peace's paramour, betrayed her lover. But this sort of thing was an unearned bonus and most information came only as the result of carefully cultivated informers.

The issue of police informers was even more sensitive in the nineteenth century than today. The fear of the police as the enemies of individual freedoms, as they were in many repressive regimes in Europe, was standard currency among left-wing groups. There were also many liberals who were vigilant for any sign of the misuse of police powers. Informers, they argued, were a form of agents provocateurs used by the likes of the Tsar's secret police in Russia to entrap political enemies. The police, therefore, found it wise to conceal this aspect of their work and to stress their deterrent role. Even the use of plain-clothes detectives was suspect in liberal eyes and the authorities played down their importance. As late as 1870, when the Metropolitan Police Force numbered 9,000 men, Scotland Yard admitted to having only twenty plain-clothes detectives.

None of this, however, diminished the value of inside information. Reading the memoirs of any Victorian detective, it is obvious that many of the flashes of insight they put down to intuition were in reality the result of 'information received'. Yet few detectives of this era make any mention of this, preferring to maintain a tactful silence which has the additional advantage of adding to their own reputation. The peelers who threw stones at young Edward Ward were not representative of their colleagues. Generally the police were the ones who were bombarded from all quarters – assaulted by criminals, resented by the public, criticised by the middle class ratepayers, ostracised by their own class. They were in an impossible situation and the demands imposed on them were beyond them.

There were, however, other policemen whose difficulties were the result of their own deficiencies. In the middle of the century, for instance, drunkenness in the force was a major problem. In many ways this was simply a reflection of Manchester society. In one case, a member of the Salford public found on duty a PC John Pollet in such a drunken stupor, that in a reversal of roles, he carried the sodden peeler home. Nor was this an isolated instance. The problem was so great that fifteen years after PC Pollet's riotous night out the Salford Watch Committee instructed the Chief Constable Palin to lock up and then take before the magistrates any constable drunk on duty.

Needless to say, these were the exceptions. Most of the men who joined the force and stayed in it had a powerful sense of duty and high personal expectations. It was to fully utilise these qualities that during the 1870s the force was split into five divisions, with bases at Knott Mill on Deansgate, Goulden Street in Collyhurst, Fairfield Street, Cavendish Street and the force headquarters at the town hall building, which was in King Street until 1871 and thereafter Albert Square. The Chief Constable's office took up a part of the ground floor, which also housed the charge office and cells.

By 1877, however, attacks on arresting officers in the Collyhurst area occurred with such frequency that it was necessary to build a new station. For a long time Collyhurst men believed that no man worthy of the name would allow the police to take an acquaintance, and certainly not a neighbour or a 'mate', in charge without putting up a fight. Nor did the struggle end at the entrance to the lock-up. Consequently the new station in Willert Street was built to withstand the most violent siege. Metal plate reinforced its thick walls and there were no windows facing the street.

The officers besieged in the Oldham Road station in 1889 didn't have the advantage of such defences. When soldiers from the Tib Street barracks wrecked the station to avenge a slight to a comrade, not even reinforcements from other divisions could save them. The cobbles ran red with blood and it was only the Colonel of the Regiment, sword drawn, riding on horseback into the tangle of bodies, who prevented further carnage. Colonel Arbuthnot's courage scattered the rioters. But their thirst for vengeance was not satisfied and the men of the 15th Regiment of Foot Soldiers fled into the city where they converged on several police stations, dragging out the occupants and beating them in the streets. In this droves of unemployed cotton weavers, delighted to get their own back, enthusiastically supported them. The previous week the force, at the behest of the employers, had evicted them from several mills. When the weavers gathered in the nearby streets, the police hauled them before the magistrates, charged with illegal assembly. Industrial action of this sort was a major cause of antagonism between peelers and workers.

In meeting this array of challenges effective leadership was vital. Few organisations can be any more effective than their leaders. Unfortunately for the Manchester force those charged with ultimate responsibility were not of the necessary quality. Captain William Palin was universally popular with those he commanded. He was a forceful and effective leader and a vigorous defender of his men. Unfortunately the same cannot be said for his successor, Charles Malcolm Wood, who was only thirty-four at the time of his appointment.

Despite his youth, Wood was a popular appointment. Before serving as Palin's deputy, he gained experience in the Indian Civil Service and as Assistant District Superintendent in the Karachi Police. He presented himself as the candidate of continuity, a man who would maintain the traditions nurtured by Palin, rebuff unjustified criticism and strengthen the force's status. He failed to deliver on all counts. A uniquely troublesome subordinate mired his entire period of office in scandal.

In 1882 the Watch Committee promoted John Bannister to Superintendent of D division, though there was nothing in his career to suggest he was suitable for such a post. In fact, Bannister was the least experienced inspector in the division and therefore, according to established precedent, not eligible for such a post. But what Bannister lacked in qualifications he made up for with friends in high places. In Alderman Bennett, Chairman of the Watch Committee, he had a determined advocate. Though Wood fought Bannister's appointment, Alderman Bennett persisted and, despite resentment among his colleagues, Bannister took up his new position. Wood never recovered from this error. His acquiescence in the appointment irretrievably damaged his authority and made it clear that the Watch Committee could impose appointees in whom he had no confidence.

Nor was Wood the only one to doubt Bannister's suitability. Not only was he lacking experience, he was extremely volatile. Worse still his integrity was questionable. Yet with such powerful supporters, he acted as if he were invulnerable. His division became notorious as a haven for the feckless, the dishonest and the timeservers of the force.

By 1892 Bannister's behaviour was causing such public outrage that it was impossible to ignore. In particular, his fraternisation with one of the city's most infamous madams, whose brothel in Shepley Street was his favourite haunt, led to an inquiry by the Watch Committee. Contrary to all expectations, Bannister managed to muddy the water sufficiently to avoid outright censure. Nevertheless, Wood was confident that his demand for Bannister's resignation, backed as it was by most of the Watch Committee, would mark the end of the troublesome superintendent. But Bannister decided to brazen it out. The Watch Committee let the matter drop in the hope of limiting the damage to the force's reputation. Bannister had shown that he was answerable to no one. He continued to act much as he always had.

In 1897 matters again reached a crisis. D division was an open sewer, infecting the morale of the entire force. The Lord Mayor bypassed the tangle of procedural obstacles and initiated a special inquiry. The report revealed fundamental weaknesses in the management of the force. The nub of the problem was the Watch Committee's insistence on making appointments in the face of the Chief Constable's opposition. Among instances of this that came to light was one involving a man Bannister had recommended for promotion. Wood had objected on the grounds that the candidate's record showed he had been fined on five occasions for being drunk on duty – a dismissal offence. Yet an alderman strongly supported Bannister's nomination and, backed by other members of the Committee, secured the appointment.

Though the report did not state as much, it is clear that the Committee's actions were not motivated by the best interests of the force or even by what was reasonable and fair. Corruption, or at least blatant nepotism, was at work.

Or was it blackmail? Among other things, the inquiry revealed Bannister's links with many brothels throughout the city. He acted as the protector of several. It is possible that through these connections he found out certain things about members of the Watch Committee, things they desperately wanted to conceal. Nothing about Bannister suggests he would have had any qualms about using such information to his advantage.

The manner in which he ran D division was certainly not to the advantage of the Manchester public. Drunkenness was common among officers on duty and there was a culture of senior officers borrowing money from their juniors and never repaying it. What was perhaps most embarrassing for the Watch Committee was evidence of malpractice extending beyond D division to all areas of the force. Several witnesses spoke of the systematic doctoring of statistical returns, especially with regard to beerhouses and brothels. Bannister was not the only peeler whose relationship with pub and bordello was a little too cosy.

The scandal undermined the integrity of police management. Eventually the council swept away most of the old Watch Committee and sustained press criticism drove the chairman from office. The Chief Constable dismissed thirteen constables from D division and as many more resigned. The report marked the end for Wood. His feeble leadership had resulted in a steady decline in the force's morale, worsened by long hours, poor pay and appalling conditions.

Wood's successor, Robert Peacock, found he also had other

problems. He admitted in 1900 that many officers were incapable of writing a coherent report. Judging from the number of complaints against peelers for using violence against men in custody, there were many among the Manchester constabulary who did not put their trust in paperwork. Given the derisory penalties imposed on those convicted of assaulting the police – even when offensive weapons were used – it is hardly surprising that many officers agreed with the famous American Inspector, Alexander S. Williams. Known as 'Clubber' Williams, his philosophy was, 'There is more justice in the end of a nightstick than in any court decision.'

Despite all these difficulties, there is no doubt that crime in Manchester was less conspicuous in 1900 than 1870. Caminada, looking back on a long and distinguished career, pointed to the demolition of the labyrinth of Deansgate slums and the sweeping away of the droves of bogus beggars as clear evidence that crime was on the wane. Many of the seediest drinking dens had gone. *The Manchester Evening News* of 12 July 1895 struck a similarly smug note. Writing of crime over the previous twenty years, the editorial purred, 'One cannot compare the present and past state of the city without recognising the wonderful improvement.'

There were many conscientious and public-spirited men who did their duty to the best of their ability. They held back and even reduced the advance of crime. But the insurmountable obstacles confronting the Manchester peeler were such that crime retained its special significance in the life of the city.

For this the ineffectiveness of the courts must take a large share of the blame.

13

Punishment

More Than the General Mass of Labourers

One of the major reasons for the high level of crime in Manchester was the failure of the courts to impose deterrent sentences. A court appearance held no terrors. This was partly because the living conditions of most of those imprisoned were so poor. Inside they ate well, washed and were better clothed than many could afford when free. The average convicted criminal had already served eight previous terms of imprisonment – which suggests that a stint inside was no more than a minor irritant.

The belief that courts are too soft on criminals is nothing new. People have been saying this for the best part of two centuries. Unless a convict faced the possibility of execution or whipping, he stood before the courts with equanimity, certain that any sentence was no more than a minor inconvenience and unlikely to make him turn away from crime. Then, as now, the legal system was stacked in favour of the accused. The police frequently failed to get a conviction because witnesses who were prepared to appear at a magistrate's court refused to appear at Quarter Sessions or Assizes as it frequently involved loss of pay because of days off work. Remuneration for travel and loss of pay was miserly.

Interference with witnesses was common in Manchester at this time. The Hebron brothers clearly threatened witnesses when they were charged with drunkenness. A number of frightened witnesses went to the police and the Hebrons were warned that they would be held responsible if any harm came to those who had given evidence against them. It is clear from reading the evidence that the Hebrons persuaded people to give false testimony on their behalf. Under cross-examination several admitted as much. Besides, many witnesses were quite happy to be bought off and no one thought any the worse of them. Lots of witnesses made a poor showing when questioned by a competent defence solicitor. Often ill educated and overwhelmed by the court, for many it was a daunting experience. If neighbours were involved, they often found it difficult to deliver what they had earlier promised the police. When prosecution witnesses were convincing, juries were often reluctant to convict children and other sympathetic defendants, even in the face of overwhelming evidence. Even when convicted, many criminals showed their contempt for the court by swearing vengeance against the police officers involved. Many of the Manchester crooks who threatened retribution were hardened criminals whose habitual criminality was a key factor in their conviction. This was largely due to the 1869 Habitual Criminals Act, which established the practice of compiling files with photographs and descriptions of offenders. It led to a national register of all those with more than a single criminal offence. Aliases were no longer enough to avoid punishment as a repeat offender. Police now targeted known criminals in the hope of linking them to stolen goods.

The problem was that when police brought them before the court, criminals often received derisory penalties. This trend of ever more lenient penalties started in the 1830s.

In 1800 there were more than 160 death penalty offences and even children faced execution for minor thefts. In practice, however, the main sanctions against serious crime were transportation and imprisonment. Until 1868 there were still public executions.

Changes in the law, which reduced the number of capital crimes, were merely reflecting what had long been the case. Between 1828 and 1834 only 355 of the 8,483 people sentenced to death in England and Wales were actually hanged – less than five per cent. And even this small percentage decreased as the century progressed. By 1837 murder was in practice the only crime that incurred the death penalty. Many crimes that had previously carried it such as most forms of theft were now punishable by transportation and, after 1857, when transportation was in decline, penal servitude.

Despite all the mythology surrounding transportation, both criminals and the honest poor regarded it as a soft option. The transported convict got the opportunity to start a new life in a country where he had every hope of becoming a free labourer and a landowner. This was beyond the wildest dreams of most of the honest poor who could not afford the cost of emigration. Most criminals, however, received lesser sentences. Eight out of ten criminals who came before the Manchester courts in the second half of the nineteenth century received terms of imprisonment of six months or less. By 1860, however, most of those who went to prison were habitual criminals who accepted short periods of imprisonment as an unavoidable part of life. Such was the middle-aged Annie Turner. When she appeared in court on 8 November 1889 charged with being drunk and disorderly, it was hardly necessary for her to give her name as she was a frequent visitor. In fact, it was her sixty-first appearance. With a weary sigh the magistrate gave her seven days.

By then there was a great change in the criminal justice system, a turning away from hanging, whipping and transportation towards a new approach – reforming the criminal. For young offenders the key institution was now the reformatory, its very name redolent of the optimism of the age. For adult prisoners there was a new prison regime – the solitary and silent system.

In 1853 the government introduced penal servitude, designed to replace transportation. The Australian government was no longer prepared to act as Britain's dumping ground for an average of 2,500 undesirables every year. The key institution for bringing about this transformation in adults was the penitentiary. Again this term, with its religious connotations of acknowledging and rejecting one's sins, reflected this new idealistic approach to the remaking of criminals. Many conservative politicians and newspapers saw this new liberal approach as surrendering to the criminal. They made dire prognostications, predicting a great increase in crime.

The separate and silent system, designed to stop mutual corruption and put an end to prisons as universities of crime, was the key to the new convict prisons. The Prison Act of 1865 required all local prisons to provide each prisoner with a separate cell. It was only in 1879, however, that prisoners actually received rigorous treatment in accordance with current penal philosophy. Prison Commissioners prescribed 'a uniform application of cellular isolation, absolute non-intercourse among prisoners, the rule of silence, oakum picking and the tread wheel'. The separate provision soon became the rule, though other aspects of the regime varied from prison to prison. By 1900, however, all prisons came under the control of the Prison Commissioner and became institutions of unbending severity.

Prior to this it is doubtful that prison served as an effective deterrent. What is certain is that during the nineteenth century prison food was a great deal better than that of the average working man. The new system only increased the extent to which the prisoner ate better than the honest workman. William Augustus Guy, an eminent pioneer of the science of medical statistics and Medical Superintendent of a new penitentiary at Millbank, writing in 1863 in the *British Medical Journal*, had no doubt that 'prisoners in all categories receive more than the general mass of labourers throughout the country and those in convict establishments receive at least as much as the well-off labourers'. Not only were prisoners better fed than free labourers, they often did less work. Prisoners serving hard labour in Holloway in 1868 – which set the standard for other prisons – had to pick three pounds of oakum during a ten-hour working day. A woman working as an oakum-picker, however, had to pick twice that amount to earn a shilling – an extremely poor wage.

Prisoners were also better off than workhouse inmates. Many commentators believed that paupers deliberately committed crimes in order to access prison's preferable conditions. An American visitor summed it up when he said, 'In England, the pauper lives better than the free labourer; the thief better than the pauper and the transported felon better than the one under imprisonment.'

By the 1870s a Manchester criminal charged with a crime was likely to end up before a magistrate. This was certainly the case for children. The Petty Sessions dealt with minor criminals, such as most thieves, drunks, prostitutes, beggars and vagrants.

At this time Petty Sessions heard on average 10,000 cases a year, about 6,000 of which they referred to a higher court – the Assizes or the Quarter Sessions. In practical terms this meant that on an average day they dealt with about forty cases, more than enough to overwhelm all concerned. And contrary to the popular image of nineteenth century justice as harsh and heartless, the majority of Manchester magistrates were sensible and compassionate men. They were ready – far too ready in the eyes of the police and many members of the public – to take into consideration extenuating circumstances, particularly youth and previous good character.

Even if the police managed to pick their way through this minefield of obstacles and achieved a conviction, the result was often disappointing. The majority of sentences were short and acted as no deterrent – yet another perennial complaint against the criminal justice system. At the Manchester Assizes of 1875 half the sentences handed out were less than ten months and of 477 convictions, only eighty-nine led to terms of penal servitude. Most juveniles sentenced to prison were back on the streets within two months.

What happened to them during those two months and what was its effect?

Six Strides Long

He looked up the wall of the exercise yard, its sheer face broken only by the courtroom windows, protected by iron spikes. With the litheness of a rat, Braithwaite scuttled up the wall to the window and yanked himself precariously onto the spikes, swaying like a man on the high wire.

Stretching the full length of his lithe body he reached the top of the wall with his fingertips. Somehow he gained purchase, pulled himself up onto the wall, scrambled along until he was opposite the Bolton Arms on New Bailey Street and leapt to the street below, landing on flexed knees like a cat. No one had ever done it before. Braithwaite, famed for his ability to shatter any mantelpiece with his forehead, escaped from the New Bailey just before it closed in 1867.

Unfortunately for him his freedom was short-lived. A red-faced Chief Constable Captain Palin promised James Bent £5 reward for the capture of the acrobatic fugitive, which he duly achieved simply by watching Braithwaite's usual haunts. On his return to the tender care of the New Bailey, a warder flayed Braithwaite's back with thirty-six lashes.

For most of our history physical punishment, execution, public humiliation and transportation were the standard penalties for serious crime. Imprisonment was deemed both expensive and ineffective, a view regaining popularity today. The burgeoning industrial towns of the late-eighteenth and early-nineteenth centuries generally had two prisons. In Manchester there was the House of Correction, known as the Bridewell – housing mainly paupers who refused to work – and the dungeon, known as the 'Old Bridge'. Gradually the distinction blurred and all prisoners spent their days at the prison bars begging from by-passers. Inmates were debtors, those serving short sentences for minor crimes, remand prisoners and those awaiting transportation and execution. Conditions were appalling. Regardless of habeas corpus, the law that obliged police to present a suspect to the magistrates before imprisoning him for more than a day, the police locked up petty criminals for a short time without them ever appearing before a magistrate.

Transportation came to an end just as Strangeways first cast its shadow over the city. The final shipment of 800 felons landed at the Swan River in Western Australia in 1867, the last of approximately 150,000 transportees. Until 1867 the New Bailey in Salford provided for the needs of the two cities. Remodelled in 1790, the number of New Bailey inmates grew from fifty-one in 1823 to 8,407 in 1847. For most of the nineteenth century, women – often prostitutes and drunkards – were almost as likely to find themselves in prison as men. The prison was so overcrowded that conditions were life threatening. Behind its walls lunatics, debtors, prostitutes and thieves jostled for space. Such labour as they undertook produced little and discipline was insufficient to prevent prisoners preying on each other. Once the turnkeys locked the cell doors the weakest were at the mercy of the rest for the next seventeen hours.

The fabric of the prison was equally squalid. Cells had no lighting and were so cold that prisoners stuffed up the unglazed windows with rags. The food was poor. But worst of all was the systematic bullying of minority groups and the vulnerable – Catholics, Jews, the deformed, the feeble-minded, the Irish and foreigners. When things threatened to get out of hand, the overwhelmed staff – in 1847 there were thirty-seven for 700 inmates – resorted to whipping and solitary confinement. Solitary meant three days on bread and water locked in total darkness.

Strangeways was the city's first recognisably modern prison. The great Victorian monolith embodied a new principle in criminology, the belief that given the correct environment and a rigorous regime, the wrongdoer would reform. It was designed to implement the new penal servitude regime. Since first closing her forbidding gates behind the first inmate, the stern stronghold has glowered over the city, its ventilation tower giving Manchester her distinctive skyline. Yet even when new, Strangeways' bricks were never clean. Ever conscious of cost, the city fathers had recycled the scarred bricks of the recently demolished New Bailey. Appropriately, Strangeways' first inmates were already dead. The builders dug up the remains of those hanged at Salford, including the Manchester Martyrs, and carried them across the city to Southall Street.

The new Strangeways was really two separate gaols, the men in one tantalisingly close to the women in the other. It had accommodation for 744 men and 315 women.

Each cell was six short strides long and seven feet wide. Though the ceiling was nine feet from the tiled floor, the cell was both warm and well ventilated. The plank bed folded into a table while a gas jet provided good lighting. Every cell had a water tap and a WC.

A table and artificial light were essential for what was intended to be an individual workshop, giving men the opportunity to work at carpentry, cobbling, tailoring or mat weaving. The women worked sewing, laundering and cleaning the building. This gave them the chance to do something more rewarding than turning the crank, a soul-destroying punishment which involved labouring for eight hours a day turning a large handle a set number of times in order to earn meals.

On average during the 1870s there were 629 inmates, about half involved in profitable labour; 129 others worked around the prison and 114 climbed the endless staircase of the treadmill or turned the crank. Despite the central role of labour in the new penal regime, eighty-four were in effect idle. Women enjoyed far better conditions than men. Their cells were similar: white-washed, they had a gas jet and a chimney, shelves, a small table and a stool, a clothes box and a hammock. A rectangular strip of glass near the ceiling provided the only natural light. The work-house took the young children of convicted Strangeways women. By the 1860s the courts no longer imprisoned young children, though they did still remand fifteen-year-olds.

The guiding principles of both male and female sections were separation, religious instruction and hard labour. Many condemned the system as cruel. Even in the 1860s there were those who objected to punishing criminals. One of the new system's many proponents, however, was Joseph Kingsmill, the Pentonville chaplain. Its great strength, he maintained, was that it made 'the propagation of crime impossible – the continuity of vicious habits is broken off – the mind is driven to reflection – and the conscience resumes her sway'.

The other aspect of the system, silence, was supposed to prevail on all occasions. In practice it was impossible to enforce. Kingsmill complained that because prisoners spent so much time picking oakum with their heads bowed it was easy for them to carry on a conversation without detection. It was precisely to avoid this that the first stage of the sentence was separation, designed to break the convict's will and prevent the contagion that made prisons finishing schools for criminals. The Surveyor-General of Prisons, Sir Joshua Jebb, described it as a system 'in which each individual prisoner is confined in a cell which becomes his workplace by day and his bedroom by night, so as to be effectually prevented from holding communication with or even being seen sufficiently to be recognised by other prisoners'.

When he left his cell, the prisoner wore a large Scotch cap, with a peak that came down to his chin like a mask, with holes for the eyes. The numbers sewn onto each prisoner's uniform were the only means of identification. He spent at least nine months in separate confinement and received neither visits nor letters. He took his exercise in a yard, with a separate area for dangerous criminals. Each man held one of the knots in a rope and walked in circles, ensuring that at all times the rope remained taut. The knots were five yards apart. In the centre, perched on his platform, a vigilant warder maintained silence, ensuring that the only sound was the crunch of gravel under the prisoners' feet.

Privileges improved as the convict's sentence progressed so that eventually he enjoyed a letter and a visit every quarter, up to thirty shillings of gratuities a year and three exercise periods on a Sunday. He might also earn minor improvements in diet and uniform. The only way to earn remission was through hard work and good conduct. A prisoner's sentence consisted of a number of marks, which he earned by his labour. He received a maximum of eight marks for a day's hard labour.

All instruction was in the cell – not in classes – and those who did not master reading and writing according to a set schedule lost their gratuity. This system lasted until the 1890s. The regime kept inmates gainfully employed to protect them from the temptations of idleness. They rose at 6am and immediately set about cleaning their cells before starting on the corridors. Cooks and bakers reported to the kitchens. At 6.30am work began in the cells. The bright, spacious blocks echoed to the clatter of looms and the incessant tapping of cobblers at their lasts. At 7.30am prisoners breakfasted in their cells. The iron steps vibrated to the tread of the prisoners' boots as they filed down to chapel at 8am. Once there each man sat in his own individual three-sided cubicle that ensured he could see only directly in front and prevented any eye contact with fellow prisoners.

After chapel the men took exercise until 9am. From then until it was time for dinner at 1pm they worked in their cells. Supper was at 5.30pm and from then until 7pm the instructors distributed materials for the following day's work. The only period of recreation was from 7-9pm when the men read in their cells. After that the warders quenched the lights and the building fell into a profound silence. Warders glided about noiselessly in their felt slippers throughout the night.

What fascinated outsiders and deflated inmates was the treadmill, or the 'cockchafer' as old lags graphically called it. The thinking behind it is totally alien to the twenty-first century liberal penologist. Its purpose was to inflict physical and psychological pain, to exhaust the convict while depriving him of any sense of achievement. It was torture. Those condemned to it found their lungs bursting and their legs turned to mush as they tried to keep up with the 'everlasting staircase'. Its sixteen-foot circumference was like the wheel of a great paddle steamer. It had twenty-four steps, each eight inches apart and the convict, his arms balanced on a stationary bar, had to keep stepping up as the weight of his body caused the wheel to drop away. The men worked a 'fifteen minutes on, fifteen minutes rest' routine and completed fifteen sessions a day. By then they had climbed more than twice the height of Snowdon. One hundred and fourteen short-term or summary offenders drove the treadmill that pumped the prison's water from a deep well. Those sentenced to hard labour spent part of every day on it.

The equivalent in-cell punishment was the crank, a large handle like that on an old-fashioned mangle that required considerable effort to turn. A day's labour consisted of turning it 10,000 times. Given average strength and reasonable application a man could achieve this total in about eight-and-a-half hours. The far more famous treadmill was not quite as bad. It was infinitely preferable to the solitude of the cell-based crank. Each man occupied a small compartment, which on a warm day became so hot that it was difficult to breathe.

Corporal punishment, reduced food and the punishment cells were common sanctions against those who refused to conform. The most dreaded punishment was the cat o'nine tails, which had such a profound impact on those who received it that they produced many accounts of the experience. The turnkeys frog-marched the prisoner to the exercise yard and stripped him to his trousers. They tied each wrist to a metal ring set into the wall at shoulder height and clamped his feet into a box. Then they strapped him by a belt around the chest to a timber frame that made it impossible for him to move any part of his body.

Each lash of the whip with its nine leather strips was like a red-hot iron laid across the flesh. After a few stripes the whole back felt puffy and sensitive, like a septic finger. At each lash the victim felt the blood running down his trousers onto his buttocks. Worst of all was the sensation when the cat lapped around the chest and crushed the breath from his lungs. Regulations permitted a maximum of thirty-six lashes, for weeks after which the prisoner was unable to button his trousers or wear braces. Old lags advocated shouting in response to each lash in the hope that the watching doctor might shorten the ordeal. Psychological agony was added to the physical pain. There was a gap of a count of thirty between each lash. The doctor pointed out where each lash was to fall and the turnkey aimed for the spot. All who endured the cat agreed: there was no other punishment that came near it.

Apart from corporal punishment there were the punishment cells in the basement. There inmates squatted in total darkness, something city dwellers had never experienced. With nothing to do they contemplated the gnawing hunger that several days on bread and water ensured.

Charlie Parton left an account of his nine months in solitary confinement under the Silent System (reproduced in the 2005 book *Strange Tales from Strangeways* by Sara Lee). He got out of the cell for one hour in every twenty-four. For the rest he was alone and not allowed any books. The only break was when the warders brought his food. During the day he was kept working making slippers. For his first six months he got neither letters nor visitors.

Many penologists agreed with the Pentonville cook who said, 'There are few who can hold out against short commons. The belly can tame every man.' By the 1860s corporal punishment was rare and the only Holloway prisoners flogged during the decade after 1852 were those sentenced to it by the courts. Reducing rations was far easier and when a bread and water diet was combined with being locked in a cell without light it became a powerful deterrent.

A minority of commentators believed that the normal prison diet was itself a deterrent to crime. The Strangeways diet of the 1870s was three-quarters of a pint of cocoa and eight ounces of bread for breakfast; a dinner of five ounces of meat, one pound of potatoes and six ounces of bread and a supper of eight ounces of bread and a pint of oatmeal gruel. The punishment diet reduced food to one pound of bread a day.

Even when in the punishment cell the convict knew his position was not the worst. The man in the basement cell in B wing, who was awaiting execution, held that distinction. For a short time he enjoyed the luxury of a cell twice the normal size. It had two doors. One led to the visiting area where the condemned man, forbidden to touch his family, stood separated from them by bars. As for the other, he knew that those who passed through it never returned.

Epilogue: Bang! Bang!

The sunlight glistened on his perfect incisors. He drew his thumb up to his nose and aimed along the barrel of his forefinger. His eyebrows were white bristles of perished fuse wire but there were still daubs of ginger in his hair.

'Bang! Gotcha! Bang!' He laughed through his vulpine mouth, the laugh of a diesel engine catching on a winter's morning.

'Where's yer bullet-proof vest, man?' he demanded.

What's he on about? I wondered. Are these the ramblings of the geriatric mind?

Then the penny dropped. The uncle I had come to visit in this retirement home in Durham had told the other residents I lived in Manchester. And when people think of Manchester they, like my uncle's friend, think of gun crime. Crime and Manchester, it seems, are destined to be for ever linked.

The roots of lawlessness go deep into the red sandstone on which Manchester rests. Yet between 1870 and 1900 Manchester's most conspicuous crime diminished. The families unable to support their children, the beggars clogging the city streets, the impenetrable Deansgate rookeries, the droves of itinerant workers – all disappeared. Redevelopment, especially that which swept away the worst of the Deansgate rookeries, revolutionised the appearance of the city centre. Changes in the way courts treated juveniles greatly reduced the number of young beggars. The improvement in the working man's living standards did away with many of the outward signs of crime. It was not because of any improvement in the efficiency of those forces working against the criminal.

The criminal justice system of the second half of the nineteenth century was by no means as brutal as many people believe.

In many ways it was extremely lenient, particularly in its indulgence to those who attacked the police. Nor was it only violent thugs who escaped with derisory sentences. Frauds such as William Chadwick, who made a career of systematically cheating generous people, also enjoyed the leniency of judges. Chadwick and his sort were as despicable as any modern shysters operating a fraudulent cancer charity. It is easy to romanticise our ancestors, to attribute to them a decency they didn't have. As far as Manchester's nineteenth century criminals are concerned there is no evidence for this idealised view. There is no depravity, no cowardly or contemptible act they didn't commit. There is no area in which the modern sociopath outdoes them in infamy.

The vast majority of Manchester criminals, however, did not require the mercy of the courts to protect them from the force of the law because the police failed to catch them. In the battle between the criminal and the police all the advantages lay with the former. So many obstacles handicapped the efficient operation of the police during this period that it was usually only the inept and the outrageous who appeared before a court.

Even then, if the worst came to the worst and a criminal faced prison, he had little to fear. Unless sentenced to flogging he was unlikely to be dismayed by a short sentence. Despite all the best efforts of penology, prison conditions remained better than those in the slums and rookeries of Manchester and Salford. The worst thing about prison was the shame it brought on a respectable man. Those who had no aspirations to respectability were immune to prison's deterrent effect.

Underpinning and sustaining crime were the great pillars on which it rested: the pub, the pawnshop, the lodging house, the workhouse and most of the rookeries. They nourished criminals as the sun and rain of the Amazon jungle nurture a venomous plant. The forces ranged against them were no match. The gallows remained hidden in the bowels of Strangeways and the lash gathered dust. Though corporal punishment in prisons was not formally abolished until 1964 its use became progressively less frequent from the 1870s.

Epilogue: Bang! Bang!

The appeal of respectability and the incompetence of criminals were more effective barriers against lawlessness than the efforts of police, courts and prison.